hy

American Research on Russia

EDITED BY HAROLD H. FISHER

American
Research
on
RUSSIA

INDIANA UNIVERSITY PRESS

Bloomington

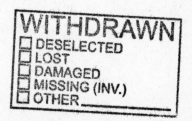

Copyright © 1959 by Indiana University Press
Manufactured in the United States of America
Library of Congress catalog card number: 59-10870

PREFACE

A GREAT DEAL of research on Russia has been done in the United States since World War II. This is a matter of common knowledge, but many of those who have been doing this research have little or no notion of what has been accomplished in fields of specialization adjacent to their own. Others who are not specialists but for one reason or another are interested in Russia, the Soviet Union, and the Communist movement, have even less reason to know what subjects have been investigated, what has been written about these subjects, and where these writings may be found. At the same time, the lack of this information makes it difficult to know the topics on which further investigation is most urgent or most promising. Furthermore, without knowledge of what studies have been made, it is impossible to make the best use for general education and public enlightenment of the truly impressive scholarly work of the last few years. The essays in this book are intended to provide this information, first, by reviewing American research on Russia during the years since World War II and, secondly, by indicating some of the topics on which further research would benefit the specialist and the nonspecialist and add to our knowledge of an important area.

v

The essays were written at the suggestion of a subcommittee of the Joint Committee on Slavic Studies of the American Council of Learned Societies and the Social Science Research Council. This Subcommittee on the Review of Russian Studies has conducted a general survey of Russian studies in the United States, which has covered not only research but also the organization and development of Russian area studies and the impact of these studies on general education.* A complementary survey of library problems and needs has been made by a committee of the Association of Research Libraries. The purpose of these surveys is to present information on recent experience and to stimulate thought, provoke discussion, and draw out suggestions regarding the direction and methods of Russian studies during the next decade.

The authors of the eleven essays in this book prepared their first drafts as discussion papers for a conference held under the auspices of the Joint Committee at Cambridge, Massachusetts, January 30-31, 1958, in conjunction with the tenth anniversary of the Russian Research Center of Harvard University. The draft of each paper was read and commented on by specialists in the respective fields and, in most cases, by at least one other scholar in the discipline who was not a Russian specialist. The authors have taken into account these comments and the Cambridge discussions, but the final versions are the views of the individual authors.

The introductory chapter by Dr. Philip E. Mosely is based on an address made at the Cambridge conference. Dr. Mosely, now Director of Studies at the Council of Foreign Relations, was formerly Director of the Russian Institute of Columbia University, and is one of the founders of Russian area studies in the United States and a leader of great influence in their growth. His observations on interdisciplinary, cooperative, and group re-

* The reports on education will be published in a volume on *The Study of Russia in American Education* (Indiana University Press).

search, on government and privately sponsored research projects, and on the peculiar difficulties and achievements in this field of scholarship are based on a wide acquaintance with the work of the individuals and institutions which have accomplished so much in the study of Russia.

As will appear, the authors place the principal focus of their essays on research by American scholars outside the government. They also discuss the different kinds of research that have been done in their disciplines, and refer to certain titles that illustrate these trends or are otherwise significant. None of the contributors attempts to cover all research done in his field or to present a comprehensive bibliographical survey of that research. They all, however, suggest topics, periods, and methods to which more attention should be given.

The writers have approached their subjects in a variety of ways. Some have surveyed the work in their fields by topics, others by major works; some have listed a good many titles, others only a few which they considered representative. Some have given more and some less attention to published articles and to studies in progress. Some have had more occasion than others to refer to work done before World War II, to research by other than American scholars, and to studies made under government contract. All have dealt to some extent with topics of both the Imperial and the Soviet period, the amount of attention being determined by the amount of research, which, in turn, has been largely determined by the nature of the discipline. For example, in such disciplines as economics, political science, and social relations, the analysis of pre-Soviet materials has been considered by most of the contributors to be the business of the historian, and the review of historical research refers to several studies of this type.

Most of the essayists have discussed area-oriented interdisciplinary research and discipline-oriented individual research together. Since much research has been done under the sponsorship of the various Russian area programs, considerable emphasis has been put on an integrated outlook in the study of Russian society through drawing upon the insights and techniques of several disciplines. Sometimes this has turned out very well; sometimes not so well. The evidence is not sufficient to determine whether the occasionally unsatisfactory result is due to something inherent in the "integration" approach or to failure, as yet, to solve some of the problems involved in this seemingly promising method. In the meantime there has been a substantial increase in the research done in the spirit and according to the rules of traditional discipline study. The essays do not examine the relative merits of the integrated and the non-integrated method, but the reviews of what has been accomplished and the suggestions of what needs to be done indicate that both methods should be encouraged.

The eleven fields surveyed—history, geography, political science, economics, social relations, philosophy and religion, literature, linguistics, music, fine arts, and science—do not include all the fields of specialization in which work on Russia has been or is being done. No separate surveys have been made of the research done on the history and structure of Russian and Soviet education, or on painting, sculpture, choreography, and the dramatic arts. Some reference is made to these aspects of Russian life in the essays, but the absence of separate surveys is an indication that very little research has been done in these fields. Some investigations have been made of and much has been written about Soviet education, especially since Soviet scientists and technologists made such a sensational demonstration of the high quality of their work, and some of these studies are mentioned in the chapters on history, social relations, and science.

In conclusion I know that I speak for the contributors in acknowledging the assistance of Professor C. E. Black of Princeton University and Mr. John M. Thompson of the Social Science Research Council, chairman and staff assistant of the Subcom-

mittee on the Review of Russian Studies, in the preparation of
these essays. I wish also to express the thanks of the participants
in this undertaking to the scholars who commented on the original
drafts of the papers and especially to the Subcommittee on Grants
of the Joint Committee on Slavic Studies, whose generous aid
made this publication possible.

H. H. F.

CONTENTS

xi

CONTRIBUTORS

JOHN A. ARMSTRONG is associate professor of political science at the University of Wisconsin and the author of *Ukrainian Nationalism 1939-1945*, and *The Soviet Bureaucratic Elite: A Case Study of the Ukrainian Apparatus*.

ARTHUR S. BARRON studied at the Russian Institute of Columbia University and received his doctorate in sociology at Columbia. Formerly with the Research Institute of America, he is now on the staff of CBS News.

EDWARD J. BROWN is professor of Russian at Brown University and attended the Fourth International Congress of Slavists in Moscow in September, 1958. He is the author of *The Proletarian Episode in Russian Literature, 1928-1932*.

JOHN S. CURTISS is professor of history at Duke University and has written two studies of the position of the Orthodox Church in modern Russia, *Church and State in Russia* and *The Russian Church and the Soviet State*, as well as a brief interpretation of *The Russian Revolutions of 1917*.

HAROLD H. FISHER is professor of international relations at San Francisco State College. He was an officer of the American Relief Administration during its operations in eastern Europe after the First World War and during the Russian famine of 1921-23. He was for many years professor of history and chairman of the Hoover Institute and Library at Stanford University.

GREGORY GROSSMAN is associate professor of economics at the University of California, Berkeley, and the author of articles on the Soviet economy.

W. A. DOUGLAS JACKSON is associate professor of geography at the University of Washington and has written on Russian agricultural geography.

GEORGE L. KLINE is assistant professor of philosophy at Columbia University. He has translated V. V. Zenkovsky's *A History of Russian Philosophy* and has selected, translated, and written an introduction for a series of essays published under the title *Spinoza in Soviet Philosophy*.

PHILIP E. MOSELY is director of studies at the Council on Foreign Relations. He served with the Department of State during the Second World War and was director of the Russian Institute at Columbia University from 1951 to 1955. He is the author of *Russian Diplomacy and the Opening of the Eastern Question in 1838 and 1839* and has written extensively on Soviet foreign policy and international affairs.

ROBERT M. SLUSSER studied at the Russian Institute of Columbia University. From 1953 to 1956 he was associate director of the Research Program on the U.S.S.R. of the East European Fund, and since that time he has been co-director of A Study of Soviet Treaties at the Hoover Institution, Stanford University.

JOHN TURKEVICH is professor of chemistry at Princeton University. His avocation is the study of the development of Soviet science. He has frequently served as a consultant to the government and has contributed a number of significant articles in this field.

FRANCIS J. WHITFIELD is professor of Slavic languages and literatures and chairman of that department at the University of California, Berkeley. He has written *A Russian Reference Grammar* and prepared a one-volume abridgment of Prince Mirsky's *History of Russian Literature*.

PAUL WILLEN is an architecture student at Pratt Institute, Brooklyn. He also studied at the Russian Institute of Columbia University and has been on the staff of Radio Free Europe. He has written articles on Soviet and East European affairs and prepared for the Free Europe Press a volume entitled *Satellite Agriculture in Crisis*.

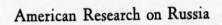
American Research on Russia

Philip E. Mosely

1. THE GROWTH OF RUSSIAN STUDIES

I

THE FIRST BEGINNINGS in the continuous and systematic study of Russia by American scholars date back to the years before 1914, when the United States was groping toward an understanding of its emerging role in world politics, and therefore felt a need to enlarge its intellectual horizons beyond the traditional fascination with the literature, the arts, and the history of western Europe and the Mediterranean. And this was the decade in which Tolstoy and Chekhov, Stanislavsky and Diagilev, Musorgsky and Tchaikovsky became familiar and exciting spirits throughout the West, returning to the older centers of science and culture the new and challenging gifts of a Russian renaissance. Prior to these years, it is true, talented individuals—Eugene Schuyler and George Kennan (uncle of George F. Kennan), among them— had sporadically "discovered" Russia for Americans, but the "naturalization" of Russian studies could begin only with their anchoring in universities and their curricula. By 1914 there were three chairs of Russian language and literature—at Harvard, Columbia, and California—and courses in Russian history were being taught at California and Harvard.

I

A new stage in the study of Russia began with the dramatic and perplexing events of the Russian Revolution. The emergence of an entirely new and, for the West, unforeseen system of ideas and power aroused an unceasing if unfocused curiosity about Russia's origins and much speculation about its future. The same upheavals also brought to our shores a number of talented Russian scholars who, together with American-born scholars, did much, during the 1920's and 1930's, to nourish a slow but steady development of Russian studies, primarily in the traditional fields of history and literature. During these two decades a few American-trained scholars, not more than a dozen or so, were also equipping themselves for research and teaching, through systematic training in the Russian language and in their disciplines as applied to Russian studies. By 1937, when access to the Soviet Union became almost impossible, most of them had benefited, and benefited greatly, from varying periods of intensive research and direct experience in Russia.

Meanwhile, several modest steps were being taken to establish a wider framework for scholarly work related to Russia. In 1934, on the initiative of the American Council of Learned Societies and with the support of the Rockefeller Foundation, a first and very useful experiment was launched in the improved teaching of the Russian language. Three intensive summer courses, held at Columbia, Harvard, and Berkeley, helped lay to rest one persistent bogy, proving that with the right methods a reading knowledge of Russian can be acquired in a relatively few months. This experience, and the materials and methods developed from it, provided a springboard for the war-time and postwar programs for the intensive teaching of Russian. For the head start of Russian area studies in the intensive teaching of the language, scholars in this field are deeply indebted to the efforts of the American Council of Learned Societies and particularly of Mortimer Graves, its executive secretary.

The ACLS, through Mortimer Graves, also took the first

initiative in providing a focus through which the opportunities and needs of Russian studies could be studied and presented in a wider setting, by appointing, in 1938, a Committee on Slavic Studies.* In reviewing the prospects and requirements for this infant field of study, the committee emphasized the importance of intensive language training and of building up research materials on a systematic basis. It pointed out some of the major gaps in our research personnel and resources, and outlined some of the main requirements for the effective study of Russia, for example, the need for economists and political scientists, geographers and sociologists equipped in this field. As a stimulus to the setting up of college courses on Russian history and literature it arranged for the preparation and publication of a 1,500-item selected *List of Works on Slavic Civilizations, in West European Languages,* and followed this with a 500-item basic list of Russian books essential to college teaching in this field. To fill some of the gaps in library resources, it undertook the offset reprinting of several scarce books of special importance to research training, and it encouraged the ACLS to set up an extensive and very useful Russian reprint program, conducted mainly through the University of Michigan Press. Through an intellectual offshoot, the Russian Translation Project, conducted in 1942-48 by a devoted editor, W. Chapin Huntington, some twenty-five important Russian books of political, economic, and intellectual history, as well as geography and political science, were translated, carefully edited, and published in English.

From its inception the Committee on Slavic Studies, without in any way depreciating the cooperation and hospitality which the editors of the *Slavonic and East European Review* (London) had always shown their American colleagues, had stressed the need for an American journal to serve as a focus and stimulus to

* George R. Noyes, chairman, 1938-39; Samuel H. Cross, chairman, 1939-46; Philip E. Mosely, chairman, 1947-48; others members for varying terms: Geroid T. Robinson, Alfred Senn, Ernest J. Simmons, Marvin Farber, Francis J. Whitfield.

research and publication, and in 1939 it undertook to establish
the *American Slavic and East European Review,* with assistance
from the Curt H. Reisinger Foundation. After drawing up a
comprehensive list of some 300 people teaching in the Slavic
field, the committee arranged for this constituency to nominate
and then elect a board of editors, who then elected Samuel H.
Cross as the first editor of the *Review.* Plans for a first issue had
been completed, and the articles and reviews received or promised,
when, in December 1940, Cross received a heart-rending cable
from Sir Bernard Pares. Because of the savage fire-bombing of
London, the *Slavonic and East European Review* had been
crippled and Pares asked his American colleagues to carry on
the *Review* until the war was over. Naturally, there could be
only one response, and therefore the war-time issues of the
American *Review* bear the title and numbering of its British
elder brother.

During the period until 1941 most studies by American scholars
dealt with the history and literature of Russia prior to 1917. One
prominent exception was the work of Samuel N. Harper and
of several of his pupils at the University of Chicago; a beginning
was also being made at Harvard and Columbia in the fields of
political science and economics. However, with a few exceptions
most of the efforts to study contemporary Soviet Russia were
carried on, not by university scholars, but by talented journalists,
such as William Henry Chamberlin and Louis Fischer. Some of
the "schoolmen" felt, however, that a systematic study of contemporary foreign civilizations was both possible and necessary,
and in the years 1938-41 there was some discussion of setting
up Russian and other "area programs." Several of these proposals
had a markedly linguistic flavor, assuming that the study of the
history, institutions, and culture of Russia should proceed from
a perfect mastery of the language, both printed and spoken. On
the other hand, the organized social science disciplines, except
history, were then unsympathetic to the concept of area studies;

for them, a discipline could only be universal in validity, and "area studies," largely untried as yet, seemed of doubtful scholarly value or promise. Still, many future Russian specialists received indispensable fellowship support from 1924 on through the programs of the Social Science Research Council, in addition to fellowships provided by the ACLS.

Another difficulty sometimes hampered Russian studies in their early development. Sometimes the general public, and occasionally even college administrators, found it hard to believe that Russia could be the subject of objective teaching and research. Scholars interested in studying Russia not infrequently were asked: "Are you for it or against it?" As a result of an unrelenting emphasis upon careful and systematic research achievement, this naive assumption that in one way or another one must be "for" or "against" has been almost completely dissipated. Today any conscientious scholar can state his strong attachment to the liberal values of our free society and at the same time calmly pursue his researches to their own factual conclusions, however discomforting these may be to him and his readers.

II

The cataclysm of World War II, in shaking the world, also shook up the small world of Russian studies. The national interest, indeed, the national survival, brought new needs and demanded urgent and accurate answers to many difficult questions. One requirement, which some scholars foresaw many months before the national government, was to provide at least small numbers of people trained in languages, from Japanese and Burmese to Urdu and Swahili, and versed in the history and culture of many peoples in many distant parts of the world. The ACLS Committee on Language Instruction in the Emergency, created within a few days after Pearl Harbor, did yeoman service, with support from the foundations, in identifying scarce resources in teachers and informants and in filling many gaps in teaching materials and methods. Although the teaching of more than forty "unusual" languages was eventually introduced or strengthened under this program, Russian, with its head start, was the first to be taught, from late January 1942, in a new "super-intensive" course, first at Cornell and then elsewhere.

It was also clear from the start of hostilities that the knowledge of a "strange" language must be backed by at least some familiarity with the culture and institutions, customs and thought-patterns, of the peoples studied, and again it was a Russian Area Program, also at Cornell, which pioneered in the first area studies program, with the support of the Rockefeller Foundation. At first government agencies insisted stoutly that there was no possible utility in these and similar "boondoggling" programs, but by 1943, convinced by experience of the crucial need for interrogators, intelligence specialists, liaison and military government personnel, the Army and Navy set about developing numerous Area Studies Training Programs of their own on a scale which dwarfed the modest efforts of the ACLS, the foundations and universities. From these programs, and from the experience the Army and Navy area students had subsequently gained in many far-flung corners of the globe, came the inrush of able, enthusiastic, and mature young men and women who made the new postwar programs a dynamic addition to our educational and research resources. From this war-time experience have come also the excellent postwar language schools of the Army and Air Force, as well as continuing programs of the services for training groups of selected officers in the universities' area programs.

The central authorities of a government waging war around the globe needed expert area information on an entirely new and unprecedented scale. Was the entire Japanese nation inspired by a *kamikaze* psychology? How could the Arabs of the Maghreb be persuaded to contribute to an early Allied victory? How could friction be minimized between the masses of American servicemen and their friendly but often exasperated host peoples in Britain, France, and elsewhere? Clyde Kluckhohn, Ruth Benedict, and their colleagues proved by their incisive studies that it was possible, working at a distance and relying on the raw materials at hand, to analyze the Japanese institutional and psychological structure to great effect. The same desperate need for accurate information and reliable forecasts also applied to our relations with the Soviet Union.

Although Russia was an ally, its rulers were even less communicative than in peace-time when it came to supplying information needed in Washington to make vital decisions or establish painful priorities. Yet it was important to know whether Murmansk and Vladivostok could actually handle great amounts of supplies and equipment, or whether the upshot of meeting the vast Soviet demands would be to leave scarce shipping riding idle in roadsteads for many weeks while other fronts were starved of supplies. How far could the unoccupied areas of the U.S.S.R. feed the people and the army, and how much food should the United States and Canada supply? And what were Soviet intentions toward the not yet occupied countries of east central Europe? Was Tito likely to be a national or a Muscovite Communist? The range of questions was almost infinite, the research resources sadly limited, and the conviction grew among the overworked area specialists that systematic steps must be taken after the war to plug these gaps in the arsenal of national policy.

Among many agencies which attempted to provide informed answers—ranging from "hard" answers on logistics to "soft" ones on intentions and attitudes—the Research and Analysis Branch of the Office of Strategic Services rendered pre-eminent services. Geroid T. Robinson served as the Chief of R & A, U.S.S.R., with John S. Curtiss and Abram Bergson as his immediate assistants. Despite the glamorized notions which have gathered about some of the activities of OSS, the work of R & A was a real research slugging match, mustering the inadequate data as carefully as possible, and interpreting them with the combined analytical techniques of historians, economists, sociologists, oil and food specialists, and engineers. The answers, demanded with a deadline attached, were cranked into the machinery of state, which spewed forth its crucial decisions of policy and operations. The field of inquiry was, if anything, wider-ranging, more recalcitrant, and more poignant in its meaning for human lives than even the broadest academic program of today. The R & A experience showed that analysts of many different skills not only could but must work in harness to accomplish many types of research. While neither R & A nor the present area programs have broken down the walls which separate the social sciences, they have broken through many new channels of mutual comprehension and cooperation. Thus the determination to establish graduate programs of interdisciplinary teaching and research on Russia and the U.S.S.R. grew out of both prewar hopes and war-time urgencies.

Just as the war came to a close, farsighted university administrators and foundation officials were debating the meaning of the United States' world-wide contacts and responsibilities and the ways in which the universities could help promote a new level and range of information and understanding of distant areas and unfamiliar peoples. Because of the prewar pioneering in the Russian field, and because of the availability of a small reserve of senior scholars in a variety of disciplines, the field of Russian studies was better equipped than most others to press forward in this new initiative, and in the first two years after the war five new or enlarged programs received substantial university-plus-foundation support for greatly strengthened work in Russian studies. Returning enriched in mind by their war-time experiences, both teachers and students plunged with enthusiasm and conviction into this challenging experiment.

In the rapid growth of Russian studies after 1945, organized channels of research effort, interpreting to universities and foundations the needs as the scholars saw them, again played an active part. The main difference now was that the social sciences were adding their backing to the continuing contributions of the humanities. It was, for example, the World Areas Research Committee of the Social Science Research Council which in 1946 laid down the basic criteria for defining an adequate graduate program of area studies: five disciplines or more, working closely together, intensive language training, substantial library resources, administrative recognition of the program within the system of instruction. The SSRC program of postwar "reconversion" fellowships enabled many area specialists to turn from wartime service to productive research during their transition back to academic pursuits. The SSRC program of Area Research Fellowships, inaugurated in 1947, for the first time gave specific recognition to the opportunities and needs in this field. At the end of 1946 the *American Slavic and East European Review* surveyed its role afresh and adopted new policies, emphasizing new areas of interest. Under the editorship of Ernest J. Simmons and John N. Hazard, it has both reflected and stimulated a rapidly growing maturity of research. The Committee for the Promotion of Advanced Slavic Studies, Inc., inspired and guided by R. Gordon Wasson, has made many contributions to research and publication, with special attention to the culture and history of pre-Soviet Russia and to the needs of Slavic linguistics.

In 1947 the ACLS Committee on Slavic Studies was enlarged and strengthened by becoming the Joint Committee on Slavic Studies, appointed concurrently by the ACLS and the SSRC. A major part of its work has been to improve and broaden the flow of published research materials in many ingenious ways, to make west European repositories more accessible to scholarly use, to recommend the completion of the Cyrillic bibliography of the Library of Congress, to expedite the distribution of Library of Congress duplicates, to encourage the publication of the Library's *Monthly List of Russian Accessions* and the parallel bibliographies on east central Europe. A special concern of the Joint Committee has been the establishment and operation of the *Current Digest of the Soviet Press*, an invaluable tool for both teaching and research.

The Joint Committee has also advocated successfully the enlargement of programs for the support of research training, for advanced research leaves and other grants-in-aid. Under four successive chairmen and with a membership reflecting the insights of several disciplines, the Joint Committee has labored long and hard to strengthen the resources of Slavic studies. The Inter-University Committee on Travel Grants has moved energetically, once the barriers were lowered in 1954, to enlarge the opportunity for scholars to see something of the Soviet Union at first hand and, under the U.S.-Soviet cultural exchange agreement of January 1958, to enable American graduate students to take advantage of the opportunity to do research in the Soviet Union, while arranging reciprocal opportunities for advanced Soviet students in American universities. Finally, no review of Slavic studies can fail to pay tribute to the many and great contributions which the Library of Congress, wisely advised by Sergius Yakobson, Chief of its Slavic and Central European Division, has made and is making to the advancement of this field of research.

III

Russian area studies may be experimental, but there is nothing unique or mysterious about their purpose or their methods. The function of area studies is the same for Russian studies as for the study of China or Japan, India, the Moslem world, Africa, or Latin America. Their educational purpose is to help people see a society, a system of power, or an economy, or all three interacting together as they do in real life, and to see them both in their interconnections and as a whole.

In an age of scientific specialization this is not an easy task. As our various disciplines have broken away, since the eighteenth century, from their stern parent, Moral Philosophy, they have often tended to emphasize their separateness from each other, the unique validity of their exclusive methodologies, and even the mutual incomprehensibility of their vocabularies. The area studies approach can, as I see it, help to pull the fissiparous disciplines back together again, not by administrative fiat but by a common dedication to the study of a single civilization or area. Like all educational enterprises, this is a difficult and never finished one, but the effort to see any human society and see it whole is in itself an exciting experience in self-education.

Viewed in this perspective, area studies are not a real innovation, a "sport," within education. For several centuries the interdisciplinary study of ancient Greece and Rome provided the central core for the training of minds in the West, and classical training has today a high prestige in Britain and France. In addition to mastering grammar and vocabulary, a student of the classics must understand the philosophy and logic, the literature and history, the political, economic, and social institutions, the religious beliefs and military strategies of the ancient world, and, above all, the interconnections among them. The peculiar feature of classical studies is that they deal with a civilization which in its fully developed form seemed relatively stable for several centuries and which can no longer be studied *in situ* today. In contrast, area studies aim to study and interpret living societies, all of which are developing, some slowly, some tempestuously, but none without profound implications for the future of mankind.

In the few years since 1945 a number of factors have favored the emergence of Russian area studies as a relatively strong segment within the widening field of area studies. For one thing, no one can go far in studying Russia without realizing how closely different aspects of its life interact. The Soviet leadership aims to create a monolithic system, embracing potentially all activities. What happens in the economy interacts with, and is affected by, changes in the structure of political power. Literature is influenced strongly by the changing demands of the ruling party and in turn reflects changes in the purposes and expectations of the Party. This factor of interaction, which is displayed in varying degrees in both Soviet and earlier Russian development, makes it natural for students of Russia to attempt to apply a coordinated or multidisciplinary approach, more so than would be easy in analyzing a highly dispersed system with many interacting centers of power or resistance.

A further advantage in the impetus given to Russian studies has been that one major and not very difficult language opens up the study of the principal forces and actions of the system of power and the economy. The languages of the non-Russian peoples unlock other cultures and problems for study, and there is an encouraging widening of our research focus to include study of the non-Russian peoples. In this field, as well as in comparing these forces and factors with what is happening within the Soviet-dominated satellite countries, there are many urgent themes of research. Nevertheless, unlike the situation in Far Eastern, Moslem, and Indic studies, the beginning specialist on Russia can accomplish a great deal after learning one principal language well, and this has made possible a relatively short period of basic area training, compared with the study of most other non-European areas.

The challenge of Soviet secretiveness has certainly added a special zest to research in the Russian field. If the Soviet leadership should open up many more aspects of its system to easy study, perhaps scholars would not feel to the same degree the challenge to probe the obscurities of Soviet data, to piece together the confusing and conflicting figures on the growth of the Soviet economy, to penetrate the workings of the Communist Party and the political police. To the student of the Soviet system the excitement of discovering the bits and pieces and fitting them into meaningful patterns is as stimulating as a similar task is to the archaeologist, except that new "artifacts" are turned out every day by the Soviet press and radio instead of being dug laboriously out of ancient ruins or kitchen middens. The unceasing effort of research is spurred on by the need to analyze, urgently and objectively, what the Soviet system is, how it is evolving, and how the Soviet leaders use their growing power, at home and abroad.

To meet this need, Russian area studies centers and institutes have endeavored, within the limits of trained personnel and budgets available, to provide an essential framework for systematic research, backed by growing but far from adequate facilities. They have elaborated programs of necessary research, identifying gaps and encouraging promising students to fill them. They have trained, far better than was possible before the war, substantial numbers of teachers, government officials, and journalists. Like scholars in other fields they have worked hard to build a solid body of verified knowledge. When solid data fail, they point out the role of projection and conjecture, thus widening the areas of systematic and verifiable knowledge and diminishing gradually the necessity to rely on personal hunches and insights, however inspired. That great strides have been made in building up this body of knowledge and that much more must be done is confirmed in the reports that follow.

Merely to accumulate research bricks, however workmanlike each may be, is to stop far short of our duty to scholarship and to an informed public opinion. Area studies offer a special opportunity to work out a systematic framework of interrelated concepts to explain the strengths and weaknesses, the forces and the resistances, of the society under study, and ultimately to predict within broad limits the directions in which it is moving. Some important efforts have been made to analyze the broad structures and dynamics of the Soviet system, but more efforts are needed. Remembering the influence which personal and political predilections exercised in the 1920's and 1930's on the interpretation of Soviet events, postwar scholars have understandably preferred to prove their mastery of method and to leave the more massive enterprises until later. In the next decade, I predict, students of Russian affairs will be better equipped to devote more attention to the dynamic aspects of the Soviet society and system, and they will be the more encouraged to do so if that society, after appearing almost frozen for so long, continues to display signs of gradual change.

IV

Because area study programs strive, however imperfectly, to look at a society or a system of power as a whole, they have a special opportunity and duty to pioneer in projects of multi-disciplinary research. In this part of our research there have been some notable efforts and some solid achievements. The Harvard Russian Refugee Interview project showed that scholars of different disciplines can work together fruitfully, learning a great deal from each other and about each other's methods in the process. If the successive steps from raw data to broad conclusions about the nature of the Soviet system proved not quite as simple and direct as had been assumed in the beginning, both the experience and the products of this project have added a great deal to the realism of Russian studies.

The study of Russia in Asia, carried on at the University of Washington, has brought together scholars of several disciplines and of very different if contiguous areas, and its results, for both Russian and Chinese studies, are of great interest. A somewhat different, more contemporary, study of Russian and Asian interactions is progressing favorably at the University of Southern California, and Stanford and Columbia have been hospitable to work in this difficult field.

The studies of the RAND Corporation on the Soviet economy have shown the great importance of intensive full-time research in a stimulating and self-critical environment, if we are to plumb successfully the mysteries of deceptive or self-deceptive Soviet statistics. Similarly, the studies of Soviet politics at RAND, by Nathan Leites and others, have opened up new techniques of analysis and emphasized the need for more experimental approaches. The War Documentation Project of Columbia University attempted to bring several disciplines to bear on the study of the behavior of the Soviet population under German occupation, as a means of investigating the impact of Soviet rule on the people governed. The studies of the Massachusetts Institute of Technology on the working of Soviet society, on the economies of the east European satellites, and on Soviet education have similarly brought together a wide variety of skills and professions.

While our scholars have learned a little about interdisciplinary research, there is, I am sure, no single or preordained pattern to serve as a guide. A new pattern has to be worked out, by trial and error, for each new major problem. Russian studies, nevertheless, have developed a substantial body of scholars who have learned to work together, combining their different skills and insights to tackle problems which would leave an individual researcher dazed and helpless. Side by side with interdisciplinary efforts, cooperative research of a more customary variety has also been practiced on a fairly wide scale. In the Research Program on the U.S.S.R., a part of the East European Fund, Inc., some of the ablest of the ex-Soviet scholars worked closely with American-trained scholars expert in their own fields; the new arrivals learned a great deal about Western standards of research and American scholars learned much about life and research within the Soviet Union. In a related field the Mid-European Studies Center of the Free Europe Committee, Inc., brought together much systematic information on east central Europe. Working under a still different pattern, the Institute for the Study of the U.S.S.R. in Munich offers an outlet for research talents among the ex-Soviet refugees. Its resources could be utilized to greater advantage by west European and American research workers. The Research Program on the History of the Communist Party of the Soviet Union is similarly an attempt to identify our resources and fill some of the gaps in the study of the Soviet system of power and ideology.

Interdisciplinary, or as I prefer to call it, multidisciplinary research is neither an open sesame nor a nostrum. It is not a prescription which can be filled by rote. It can be very rewarding if it allows time for individual minds to understand and adopt the underlying concepts and apply the methods of related fields of work. Unless the economist is paired with a sociologist or a social psychologist it is going to be difficult for him to measure the role of incentives and deterrents within a Soviet scale of satisfactions. Similarly a student of Soviet ideology needs a long background of Russian history and a sensitivity to what is "façade" and what is a genuinely motivating force in Soviet statements of value. Meanwhile, the student of Russia has strong incentives to open up channels of communication with his colleagues in other disciplines and to help some of the ablest students press on from the multidisciplinary program of training to build effective habits of multidisciplinary research as their abilities mature.

v

If present trends continue, American scholars will find increasing opportunities to do research in Soviet libraries, to consult Soviet colleagues on problems of common research interest, and perhaps to make some use of archival and statistical collections. Perhaps there will be some opportunities to do archaeological field work, perhaps later, ethnographic studies. Other types of field studies, such as are widely practiced in our own society, seem remote today. Any type of study and research in the Soviet Union is going to be expensive, and is going to require much greater proficiency in understanding and speaking Russian than most of our scholars have acquired. Whatever the cost, ways and means must be expanded to give our area specialists a firsthand experience of Soviet life. During the postwar years, those senior scholars who had done research in prewar Russia have been more and more distressed as they watched the growing number of people who must study Russian subjects without ever having lived in Russia and among Russians. They often wondered whether a high standard of realistic understanding could be maintained indefinitely under conditions of isolation. The new opportunity for research in the Soviet Union must be utilized to the full, and reciprocal hospitality extended freely and cordially to Soviet scholars, if our resources are to expand in quality as well as quantity.

In order to meet more effectively the growing demands which are placed on Russian and Slavic studies, our field of study needs even more research opportunities than it now offers. Much more must be done to strengthen our research collections, and efficient and rapid means must be found to reproduce unique or rare books at low cost. If this obstacle can be removed, research opportunities can be expanded rapidly and brought within reach of many score of able young scholars who now feel cut off from the resources of the few major repositories. Our field needs many more oppportunities for people already engaged in teaching to return to major centers or to go to the Soviet Union or other countries of eastern Europe in order to carry on their research systematically. Younger scholars, with good research skills and research ambitions, should be able every third year to go where they can pursue their research interests full-time and in a stimulating environment, and not be forced to let that research skill wither for lack of adequate research time and research resources. We need more encouragement and support for the publication of the best research studies. A useful program to this end is being carried on by the SSRC Grants-in-Aid program, but more can profitably be done, perhaps through endowing prizes to finance the publishing of the best studies.

Much more can and must be done to study the history and literature, the social and cultural conditions and prospects of the non-Russian peoples constituting almost one-half of the population of the Soviet Union. As our students gain a firm footing in Russian studies, a few of the ablest are adding to their tool kits a knowledge of one or more non-Russian languages of the Soviet Union. In particular Soviet studies need more researchers who can do original work in the history and culture of Ukraine and the Baltic states, of Georgia and Armenia, Azerbaijan and Central Asia. Because of their own multi-ethnic origins, American scholars are perhaps especially interested in the very different situations and forces which shape the relations among the various nationalities in the Soviet Union. To what extent are the Russian language and a basic Soviet culture being accepted as a convenience and a means of vertical mobility? In what measure do national cultures subsist or develop further within a common ideological and political framework? What are the effects of industrial development and geographical mobility on long-settled peoples? Even some of the basic facts are obscure. Perhaps, for example, the census of 1959 will at least open the way to a fuller description of the new patterns of ethnic settlement and occupations.

An important task which has hardly been tackled at all is the comparative study of Communist systems, their economies, their political organizations, and the channels of communication between different layers of the population and among different nationalities. This type of study, resting first on intensive investigations of these problems within the Soviet Union and the countries of east central Europe, should be enlarged to a comparative examination of social and political dynamics in the Soviet Union and Communist China, and North Korea and North Vietnam should not be overlooked. Many concepts and insights can be sharpened by applying acquired research skills to similar problems elsewhere within the bloc. Here a genuinely cooperative effort on a substantial scale is needed.

Perhaps we need to undertake "bloc-wide" studies of the opera-

tions of the Communist Parties, which, despite a common ideology and a common reliance on totalitarian dictatorship, show today some significant differences. Do we know which of these
differences are really important and which are transitional? In
the various systems there are presumably some differences in the
composition and intellectual inheritance of the elites and in the
methods of communication between them and the peoples they
rule. What is meant by the "communization" of culture in each
Communist-ruled country, and what social and cultural factors
favor or resist it? The events of 1956 in Poland and Hungary
showed how superficial the penetration of the popular psychology
had been. What is the role of simulated and "guided" voluntar-
ism? And how far are controls tempered to fit different national
conditions? These and many other subjects invite intensive comparative study today.

VI

Building on a modest but strong prewar foundation, Russian
and Soviet studies, since the war, have attracted a strong core
of able graduate students. To a remarkable extent unequal twin
challenges—a difficult field of investigation and the emergence
of a bipolar world—have recruited a considerable share of the
pick of the crop. During these years several new fields, in addition to history, literature, and language, have matured to a high
level of achievement. Economics has had a startling growth in
the scope and effectiveness of its researches. The study of political
institutions and ideology has advanced greatly. Sociology has
made a good beginning. International relations, dealing with
actions and aims of Communist states and parties, has made a
strong place for itself in teaching, research, and policy study.
Much remains to be done, however, not only in more or less
established fields of investigation, but especially in the study
of geography and natural resources, of psychology and mass cultural changes, of law and institutions, of propaganda and educa-

tion, and of the various institutional and psychological channels through which the Communist leadership exerts its influence upon the peoples it rules and outside the bloc. Many solid achievements, as well as great unfilled needs, are described in the following chapters.

Scholars working in the Russian field can review with some confidence the healthy way in which, on the whole, they have taken in their stride the adjustment to the polarization of power in world politics. One can imagine situations in which serious damage could have been done, from within and without the academic community, to the integrity and self-respect of the scholar-citizen. In fact, however, the basic effect of this polarization has been to lend greater urgency and inspire greater efforts to advance Russian studies. The spirit of scholarly endeavor, the ambition to serve our democracy by striving for objectivity of analysis, has been a strong armor against the risk of non-scholarly and even anti-scholarly interference.

Some people argue that the expansion of Russian studies has been a by-product of the "cold war." As a matter of record, several of the basic decisions to develop this field of study more effectively were taken before the outlines of the postwar division of the world had become clear. In 1945-47, in planning the first major steps, American students of Russia hoped that we could have, if not intimate, at least regular and continuing intercourse with Soviet scholars in related disciplines. The planning of Columbia's Russian Institute, for example, included provision for inviting a visiting historian from the Soviet Union. In 1947 Ernest J. Simmons visited Moscow, armed with a basketful of useful proposals for scientific cooperation and cultural exchanges. These and other proposals, even if rebuffed by Soviet officialdom, testify to the desire, on the part of our leading scholars and institutions, to enter into mutually beneficial cultural and academic exchanges even as the cold peace was turning into a cold war. And this desire remains strong today. Russian studies have not become a permanent part of the academic landscape because of the cold war or despite it. They are here because it became clear by 1945 that Russia is one of the great powers, with a powerful system of its own, with a great impact in world politics. Scholars and academic statesmen realized that we needed to learn far more about Russia, to study it more tenaciously and more systematically than we had previously studied any other system of power.

An important by-product of the development of Russian and Soviet studies has been the strengthening of the research function within government. This has been accomplished in large part by younger scholars who have gone from the area centers into government research posts; within government their reputation stands high and they have made valuable contributions to the background of policy, some also in the formulation and execution of policy. Government agencies have come to feel that they can benefit a great deal in meeting their responsibilities through sending selected officers to the major centers for advanced training in research, and they have done so on a substantial scale. Finally, many individual scholars, in their personal capacities, have been called on by government agencies to advise them. The strength and flexibility of our democratic system is illustrated by the way in which, from the founding of the Research and Analysis Branch of the Office of Strategic Services in 1941, and the many other war-time demands for the expert services of area specialists, there has been a steady strengthening of systematic research within government, often paralleling that done in the university centers. The interchange of research experience and sometimes of research materials has been beneficial to both.

One of the strengths of Russian studies is that, whatever fears and hopes its practitioners feel as citizens, they have worked long and hard to make sure that their conclusions are founded on solid research. Compared with the value-laden judgments and predictions emanating from many non-research sources, the sober findings of our Russian area specialists stand up well. No one, even the detached scholar, can or wants to live and work without expressing his deep-felt values as a member of a democratic society. But, by stating those values explicitly, he can go on to fulfill his special role, that of strengthening the democratic world, helping it to take better informed and more farsighted decisions, by providing it with the best fund of systematic knowledge which he can work out, without regard to whether he or others like or dislike his findings.

A scholar has a special duty to be vigilant against his own preconceptions and preferences and to be willing constantly to test his previous conclusions against new evidence or data previously neglected. In this way he serves both as a scholar and as a citizen. As a citizen he takes part in many non-research activities. As a scholar he always returns to that central purpose of making his research as nearly objective as possible, not by renouncing values, but by making them explicit through his self-disciplined effort to rise above them as he studies and analyzes a system which, very different from our own in its values, constitutes, in the world of today, a dynamic and challenging focus of power.

John S. Curtiss

2. HISTORY

I

A STRIKING FEATURE of historical studies in the United States before 1917 was the very slight interest in Russia. American students who worked in the field of European history turned chiefly to England and France, and to a lesser degree to Germany and Italy. The vast area east of the Elbe and the Adriatic was largely *terra incognita*. Eugene Schuyler's work on Peter the Great remained an isolated landmark for thirty years.[1] Archibald Cary Coolidge vigorously promoted Russian history at Harvard University, and took the initiative in building up one of the first large libraries in this field.[2] His student, Robert J. Kerner, produced an outstanding bibliography of Slavic Europe.[3] A few years earlier another student of Coolidge, Frank A. Golder, had published his volume on Russian expansion on the Pacific.[4] At about the same time, Samuel N. Harper of Chicago was investigating Russian life and politics on the spot in the company of Bernard Pares.[5] George Kennan had aroused special interest in one aspect of Russian life, the exile system, and ten years later Senator Beveridge wrote eloquently of Russian imperialism for the *Saturday Evening Post*.[6] There was little demand for Russian history, however, among university administrators, professors, or students.

It was the events of the First World War and the revolutions of 1917 that definitely brought Russia into the forefront of American interest. During this period a considerable number of Americans were present in Russia in various capacities and, as our citizens realized their ignorance of this now vital area, the ground was prepared for scholarly work. The events of the Russian civil war did much to stimulate the growth of Russian studies in this country, as Russian scholars, uprooted by the revolutionary turmoil, began to make their way to our shores to find places in academic life. In addition, a small band of young men, after serving in various missions in Russia during the immediate post-war period, returned home with some knowledge of the language and the people and entered academic life. Thanks largely to these two sources, Russian historical studies in the United States began to develop and it became possible to train graduate students in the field. Nevertheless the progress was far from rapid, as few students took the trouble to learn the language and there were few academic opportunities for scholars in the field of Russian history.

Able journalists helped to supply the need for historical works, with little competition from the academic historians. By 1941, however, the second generation of historians in the Russian field, chiefly trained in this country, had begun to reach respectable proportions, only to have their historical studies almost completely cut short by the demands of World War II.

Russian historical studies in the United States before 1945 were thus limited, both in volume and in scope. There was a considerable flow of memoirs of Russians who had fled their homeland, among them Kokovtsov, Rodzianko, Sazonov, and Kerensky. Among the Americans who published their memoirs of experiences in Russia were Ambassador D. R. Francis, Major General William S. Graves, and Raymond Robins. The Economic and Social History of the World War sponsored by the Carnegie Endowment for International Peace published a dozen very useful volumes on various aspects of Russia's participation in the conflict, written by competent Russians.[7] Furthermore, valuable works were produced by men who were not professional historians: Louis Fischer's *The Soviets in World Affairs* (2 vols., 1930) and W. H. Chamberlin's *The Russian Revolution* (2 vols., 1935) are notable examples.

The historical monographs of the period between the World Wars deal with both the Imperial and the Soviet period. In the former group are studies of limited aspects of Russian foreign policy,[8] and on a wide variety of domestic problems.[9] For the postrevolutionary period there have been studies of the famine of 1919-23, of Soviet policy in the Arctic, of the economics of the First Five-Year Plan, and of the development of the Red Army; and works on the Soviet government, the church, the Revolution, and foreign policy.[10] Work was also done on the intellectual history of the two periods.[11]

II

When the Second World War ended the number of Americans interested in Russia had greatly increased. Many who had learned to use Russian during the war took up the study of Russian history and institutions at the newly established university centers for area studies. Russian specialists who had been in government service returned to academic life. In a few years these developments were reflected in the publication of increasing numbers of books and articles dealing with the entire range of Russian history.

The most impressive general works to appear since World War II are the three volumes of George Vernadsky—*Ancient Russia, Kievan Russia,* and *The Mongols and Russia*—and Michael T. Florinsky's two-volume *Russia: A History and an Interpretation.*[12] Shorter studies have dealt with the Slavs and the history of early Russia;[13] with the rule of the boy Tsars Ivan and Peter; with British travelers in eighteenth-century Russia; and with Siberia.[14] Many of the writings on the last century of the Tsars have dealt with aspects of Russian intellectual history, and especially the Marxist movement and its leaders in Russia.[15] In addition, there have been monographs on Alexander I, Speransky, the reformed Russian law courts, the school system, the end of the Georgian monarchy, and the Socialist Revolutionary Party during the revolution.[16] In the realm of foreign affairs there have been works on Alaska and on Russian policy in Asia; on Russia and Europe from 1789 to 1878; on the Baltic question; on Tsarist policies during the war; and on Russian influence in the Balkans.[17]

Among the books dealing with the Soviet era two that treat the revolutions of 1917 are in the form of memoirs.[18] Apart from college textbooks, with which this essay is not concerned, a number of general interpretations of the Soviet regime have been published which are at least partly historical in character.[19] There are also several studies devoted to various aspects of the political and social system.[20] An important group of studies has been concerned with the workings of the Soviet regime in certain local areas: the Ukraine, Turkestan, Transcaucasia, and Belorussia.[21] In addition, there are accounts of the Russian Orthodox Church, an analysis of the Vlasov movement, and several studies of Soviet historiography.[22] Attention should likewise be called to the significant treatises, many of which are historical in character, in the fields of political science, economics, literature, and social relations.[23] A good many historians have been drawn to the study of Russian-American relations. A number have concentrated on the period immediately following 1917,[24] while others have selected a broader period or have emphasized relations during World War II.[25] Several studies have also been written on other aspects of Russian foreign policy.[26]

In addition to the above works by American authors during

the period under consideration, another group of books has become available through the Translation Project of the American
Council of Learned Societies. These are works by Soviet authors,
a few of which are of special interest to historians. Research by
recent refugees from the Soviet Union, some of which is historical in character, has been made available in English by the Research Program on the U.S.S.R. Of particular interest to historians of the Soviet period will be the studies which are being
prepared under the auspices of the Research Program on the
History of the Communist Party of the Soviet Union.

Brief mention should also be made of the work of British,
European, and Asian scholars, in order to place recent American
scholarship in its proper setting. Significant historical studies
published abroad have dealt with the period before 1917, but
the principal interest has inevitably been in the Soviet period.
The contribution of Canadian, British, and European scholars
has indeed been so extensive that space does not permit a discussion of individual authors and works. These can be followed,
however, in the various Canadian and European journals devoted
to the field of Russian studies.[27] Well-informed studies of various
aspects of Russian affairs have also been published by specialists
in Turkey and India.[28] At the same time, there is a growing interest in Russian history on the part of Japanese scholars.[29]

III

Impressive as is this list of achievements, one is even more
impressed by the opportunities and needs for further work in
this field. Much more has been written about the early Russian
Marxists than about their predecessors, the liberals and radicals
of the mid-nineteenth century. We have no satisfactory treatment of Petrashevsky, Chernyshevsky, or the Land and Liberty
Society. No one has produced monographs on the Imperial administration, the censorship, the nobility, the *zemstvos*, the mer-
chant class, or the towns. Little or nothing has been written on

the taxation system, the liquor problem, foreign trade, or the development of the railways. Russian military history remains to be written. We lack satisfactory biographies of most of the Tsars, to say nothing of statesmen and politicians like Gorchakov, Miliutin, D. A. Tolstoy, Plehve, Stolypin, and Sazonov. There are no effective studies of the political parties such as the Mensheviks, the Cadets, the Octobrists, and the Union of the Russian People. There is no good history of the Revolution of 1905. The Duma as a whole has not been properly studied. Little has been done on the Ukraine, the Caucasus, Siberia, and the Baltic states under the Tsars or on the major Russian cities. There are no comprehensive studies of Tsarist foreign policy in the nineteenth and twentieth centuries.

Some may object that sources are lacking for many of these topics: few memoirs are available; there were no parliamentary debates before 1906; a free press did not exist. Nevertheless, the Russians expressed themselves abundantly, in spite of the censorship, and much source material has been printed in historical journals. We have in this country magnificent libraries that contain extensive collections of Russian books and periodicals.[30] In addition, there are the resources of the European libraries to supplement ours. Finally, it may be possible in the future to have access to Soviet libraries and archives. Much of the pre-Soviet period is no longer particularly controversial, and Soviet authorities may be willing to permit research by American scholars.

One may ask whether Americans can add significantly to work already being done by Soviet historians. Much historical writing has indeed been done in the U.S.S.R., of which a great deal, especially since 1934, displays abundant documentation and analysis of evidence. Certain Soviet historians, whose skill and scholarly ability are unquestioned, have produced excellent studies dealing with early Russia up to the middle of the nineteenth century. On the other hand, Soviet historical writings on the last one hundred years are rarely satisfactory to Western scholars.

The chief criticism is that they are subject to censorship by the Communist Party, which rejects findings at variance with the prevailing Party line and imposes the obligation to support its objectives. Furthermore, Soviet historians do not normally have access to archives in Western countries and are not always in touch with the achievements of Western scholarship. For these reasons, American historians feel that they cannot be satisfied with the conclusions of Soviet historians, but must themselves study the evidence and draw their own conclusions.

In studying the Soviet period students encounter greater difficulty than in research on the earlier years. Decision-making has become increasingly secretive; there is not the give-and-take of party politics; and speeches in the Supreme Soviet are remarkably similar in content. The press, which is fully controlled by the Communist Party, is used as a medium to propagate ideas sponsored by the Party and to eliminate opposing influences and ideas. When a prominent Communist is "relieved" of his duties, he does not publish his memoirs. Nevertheless, by patient, intelligent reading of Soviet periodicals and books, a surprising amount can be learned, as the excellent monographs published in this country show. The present difficulties of studying the Soviet system are no greater than in the last decade and may even be somewhat less. The importance of learning as much as possible about the Soviet regime is greater than ever.

A substantial amount of work is at present in progress, in the form of doctoral dissertations or of postdoctoral studies. Among these are monographs dealing with various governmental institutions of the Imperial regime, such as the administration, the political police, the bureaucracy, the army, and the First Duma. Studies are being made of various aspects of social and political thought in Russia, including the views of conservatives like Karamzin and Pobedonostsev, the Slavophiles, Herzen, Mikhailovsky, and Chernov. The careers of such prominent figures as Witte and Nicholas II are also being studied. Other projects analyze groups outside the government, among them the Congresses of Representatives of Trade and Industry, the United Nobility, the intelligentsia, and the Old Believers. A few works discuss Russia's foreign relations before 1917—with the Balkans, Iran, and Korea, as well as with the Dutch in the seventeenth century.

Many more scholars are at work on the period from 1917 to the present. Studies of the Provisional Government of 1917 and of the Russian peasant in revolt are in process. A relatively large number of investigations deal with Marxist ideology in Soviet Russia, chiefly as expressed by individual leaders of the 1920's and 1930's. Other subjects under study are the consolidation of the Soviet system in central Asia, the decline of the Jewish community in the U.S.S.R., and the NKVD. The problems that are presently being studied in the field of Soviet foreign relations include Allied intervention in southern Russia in 1919, the establishment of the Comintern, and various aspects of relations between the Soviet regime and Germany, Great Britain, and France. Other investigations discuss Russia at the Paris Peace Conference, and Russia and the League of Nations. Still others concern Soviet dealings with Japan, China, and India.

In spite of these undertakings, however, the catalog of important problems that still require study is long. The several studies of national minorities in the U.S.S.R. have rarely extended beyond 1927, and most of them stop with 1921 or 1922. It is highly important to know how these peoples have fared since then. Moreover, other nationalities, such as the Armenians, the Georgians, the Caucasian mountaineers, the Baltic peoples, the Yakuts, to mention only a few, should be investigated. This should be attempted in spite of the inevitable obstacles in a police state. There is need for a careful and thorough study of the fate of several important religious bodies under Soviet rule, such as the Baptists and the Moslems. An up-to-date treatment of Soviet education, as well as of the health system, would be of value. The whole field of Soviet military history has hardly been touched. Additional problems that might be considered with advantage include the history of individual Soviet cities or of individual industries, and the history of Soviet labor. Undoubtedly the list could be extended further.

Soviet foreign relations should be another fruitful field for research. There is need of a whole series of monographs on Soviet relations with individual countries: Great Britain, France, Germany, Italy, Finland, Poland, Turkey, Iran, Afghanistan, Japan, and China after 1927 are examples. Soviet relations with Yugoslavia also need further study. It also seems likely that the list will increase, with the inclusion of such countries as the Arab states, India, Indonesia, some of the new countries of Africa, and possibly some Latin American states. A monograph on the U.S.S.R. and the United Nations is near completion, but studies are needed of the role of the Soviet Union in the various councils and commissions of the United Nations and in its specialized agencies. Finally, the whole question of the relations between the Soviet Union and the other members of the Soviet orbit offers interesting problems in contemporary history.

IV

There is good reason to expect that in the course of the next generation these and many other specific problems will receive the attention of careful research. There is less cause to be optimistic, however, regarding the achievements of American scholars in examining the broader issues raised by Russian history. In the quarter of a century since the study of Russian history began to attract increasing attention from American scholars, historians in the United States have given relatively little thought to the meaning of Russian history. The predominant assumption appears to have been that Russia was following the same path as western Europe in the march toward democracy. It had for various reasons been delayed in its progress along this path, to a greater degree but in much the same way as Germany and Italy had been delayed by comparison with Britain and France. But can it not be just as readily maintained, for instance, that Russian society has always been distinct from the societies of western Europe, despite many intimate ties in space and time, and that the institutions and values of a fully modern Russia will be significantly different from those generally accepted as the basis of the "Atlantic" states?

The questioning and discussion of such assumptions is an important task for historians, and it is a weakness of American scholarship in Russian history that problems of this type are not more generally debated. The exploration of interpretive questions might serve to enrich the work of a new generation of scholars, and might have a significant bearing on their evaluation of Russian personalities and events.

One approach to general problems of this character is that provided by periodization. We have heard a great deal concerning periodization from Soviet historians in recent years, although their debates have been determined as much by politics as by scholarship. This is nevertheless an important subject, for the division of history into periods is fundamentally a question of interpretation. In the case of Russian history, a typical issue in need of further debate is the analogy frequently made between the Russian revolutions of 1917 and the French Revolution of 1789. It is often maintained that the Russian events were simply the French Revolution taking place at last in eastern Europe, and indeed it is tempting to contrast the Old Regime with the New in Russia as in France. Yet just as good a case can be made for 1861 as the dividing line in Russia between the agrarian and the industrial era, or between autocracy and the beginnings of self-government. Such choices are not only of theoretical interest, but in this instance would have a significant bearing on one's evaluation of the last years of the empire.

Another means of locating Russia's proper place in European and world history is the comparative method. Much has already been written about the relationship of Russia to Europe. One suspects that much could also be learned by comparing the development of modern Russia with that of Turkey, Japan, and perhaps other Asian states. The comparative method has many pitfalls, but it remains an essential approach to the understanding of any society. All scholars use this approach in some measure in the study of a foreign country, whether they realize it or not, and a more systematic and comprehensive application of this method in the case of Russia might well produce valuable insights.

Finally, it must be acknowledged that the interest of American historians in Russia has focused largely on political and intellectual developments. Apart from a few outstanding volumes in the field of economic history, there has been little interest in what might very vaguely be called Russian society. This attitude also underlies much American thinking about Russia. Political developments and foreign policy are often discussed without reference to the social and economic forces which form an inseparable part of any national scene. These forces are particularly significant for an understanding of Russia, because it is specifically these aspects that are so different from those familiar to American historians. Many of the limitations of American historical work on Russia may be explained by its two-dimensional approach. It is true that social and economic history requires a type of source material far less accessible than that needed for political or intellectual history, and this may to some extent explain this shortcoming in American historiography. If new opportunities for research in the Soviet Union are opened up in the years to come, it should be possible to probe into the many aspects of Russian society that remain unexplored. This would help to round out our understanding of Russian history, and would also encourage the development of interpretations embracing the totality of the Russian experience.

Gregory Grossman

3. ECONOMICS

I

THE AMERICAN STUDENT of the Soviet economy has been performing a complex role in the last ten or twelve years. As an economist working on a particular economic system, he has been concerned with comparative studies, specific institutions, their interrelationship, their antecedents, their evolution, and—last but not least—their impact upon the functioning and achievements of the Soviet economy. As a student of the Soviet Union, he has contributed—whether much or little is for others to say— to the progress of cognate areas of Soviet studies and to integral conceptions of the Soviet society and polity. His government has often called upon him to serve as an intelligence analyst, or justified its support of aspects of his research from the standpoint of some ultimate (fortunately, often very "ultimate") intelligence value. And whether he wished it or not, his work has had political implications in the world arena.

If we had the Russian penchant for marking jubilees, we should have taken note in 1957 of the tenth anniversary of the publication of a symposium entitled "Appraisals of Russian Economic Statistics."[1] While that collection of essays certainly was not the beginning of serious research in the United States on the Soviet economy, and while the contributors did (and still do) represent a rather wide range of opinion, the appearance of the symposium may well be regarded as having ushered in a new, postwar phase in study of the Soviet economy. Thumbing now through its pages, one is both comforted and disturbed by the realization that its topics—measurement of Soviet economic growth, structure of national income—are still among the main concerns of our research, and its statistical and conceptual problems are still with us. True, we now know (or think we know) much more about the Soviet economy than we did then, and there are now many more of us sharing the knowledge. Our answers have raised more questions; we know our tools better, and we trust them less; we dispose of more data, but we dispel fewer doubts. This, I suppose, constitutes scholarly progress.

It is not only, however, the distance we have traveled that prompts us to take our bearings anew. The terrain itself has changed markedly of late, and in several respects it is not as forbidding as it once was. Some of these changes are too well known to be more than enumerated here: the partial relaxation of secrecy on the part of the Soviet Union, resulting especially, from the economist's standpoint, in the publication of statistical compilations and other factual information; the possibility of traveling in the U.S.S.R., visiting libraries there, obtaining microfilms, establishing personal contacts and maintaining correspondence; and so forth. Other newly created opportunities are less frequently listed. They include: insights into the Soviet economic system through experienced Polish eyes, now that the Poles are more communicative and less constrained; glimpses of Soviet economic problems reflected in the Polish and Yugoslav attempts at institutional reform; the possibility of interviewing a more recent group of refugees from the satellite countries; and lastly, the bare inception of Soviet-American debates contained in the newly manifested readiness of Soviet economists to join the issue directly.[2]

II

Without trying to draw a sharp line between description and explanation, or between measurement and interpretation, we must recognize that the problems of data in the Soviet economic field have been no less serious than the problems of explanation and interpretation. Much of the economist's work has, therefore, been directed first to answering the questions "What?" and "How much?" before he can try to answer the questions "How?" and "Why?"

The necessity of creating its own data has left a definite stamp on the character of this branch of economics. Because the data were otherwise not readily available, or where available, not reliable, or at least had to be checked, the economist has had to dig up the basic figures and to combine them into assimilable and digestible aggregates. In moments of complacency he has compared himself with the archaeologist; probably a wishful thought, since the latter does not have to contend with deliberately deceptive materials.

Digging, whether literal or figurative, is at once ennobling and degrading. It develops one's insight, one's sense of order and proportion. But it also conduces to pedantry, to search for search's sake, to dodging larger issues, and—through an excessive spirit of competition against one's sources—to the possibility of denigrational bias. Digging takes time and energy at the expense of analytical study. It may block broader perspectives. Last but not least, it may have tended to alienate the economist from his fellow students in other disciplines, who could not share his excitement over exhuming statistical fragments and possibily even regarded it as a sign of intellectual narrowness.

Hence the partial relaxation of statistical secrecy by the U.S.S.R. is welcome for more than its own sake. Yet, withal, the economist need not be ashamed of the results of the intensive digging that dominated the first postwar decade of research. His estimates of the basic figures (index numbers are something else again, as we shall see) by and large have been closely confirmed by the statistical handbooks, which began to appear in 1956, and even by data released earlier. Indeed, it is perhaps not absurd to suggest that the success of Western students in reconstructing basic Soviet figures may have contributed to the Soviet decision to publish the data in the form of organized compilations.

Lest the reader get an unduly optimistic impression, it must also be mentioned that much important information has not yet found its way into the statistical handbooks. Such basic and, one may add, nonmilitary items as the absolute size of the grain crop,* the size and composition of the agricultural labor force, and the amount of money in circulation, to name but a few, must still be estimated from fragmentary or indirect evidence. More significantly, the mere assembling of previously scattered or unpublished figures between the covers of a few statistical abstracts in no way enhances their reliability, meaningfulness, or comparability. These problems remain as acute and time-consuming as ever.

Most of the digging, however, has not been an end in itself, but has served as a first phase for one of three types of study: construction of index numbers, compilation of national accounts, and industry studies. In the construction of index numbers— temporal series and international comparisons on production and real earnings, prices and costs, and productivity—and in the construction of national accounts, postwar American research on the Soviet economy has accomplished its most impressive volume of work, completed or well on the way. As a result, the main dimensional outline, independent of Soviet claims, of the growth in output and productivity since 1928 (over-all and by major sectors), of the movement in prices and wages, and of the structure of the economy and certain flows within it during a number

---

* Since this was written absolute data on the grain harvests in 1953 and 1958, and thereby through percentage links with other years of the 1950's as well, have been released (*Pravda*, December 16, 1958).

of "benchmark years" has emerged or is in the process of emerging. Considering the shortage of qualified personnel and the paucity and intractability of the data, this is a decade's achievement that economists—most of them American, but many of them west European—need not be ashamed of.

It would be quite impossible to subject such a large amount of quantitative work to a systematic review within the compass of this brief paper. In fact, I shall not attempt even to cite systematically all major work of this kind. Rather I shall confine myself to some general remarks regarding such studies.

(a) The results of index number studies for a country like the U.S.S.R., where the temporal and international differences in economic structure are pronounced, may be expected to vary significantly with the regimen of weights and other formal statistical properties.[3] Clear conception and exposition of the method employed by the author of any such attempt are therefore mandatory. Fortunately, this has been the case with most American work on index numbers for the Soviet economy.

(b) It follows from this, considering the different purposes for which the indices are wanted and the formidable problems of data, that a multiplicity of methods (formulae, weighting regimens) of constructing index numbers is often necessary and desirable. However, a consequence of the variety of methods used is that tests of mutual consistency are not always possible. Instead, tests of the validity of the individual computations must often rest largely on conclusions with regard to the representativeness of the sample on which they are based and the appropriateness of the formal methods of their construction.

(c) This relativism in the meaning of indices not only tends to hinder the putting together of a coherent picture of the Soviet economy over time and in relation to other economies, but may also tend to impede communication between the economist and other students of the Soviet Union, as well as between the economist and the general public. At times it seems to have hampered understanding even between economists. Similar problems arise with respect to cross-sectional accounts, whose meaning is entirely relative to the standard employed (e.g., efficiency standard, welfare standard).[4]

(d) Conceptual problems apart, and notwithstanding all the digging and piecing together, nearly all attempts at measuring the performance of the Soviet economy have, of course, been faced by serious limitations on data, especially with regard to the secret sectors. Without trying to minimize the difficulty, we may note that the limitation need not always be as severe as might be assumed at first glance, if only because data on *both* rapidly growing and slowly growing sectors and items have been withheld by the Soviets, the former generally for reasons of strategic security, the latter for reasons of prestige. Thus it is possible, at least for some subperiods and for broad sectors of the economy, that the sample of items (e.g., industrial commodities) available to us may not be too unrepresentative of the whole. Moreover, we may suspect a tendency toward inverse behavior (at least over short periods) between the secret areas at the two extremes, the lag in the low-priority items releasing the resources that permit the rapid advance in the high-priority items.

Attempts to circumvent secrecy by the deflation of current ruble magnitudes through the use of price indices[5] run into the difficulty that in the secret sectors the price indices, if at all constructible, are among the least reliable, and the current ruble figures are among the least credible. On the other hand, certain tests of plausibility can be applied to the price indices, and tests derived from the logic of double-entry bookkeeping to the ruble values. Hence this approach is certainly valuable when applied and interpreted with circumspection.

Another method of circumventing secrecy (or unreliability, or nonmeasurability) of data on output is by estimating changes in output from changes in input. (This method is, of course, applicable to international as well as to temporal comparisons.) The input-output relation may be assumed to be linear homogeneous over time or space, or may be estimated from the non-Soviet environment or from Soviet experience during less secret periods. By means of this general method, estimates have been made of the growth of industrial output, by Shimkin and by Seton (Oxford); of the magnitude of Soviet industrial output in relation to American, by Shimkin; of the growth of construction, by Powell; of agricultural output, by Johnson.[6] Although the postulate with regard to the input-output relation is rarely entirely satisfactory, although the method is at times not without recognizable statistical bias, and although the concrete meaning of the result is not always clear (which limits its use for analysis), input-derived estimates are unavoidable in some cases, and provide welcome alternative estimates in other cases. The possibility of undertaking further estimates of this nature by utilizing such input data as total caloric consumption, use of electric power for drive purposes, volume of goods carried by transport, and so forth, may be worth considering.

(e) Major statistical studies based on extensive digging are very costly and time-consuming. I am thinking not so much of the monetary expense as of the time of the senior research personnel and of the qualified junior staff. Personnel resources are scarce, their training is slow, and their attrition rate is substantial. True, the cost in lost opportunity for other kinds of work is not necessarily as great as the input of labor may suggest: some of the junior researchers are not qualified, and some of the senior personnel may not be inclined, to pursue anything but such statistical studies. Nonetheless, it is clear that there are points in all such projects where the incremental returns begin to decline, at the extensive as well as the intensive margins. The question may be legitimately raised at appropriate junctures whether additional statistical coverage, precision, or variety will add as much to our understanding of the Soviet economy as would an alternative use of the same scarce resources in a different line of investigation, such as (to pick an example) analysis of the how-and-why variety.

In raising this question, I am looking at the problem from the standpoint of the subject as a whole. I do not mean to question the individual's right to pursue research according to his own inclinations. Nor do I mean to suggest that the yardstick to be applied to returns and costs is not an ambiguous one.

(f) Lastly, there is the question of timeliness, which derives largely from the relationship of Soviet studies to the national interest. The implications are twofold: (i) Time as such, apart from money and research resources, cannot be entirely dismissed in the balancing of returns and costs (as discussed in the paragraph above). It is hardly necessary to add that this is not an argument for undue haste and sloppiness. (ii) Continual consideration should be given to bringing up to date and revising past statistical work as fuller, more accurate, and more recent information becomes available.

<h3 style="text-align:center">III</h3>

Less has been done by way of intensive and rounded monographic work on individual segments of the economy (such as industries, sectors, or regions) than has been accomplished in the accumulation of data. To qualify fully for this category, a study must be at once descriptive, historical, statistical, and analytical, and must investigate nearly every major facet of the segment and relate it to the rest of the economy.

I know of only three completed industry studies, in the full sense of the term: Jasny's on prewar agriculture, Gardner Clark's on steel, and Hunter's on transportation.[7] In addition, a small number of monographs inquire into a more limited range of problems with respect to individual industries; Shimkin on minerals, Hardt on electric power, Blackman on locomotives, and Sosnovy on housing are good examples,[8] though of varying scope and length. The extant industry studies are only a beginning of what could be done and, for a better understanding of the Soviet economy, probably should be done.

No regional economic studies, except minor ones, have been published in the period under review, to my knowledge. The limited number of substantial industry studies, major or otherwise, and the lack of major regional studies can be explained only in part. True, for the years from the middle thirties to the early fifties, the data for individual industries and regions are few. The local press for certain regions is meager, and for some years entirely lacking, while non-Russian languages present an additional barrier to the American student. In some industries the technology may be too unfamiliar and the range of outputs too great and varied to attract a mere social scientist. On the other hand, trade journals and (to a smaller extent) the local press are available in considerable volume for most years, and are not entirely lacking even for the lean years. The recent publication of Soviet regional and sectoral statistical handbooks has greatly added to these materials.

Regional and sectoral monographs are desirable not only—perhaps not even primarily—in themselves, but also as avenues of approach to an understanding of the system as a whole, and to greater knowledge of the how-and-why as well as of the what-and-how-much of the Soviet economy. It would be especially useful if the monographs covered a considerable range of industries and regions in terms of their politico-economic characteristics (priority rating, expansion or stagnation, and so forth). Of course, there would be little point in aiming at a complete set of such monographs. Even if, by dint of great cost and effort, all regions, industries, and sectors were to be represented, completeness in terms of conceptual design and up-to-dateness is never attainable anyway. Often yet another study of the same segment of the economy will contribute more than an expedition into virgin territory.

Nonagricultural labor is a case in point. Solomon Schwarz's

book,[9] the outstanding work in the field, deals essentially with the prewar period; its discussion of the postwar situation is brief and, in some respects, outdated. It would seem, particularly in view of the important developments since Stalin's death, that there is now room for a more up-to-date monograph on Soviet labor as a segment of the economy.[10] On the other hand, the updating of Bergson's statistical inquiry into the structure of Soviet wages,[11] which ends at a point even more remote in time (1934), must wait until a considerable further relaxation of Soviet secrecy takes place. However, a nonstatistical inquiry into the Soviet wage system is probably now feasible, and would be very welcome.

Another such segment is finance, where coverage has been relatively good, thanks particularly to the work of Holzman and Powell,[12] but where much interesting work remains to be done. This is also true with regard to foreign trade, on which much has been published in short pieces, but almost nothing in breadth and depth, at least for a decade.

No comprehensive economic history of any period or subperiod of the Soviet era, not to mention an economic history of the whole era, has been produced by American scholarship in the last decade. Indeed, there is hardly anything that the student can be referred to for a book-length synoptic survey of the evolution of the Soviet economy, except two British works by Baykov and Dobb,[13] both now out of date in several respects. Not only would a competent history of the entire Soviet era, or of the Plan era alone, be highly welcome, but much would be gained by the preparation of comprehensive and competent studies of shorter periods, for example, the NEP, the First Five-Year Plan and collectivization period, the war years (1941-1945), and the postwar reconstruction period.

It need hardly be added that a study of Soviet industrialization by the comparative historical method would also be timely. Such a study would presumably distinguish the elements and features that have been specifically Soviet in this development from those which have close analogues in other historical experiences of rapid industrialization. By the same token such a study would also facilitate the construction of a dynamic model of the Soviet economy, to which reference is made below.

While the shortage of materials is serious for some periods, I believe that even for the war and the postwar reconstruction periods enough data are available in this country for a useful, though more or less tentative, historical analysis. For the years prior to 1930, the availability of material can hardly be called a limiting factor. Thus there must be other reasons for the almost total lack of such works. In some cases the economist has been waiting—often, but not always, justifiably—for the completion of the massive statistical inquiries into the growth of the Soviet economy, and in some cases he has been preoccupied with their compilation. But it is perhaps also true that the American economist, because of his training and experience, feels more at home with a statistical approach than with a historical one, which often overflows into political and social realms. These he tends to consider as outside his domain. And as to the economic history of prerevolutionary Russia, this vast realm the economist (with a few conspicuous exceptions, such as Gerschenkron and Volin) has left to his gracious but somewhat undisciplined colleague, the historian.

IV

Most of us will agree that what-and-how-much cannot be divorced from how-and-why. But if we have already taken considerable strides in describing and measuring the Soviet economy, the task of understanding and explaining it still lies as a steep trail before us—or rather several trails, which, if we blaze them well, should merge into a general model of the Soviet economic system. The several paths that might take us there are partial models pertaining to identifiable sectors or processes within the Soviet economy. (I use the word "model" here broadly, as a comprehensive and internally consistent explanation of the inter-relationship of economic variables and of the behavior of economic agents, without necessarily implying a formal mathematical model.)

We need the model or models for insight into the essential operating and evolutionary characteristics of the Soviet economy, apart from and in addition to our grasp of the organizational and institutional picture. We need to know the *Wirtschaftssystem* as well as the *Wirtschaftsordnung* in order to be able to evaluate the performance of the economy, the significance of reforms such as the mid-1957 reorganization of industry, and the potential for change.

Slowly, we have begun to ascend some of the trails. The greatest progress has been made with regard to a model of the industrial enterprise, particularly in the work of Berliner, Granick, and others.[14] A considerable foundation toward a model of the *kolkhoz* has been laid, thanks to the work of a number of students in this country (Volin, Jasny, Dinerstein,[15] and others) and abroad (especially Alec Nove in London). On the other hand, little is known about the operating principles of other basic economic units: the store, the bank, the *stroika* (construction project), and those twins that have so far lurked in the penumbra of our studies, but which may, in fact, be very significant on the Soviet economic scene—*snab* and *sbyt* (supply and sales organizations).

These are, or would be, theories of the Soviet firm. We can, perhaps, apply to the Soviet scene, with certain adaptations, the Western theories of the household, especially since the abolition of rationing and of some of the restrictive labor decrees. But above and beyond these theories, we need a good analytical study, possibly leading to a model, of the Soviet planned-and-command economy. A fundamental obstacle that may be encountered in the construction of such a model or theory is a lack of systematic and orderly relationship between variables, at least at certain points. But whether this obstacle is insurmountable or not we shall not know until we have tried to build the model.

Very little has been done, in the United States or elsewhere, to investigate systematically the likely elements of such a model: the planning system, "project-making" and technological policy, the price and wage structure, the supply system, the roles of administrative fiat and of economic calculation, and so forth. Thus, apart from incidental or short pieces, there is as yet no study of Soviet planning. The same holds true for the supply system. Admittedly, meaningful information on these topics is hard to acquire. Yet whether the handicap is insuperable cannot be determined until the available data are looked into carefully. (In this connection, some information might be obtained from Soviet defectors, as well as Poles, Hungarians, and East Germans who are now in, or accessible to, the West.)

The aspect of planning known as "project-making" (i.e., engineering design) is a small, moderately explored enclave within this broad *terra incognita*, thanks to a lively Soviet controversy that attracted considerable attention in the West.[16] On technological policy—probably a significant element in the prospective model—some information has been collected and assessed in the same context, and in connection with some of the industry studies already referred to.[17] Here the problem of data is characterized by a plethora of material in the economic and technical literature; the difficulty lies in systematization and digestion. There seems to be general agreement that a thorough study of Soviet technology as, among other things, an autonomous force in the economic picture is now overdue.

That "the meaning of Soviet prices will rise to plague us in almost every study involving rubles"[18]—the last two words are virtually redundant—has been recognized for a long time, but we are still being plagued. The only two books with the phrase "Soviet prices(s)" in the title, both by Jasny,[19] are primarily descriptive and statistical. An analytical investigation of the principles of Soviet price formation and of their effects on the planning and operation of the economy remains to be made.

The recent flood of inquiry by Soviet economists into their own price system, oriented also toward the question of meaningfulness but, of course, from a radically different theoretical basis, should provide considerable new information on the problem. Several studies of the Soviet price structure and system, from different angles, are now in progress in this country, but it will doubtless be some time before the plague is conquered (or kills the patient).

In the meantime, current ruble magnitudes—whether "established" or "adjusted,"[20] as the circumstances may warrant—must be used. The strictures that have been lately raised against "adjusted rubles," and the debate that followed,[21] seem to me to have sharpened our appreciation of the conceptual and theoretical difficulties involved in the manipulation of ruble magnitudes, but not to have undermined the conceptual framework of Bergson's national accounts or Hodgman's index of industrial production, the two studies that have been criticized on this ground.[22]

Lastly, we need a *dynamic* model of the Soviet economy, a "theory of Soviet economic development" to explain the "socialist accumulation" and the specific form of "creative destruction" carried on by the Soviet regime-entreprenuer. In fact, as I have already noted, we do not even yet have a good account of *"wie es eigentlich gewesen"*—of what has and has not been accomplished, and of the qualitative and quantitative role played in the Soviet process of expansion by the various elements, such as capital investment, the transfer of labor, the training of skills, the taking over of technology, and—last but not least—the source of the drive and the mechanism of its transmission. Some valuable work on several such dynamic elements has been done;[23] much more remains to be done, particularly by way of fitting the elements together and rounding out the picture.

It is perhaps not surprising that something as sophistic, exegetic, and arid as post-1930 Soviet economic theorizing has attracted little attention from American economists, who in any event have rarely possessed the background to appreciate and assess the finer points of Marxism-Leninism-Stalinism; nor have they always been convinced of its great relevance to their analysis of the Soviet economy. Soviet economics of the twenties, particularly the great industrialization debates, is something else again. But even this literature, despite the wealth of material and the implications for a theory of economic development in general, has attracted relatively little attention in the United States, Erlich's work being the notable exception.[24]

Without either deploring or defending this neglect of Soviet economic theory, it seems likely that now, with Soviet economists theorizing (in print) much more, and somewhat more sensibly, than a few years ago, interest in what they are saying will increase on this side of the curtain.

As to ideology, this is another area which the economist has, by and large and, to my mind, unfortunately, left to the other disciplines.[25]

V

The completion of the several major extragovernmental statistical projects now under way—the Bergson-RAND deflation of national accounts to obtain a derived picture of physical growth, 1928-1955; direct measurement of Soviet economic growth by the National Bureau of Economic Research;[26] the study by the RAND Corporation of ruble-dollar ratios for purposes of international "deflation"[27]—in addition to the already published, though sometimes more impressionistic and tentative, work along these lines, will constitute a great advance in measurement. Without bringing the work of measuring to an end, it will probably mark the transition from one phase to another in American studies of the Soviet economy. Thanks in part to the digging and statistical foundation-laying, and in part to the change in environment mentioned at the beginning of this paper, students of Soviet economy will be, if they are not already, in a position to shift their emphasis from description and measurement to (what should be no less satisfying to the social scientist) analysis, cognition, interpretation, and explanation. As I have tried to point out, despite the large number of studies that have been produced in the last decade—a record that we need not be ashamed of—we still know little about what makes the Soviet economy and its components tick, what are (to continue the metaphor) its mainspring, escapement, and balance wheel. Statistical studies alone, indispensable as they are, will not give us answers to these questions. Careful empirical work, quantitative and nonquantitative, together with imaginative and perspicacious building of theories and models, "which [in Kaplan's words] we can test, revise, and then apply," may do so.

This calls for monographic studies of industries, sectors, regions, periods, and problems; and, of course, simultaneously trying our hand on the theoretical and model-building plane. Among other things it probably requires a high degree of communication not only within the field (which we have already), but also with contiguous fields in economics and in Soviet studies, and with scholars engaged in studying the other parts of the Communist world. The mechanics of this communication, however, falls outside the purview of this paper.

Needless to say, should the field develop in this direction, its requirements in research materials, in well-trained personnel, and in intellectual focal centers will assuredly not decline. It is difficult to conceive a situation during the coming decade in which the study of the Soviet economy will not elicit scholarly curiosity, or will not be in the national interest. The study of the Soviet economy is approaching not the end of its road but a challenging crossroads, with a broad and inviting panorama beyond.

John A. Armstrong

4. POLITICAL SCIENCE

I

An EXAMINATION of the progress and prospects of Russian area research in political science is complicated by the fact that political science itself, as a scholarly discipline, is hard to define.[1] The discipline has developed pragmatically rather than from a single school of thought or central theory. While there is general agreement as to the central place of some fields of study in political science, others are peripheral or, frequently, shared with other disciplines. Consequently, in this survey it seems best to consider subjects of Soviet area research to be parts of political science if corresponding subjects are commonly treated by American political scientists who are not area specialists.

It must, however, be recognized that wide differences between the Soviet system and the Western constitutional systems that constitute the main object of consideration for most political scientists mean that Soviet area research in political science must omit, or place slight emphasis on, certain topics customarily handled by the discipline, while greatly expanding or emphasizing the treatment of others which have a special relevance for the Soviet scene. For example, the studies of parliamentary organization, procedure, and tactics which form such a large part of our research on the American, British, and French governments can have little if any counterpart in Soviet studies.[2] Direct studies of public opinion, largely dependent on polling techniques, can scarcely be applied to the Soviet Union. Conversely, the totalitarian nature of the Soviet system, in which politics is the key to the understanding of vast ranges of society, means that the political scientist specializing in the Soviet area must be concerned with a large number of subjects which, in the study of Western societies, are customarily left to the sociologist, the economist, or the philosopher.

Anyone considering the state of political science research on the Soviet Union is immediately impressed with the brief period of time in which such research has been carried on. Prior to World War II, the principal contributions of political scientists to this field were sections on the Soviet Union in works on comparative government and studies of international affairs dealing in part with Soviet or Communist policy.[3] Two general treatises on government, Walter R. Batsell's *Soviet Rule in Russia* (New York, 1929) and Bertram W. Maxwell's *The Soviet State* (Topeka, 1934), together with Waldemar Gurian's *Bolshevism: Theory and Practice* (New York, 1932) were pioneering works. The historian Samuel N. Harper also made a number of contributions to the study of Soviet politics.[4]

The intensive development of Soviet area programs immediately after the war included very considerable attention to political science; the bulk of research since that time is attributable at least in part to these programs. Since the area programs were designed to overcome rapidly the alarming shortage in the United States of trained personnel and verified knowledge concerning the Soviet Union, they were undertaken with a considerable sense of urgency. After a decade in which some of the most immediate needs in this regard have been met, it may now be useful to consider the research record of the last ten years and to suggest changes in the nature and direction of political science area research appropriate to the long-term development of this field.

II

Any review of research in political science must necessarily be selective. To be sure, a comprehensive list of works on the U.S.S.R. by American scholars who consider themselves to be professional political scientists, though lengthy, would be of manageable proportions. It would be quite misleading, however, to consider the various subjects without reference to research and publications by foreign scholars, by scholars in other disciplines, and, in certain cases, by nonscholars. Consequently, examples of important books will be considered, regardless of their authorship, while specific articles, except for the most significant or illustrative, will not be mentioned. References to work in progress must also be limited, both because of the frequent difficulty of estimating in advance its nature and value, and because much of this work, especially that comprised in Ph.D. dissertations, is never completed, or completed only after a very long time. In general, all citations in the following pages are illustrative. They are by no means intended as a comprehensive catalogue, which would include many other valuable studies, particularly those prepared by or for government agencies.[5]

Ideology. Whether under this heading, or under the more customary rubric of "political theory," this is one of the core subjects of traditional political science. In dealing with this topic, the political scientist, usually concerned primarily with very recent developments, is obliged to deal with a much greater chronological span. This is true also of ideological studies by political scientists in the Soviet area. While most of the studies —too numerous to list—of Marxist and Russian political thought before the 1917 Revolution have been written by scholars in other disciplines, Alfred G. Meyer's *Marxism: The Unity of*

Theory and Practice (Cambridge, Mass., 1954), is an example of a professional political scientist's work.[6] The same author's book, *Leninism* (Cambridge, Mass., 1957), deals with the ideological background of the Soviet system, a topic also treated by scholars in other disciplines—for example, the historians Bertram Wolfe and Leonard Schapiro.[7] On the whole it seems that the pre-Leninist period and Leninism have been dealt with fairly adequately, and that no special concentration of effort on these subjects is needed.

Less adequately treated is the Stalinist period. Nathan Leites' *A Study of Bolshevism* (Glencoe, Ill., 1953) is an attempt to classify a wide range of Soviet Communist doctrine. Stalin's own political theory, however, has never been subjected to a full-scale analysis by a professional political scientist, a historian, or a philosopher. There are, to be sure, numerous shorter works on aspects of Stalin's thought, especially those by Geroid T. Robinson[8] and George Morgan.[9] Trotsky's life through the 1917 Revolution has been treated comprehensively by Isaac Deutscher.[10]

Reflections of the central ideology in related fields have keen interest for the political scientist. This is especially true for philosophy, where the principal work on the Stalinist period so far completed has been done by the Catholic priests Henri Chambre,[11] Gustav Wetter,[12] and I. M. Bocheński.[13] A recent study by Herbert Marcuse[14] represents a different philosophical viewpoint. In historiography, the reflection of ideological developments is portrayed in *Rewriting Russian History: Soviet Interpretations of Russia's Past* (ed. Cyril E. Black; New York, 1956). A somewhat similar analysis of developments in psychology is presented in Raymond Bauer's *The New Man in Soviet Psychology* (Cambridge, Mass., 1952). Similar studies for other intellectual spheres, whether written by political scientists or others, would be extremely useful.

On the whole, the study of ideology appears to have received fairly adequate attention, with impressive results in terms of completed research. Nevertheless, the rapid ideological developments since Stalin's death mean that this subject must continue to be subjected to close study and reinterpretation.

Power. The heart of political science research, according to many, if not most, members of the profession, lies in the study of power relationships.[15] Because the U.S.S.R. is a totalitarian dictatorship, power is an even more important subject for Soviet area study than it is for investigations of Western systems. Scholars in all disciplines are concerned with this problem, but its direct examination is particularly appropriate for the political scientist.

The most extended study of power relationships in the early years of the Soviet regime is Edward H. Carr's *A History of Soviet Russia* (5 vols.; New York, 1951-58). The period of the Revolution, the civil war, and to a lesser extent the struggle for power in the 1920's seems to be increasingly the province of the political historian, however, since, for this relatively remote period, a sufficient body of documentary and other source material is available to permit the writing of definitive studies.[16]

To the political scientist (and to a considerable extent the sociologist), then, falls the especially difficult task of analyzing power relationships in the obscure period since 1930. Here the Soviet area specialist can be of great use to his fellow political scientists by providing an interpretation of totalitarianism in a modern industrial society. A number of brilliant over-all studies have been completed in the last twelve years.[17] On the other hand, monographs on this subject have been fewer, and of uneven quality. In some cases, the lack of sufficient theoretical background and the inability of the authors to relate their findings to broader interests of political science—defects which some perceptive senior scholars in other branches of political science regard as the most serious confronting area research—have limited the value of the available monographs. Many studies have been reports originally prepared for government agencies.[18] The shortage of monographs on Soviet power relations is unfortunate, for in spite of the brilliance of many of the more general works, further progress in analysis would appear to depend on the development of the necessary foundation of specialized studies.[19]

The complexity of the problem of power relationships requires a slightly more detailed examination of special facets of this subject. One important topic, treated at length, of course, in the general studies and the particular subject of Nemzer's pioneering article mentioned above (see note 19), is the study of the organization and operation of the central Party apparatus.[20] Except for Sidney Harcave's study,[21] the operation and histories of the territorial Party organizations have received less attention, though as Khrushchev's triumph in June 1957 (achieved partly through the support of provincial Central Committee members) showed, power relationships at this level can be of crucial importance. This lack is particularly unfortunate in view of the existence of a vast body of newspaper and other material on the regional Party organizations, frequently far more detailed and more revealing than available sources on the central organization. The gap in intensive examination of the territorial Party organizations has been partially filled, however, by Merle Fainsod's study of the Smolensk Party, governmental, and police apparatuses, based on a unique body of documentary material seized by the Germans in 1941.[22]

Closely related to the topics just discussed are the problems of the composition and circulation of members in the ruling groups of the Soviet Union, and of Party membership in general. Little has been done on these topics, except as a part of general studies, though the same materials available for an examination of regional Party organizations have invaluable information on the composition and circulation of the elite as well. However, several studies of this nature are in preparation.[23]

Since World War II, the study of civil-military relations has been an increasingly important subject for political science. The relationship between the Soviet Army and the Party has occupied a number of scholars. In addition to Nemzer's study cited above, Zbigniew Brzezinski's *Political Controls in the Soviet Army* (New York, 1954) contributes to the topic. Raymond Garthoff's *Soviet Military Doctrine* (Glencoe, Ill., 1954), while only peripherally concerned with political relations, is valuable for background.[24] Among earlier works, D. Fedotoff White's *The Growth of the Red Army* (Princeton, 1944) and Erich Wollenberg's *The Red Army* (London, 1938), are still important. Many other significant aspects of the political role of the Soviet Army remain to be treated, however. Relationships between high-level military and political figures have scarcely been considered. The role of the army as an occupying force in eastern Europe and elsewhere needs detailed analysis.

Unlike the military, the police system is seldom considered a subject of investigation for political scientists in Western countries. The prominent role of the Soviet police has, however, made it a prime object for analysis by students in the Soviet area, in spite of the extreme difficulty of obtaining reliable information. Two recent works discuss the political ramifications of the police system;[25] a Columbia Ph.D. dissertation will deal primarily with earlier aspects of the problem.[26] A number of revealing studies of the role of the police terror in the Soviet political system have been made; Zbigniew Brzezinski's *The Permanent Purge* (Cambridge, Mass., 1956) is an outstanding example. Nathan Leites and Elsa Bernaut in *Ritual of Liquidation* (Glencoe, Ill., 1954) approach the subject from a somewhat different standpoint, while F. Beck and W. Godin in *Russian Purge and the Extraction of Confession* (New York, 1951) present a remarkably detached analysis of the operation of the Soviet terror apparatus, especially since the book is in part based on the authors' experiences as victims of the system. These studies exhaust much of the reasonably reliable material on this topic. However, Fainsod's analysis of the Smolensk documents is particularly revealing on police activities.[27]

Certain special topics in political science which have received little attention in Soviet area studies should be mentioned. Political psychology, brilliantly investigated by a few political scientists such as Harold Lasswell, faces almost insurmountable obstacles in the Soviet field because of the inability of investigators to conduct personal analyses of political figures, except for occasional defectors.[28] The somewhat greater accessibility of Soviet leaders at the present time might make possible some indirect approaches to this type of study. A second special subject, political control of communications, has received more attention.[29] Nevertheless, monographic studies of particular media would be highly useful.

Administration. Public administration is a central subject of political science. If all its ramifications—city and regional planning, local administration, etc.—are considered, it is probably the most developed branch of the discipline. Moreover, it is one in which comparative techniques are particularly appropriate. Comparison of administrative organization or practices under different systems of government frequently reveals the "marginal" effectiveness of the arrangements under consideration.

At first glance, the purposes and extent of Soviet bureaucratic operations appear too foreign to American values and practice to be of much utility for comparative purposes. Closer inspection shows, however, that there are certain administrative problems common to both advanced technological societies. Detailed examination of the Soviet experience may be of the utmost significance, if only to indicate errors (such as organizational "gigantism") to be avoided, or means which must be rejected if values are not to be corrupted.[30] Here, then, is a subject in which intensive study in the Soviet area might contribute greatly not only to a deeper understanding of the Soviet system, but to an increase in knowledge of practical importance for American institutions.

It is rather surprising that comparatively little systematic monographic investigation has been conducted on this subject.

General treatments, particularly those by Merle Fainsod and Julian Towster,[31] provide the framework for understanding Soviet administration from the political science standpoint. In his legal studies, John N. Hazard has devoted much attention to the rules and laws affecting Soviet administration, and to administrative practice as well. But most of the detailed analysis of the operation of the Soviet administration has been carried on by economists, and has only partial or indirect relevance for public administration.[32]

Law. Political scientists customarily confine themselves to the study of constitutional (public) law, except in so far as private law impinges upon political questions. The hazy line between the two types of law in a basically nonconstitutional state makes this distinction of little importance in the study of the U.S.S.R. Moreover, several of the scholars most concerned with the political and social implications of Soviet legal institutions are by training lawyers, and consequently interested in the whole range of Soviet law. Particularly important in this respect has been the work of John N. Hazard[33] and Harold Berman.[34] Several students of these scholars have already made minor contributions to the literature on Soviet law, and their research production may be expected to increase. Two émigré scholars have also made notable contributions to the study of the Soviet legal system: Vladimir Gsovski in *Soviet Civil Law* (2 vols.; Ann Arbor, 1948-49) and George C. Guins in *Soviet Law and Soviet Society* (The Hague, 1953). Soviet law will continue to require close attention, especially since it will doubtless undergo considerable change as a result of the altered political conditions in the U.S.S.R. General direction of this subject appears to be in highly competent hands, however, and no special concentration of effort upon it seems to be required.

Nationalism. The study of national movements is a subject which is rather difficult to place in the spectrum of political science, for it impinges upon the fields of ideology, power relationships, and international relations. Since nationalism is usually a complicating factor in international relations, it has customarily been studied by political scientists mainly interested in that field. In spite of the somewhat indeterminate nature of the subject, it has given rise to some of the most important recent publications in political science,[35] though the subject received a somewhat greater concentration of attention in the 1930's.

Because the U.S.S.R. is a multinational state, and particularly because national differences have played a prominent role in the struggle for power within it, studies of nationalism have been of special importance for the Soviet area political scientist. Most of the studies of Russian nationalism have been written by historians and deal primarily with the pre-Soviet period. The most important study of Russian nationalism in the Soviet period is Frederick C. Barghoorn's recent *Soviet Russian Nationalism* (New York, 1956). There is, however, room for a number of monographic studies of recent manifestations of Russian nationalism, particularly in the occupied Soviet Union during World War II; in the emigration in general; and the use of Pan-Slav ideology by the Soviet regime. Studies of the use of the Russian Orthodox Church as a political arm of the Soviet government would also be useful.[36] Material on all these topics is relatively easy to obtain.

Of the non-Russian nationalities, the Ukrainians have received the greatest attention. A series of monographic studies was initiated by the political scientist John S. Reshetar's *Ukrainian Revolution, 1917-1920* (Princeton, 1952), and followed by the present writer's *Ukrainian Nationalism, 1939-1945* (New York, 1955). Most of the intervening period is the subject of a Ph.D. dissertation (Columbia University, history) being prepared by Michael Luther. A longer period is covered by Basil Dmytryshyn's *Moscow and the Ukraine* (New York, 1956). There is certainly room for more specialized works, but as in other studies of nationalism, there is in this field a special danger of overenthusiastic and partisan efforts to draw conclusions going beyond the available evidence.

Very little has been done on the other European nationalities under Soviet rule. Nicholas Vakar's *Belorussia* (Cambridge, Mass., 1955) provides some information on the recent period. No truly scholarly studies of the Baltic nationalities during World War II have been published, though ample material is available. The other European groups—Moldavians, Finnic peoples—probably do not warrant full-scale studies, though smaller studies would be useful.

The picture is much the same as far as the Georgians and the Armenians are concerned, though these nations are much more important. Much more work has been done on the Moslem nationalities. The historian Richard Pipes' *The Formation of the U.S.S.R.* (Cambridge, Mass., 1954) is most useful on the Turkic groups. A political scientist, Alexander Park, has done a comprehensive study of the Central Asian Turkic peoples in the early period of the Soviet regime.[37] Olaf Caroe's *Soviet Empire: The Turks of Central Asia and Stalinism* (London, 1953) and Walter Kolarz' *Russia and Her Colonies* (New York, 1952) deal with Asian nationalities of the U.S.S.R. The British *Central Asian Review* has published a number of valuable short studies.

On the whole, the field of nationalism appears to have been fairly well developed, and the remaining gaps, while numerous, are at least well defined. A general study of nationality conflict in the U.S.S.R. is much needed, but should probably await the production of more monographs.

International Relations. This subject, which has steadily grown in importance in the general discipline of political science, has been especially significant in Soviet area studies, where it has occupied the attention of nearly half of the political scientists. This is, of course, due to the fact that the immediate concern of Americans with the Soviet Union arises primarily from the influence of that country in international affairs. In this connection, the work of the Council on Foreign Relations in sponsoring analyses of the Soviet impact on international relations is outstanding.[38] Philip E. Mosely, supervisor of the more recent research activities of the Council, has himself contributed what is undoubtedly the most important body of analytical articles on Soviet foreign relations.[39]

A recent tendency of political scientists investigating the foreign affairs of other countries has been to concentrate on such questions as the role of public opinion in policy formation; the process of policy formation within the government; the organization, personnel, and administration of foreign affairs; and techniques of diplomacy. All of these subjects are almost inaccessible to foreigners studying Soviet foreign relations. From his close personal contact and exhaustive study of printed materials, Frederick C. Barghoorn was able to make a contribution to the knowledge of forces behind Soviet policy formation.[40] At the present time, Professor Barghoorn is undertaking an extensive examination of the role of cultural relations, an aspect of Soviet foreign policy which is rapidly increasing in importance.

Memoirs, rather than research publications, remain one of the principal sources of information concerning Soviet diplomacy; but their value can be much enhanced by skillful assembling and editing, as in the case of Negotiating with the Russians (ed. by Raymond Dennett and Joseph E. Johnson; Boston, 1951). Still, much can be done, especially on the organization and personnel of the Soviet diplomatic service.[41]

Little need be said here about the extensive work of collecting and publishing Soviet documents related to foreign affairs, except to note that this effort, generally made by historians, provides an indispensable base for further analysis.[42] These collections are, of course, especially important for the study of Soviet relations with the major powers, and a number of comprehensive studies have been made of the pre-1941 period, where documentation is relatively plentiful.[43] It is unfortunate that full-scale analyses have not been completed on such important and relatively accessible topics of the postwar period as Soviet activities in the United Nations; Soviet attitudes toward atomic energy and disarmament; and the Paris Peace Conference.

Soviet relations with the satellite (and former satellite) countries of eastern Europe have been the subject of numerous books and shorter studies. Among the most important are Hugh Seton-Watson's *East European Revolution* (New York, 1956) and Adam B. Ulam's *Titoism and the Cominform* (Cambridge, Mass., 1952). Many more specialized studies of the imposition of the Soviet system upon the east European countries are needed, however.[44]

Almost as important as the study of the relation of the Soviet regime to its satellites is the problem of the link between the U.S.S.R. and Communist Parties which have not attained power. Important studies have been made of the west European Communist Parties, particularly those by Gabriel Almond,[45] Mario Einaudi,[46] and Ossip K. Flechtheim.[47] David T. Cattell's *Communism and the Spanish Civil War* (Berkeley, 1955) and *Soviet Diplomacy and the Spanish Civil War* (Berkeley, 1957) devote special attention to tracing the connection between Soviet policy and Spanish Communist activities. Careful studies of Comintern and Cominform activities in the European area would be especially useful.

The field of Soviet and Communist policy in the Far East is distinguished by the number of scholars who combine Russian area specialization with intimate knowledge of the language and politics of one or more Asian countries. Among them may be mentioned Paul S. Langer and Rodger Swearingen, *Red Flag in Japan* (Cambridge, Mass., 1952); Benjamin Schwartz, *Chinese Communism and the Rise of Mao* (Cambridge, Mass., 1951); Peter Tang, *Communist China Today* (New York, 1957); Allen S. Whiting, *Soviet Policies in China, 1917-1924* (New York, 1954); and James W. Morley, *The Japanese Thrust into Siberia,*

1918 (New York, 1957).[48] A similar combination of Russian and Middle Eastern specialization is perhaps even more difficult, but is especially needed at the present time.

The foregoing survey of research in the international relations field indicates that the need for specialized works is far from being met, especially in relation to Communist activities outside the Soviet Union. Undoubtedly the most urgent practical requirement of the field at the present time, however, is for an over-all study of Soviet foreign policy since the outbreak of World War II. Such a work is needed not only as a textbook, but to provide a central point for general consideration of the subject, and to point the way for further specialized research. It is probably no exaggeration to say that such a book is the greatest single need in Soviet area studies today.

III

A significant accomplishment of scholarship on the Soviet area has been the sponsorship of a large body of writing by émigrés from the U.S.S.R. Many useful articles have been produced, usually based upon the writer's personal experience or contacts, on such subjects as the police system, concentration camps, Soviet personalities, and Communist Party intrigues. Together with the extensive information collected in oral interviews,[49] this material constitutes a most important source for further analysis of the Soviet political system.

One of the greatest contributions of area studies to the growth of scholarship in the United States has been the fostering of an interdisciplinary approach. In Russian studies particularly, a willingness to transcend traditional approaches rooted in the methodology of individual disciplines has made research both intellectually exciting and fruitful in results. One does, however, often hear the complaint that area specialists who have established such a high degree of communication among themselves have failed to present their findings in such a way as to make them of maximum value to other political scientists. It is said that area specialists do not have the necessary background in theory; are unfamiliar with recent methodological advances; and disregard political developments outside their own area.

The best answer to these criticisms, if they really are significant, is the caliber of the future scholarship by area specialists who are also political scientists. If the scholar is of high intellectual competence and possesses a sound background of training, the direction of his interest is of secondary importance. In this field, as in others where basic research is involved, it would be self-defeating to prescribe subjects for investigation, for often the seemingly most remote topics ultimately have the greatest relevance for practical interests, as well as for the general advance of knowledge.

With full awareness of the overriding importance of individual choice of research interests, it does appear worth while to suggest three fields in which Soviet area research would be especially relevant for political science in general: (1) The study of power relationships in the Soviet totalitarian system should go a long way toward clarifying the general role of power in advanced technological societies. As Franz Neumann pointed out, the extreme or crisis situation often reveals trends or phenomena which are obscured in the "normal" configuration.[50] (2) The study of Soviet administration would be useful because of this circumstance, and also because the administrative experience of any country the size of the Soviet Union is bound to be relevant for other countries. (3) Unraveling the obscure but essential connections between the Soviet regime and foreign Communism is vital to an understanding of international relations in our time. But to be relevant to the discipline as a whole, such research must be reported in a manner which will make it available for comparative purposes. Fortunately, political science, unlike some disciplines, has little recondite terminology or highly elaborated theory which must be mastered as a prerequisite to communication with one's colleagues. Even if some area specialists now lack acquaintance with methodology, classic political theory, or the literature of other fields of political science, such deficiencies can be overcome with relatively little difficulty.

The need for more monographic research, stressed earlier, seems at first glance to conflict with the objective of making Soviet area investigations more relevant to the discipline of political science as a whole. But there is no reason why monographic research, if properly conceived and reported, may not both contribute to the advancement of the body of knowledge on the Soviet area and be relevant to the political science discipline. Monographs on such subjects as composition of the elite, local administration, and ties between the U.S.S.R. and foreign Communists, if properly related to broader problems in the field, should be of great interest to professional political scientists.

IV

As one looks back over the past twelve years, the progress made in the study of Soviet politics appears nothing short of phenomenal. Professional students of politics are now able to draw on a reliable and systematic body of knowledge concerning the U.S.S.R. Granting all the difficulties of exploiting Soviet materials, however, an immense field for investigation remains. During the past five years this field has very considerably expanded because of the heightened tempo of change in Soviet political conditions, and particularly the increase in material made available in the Soviet Union. To this is added the possibility of limited direct observation of Soviet conditions. Moreover, many of the students trained since the war are now approaching the status of established scholars; as a result the field is equipped with a competent staff. Consequently, there is a good prospect for still more rapid development of Soviet area research in political science during the next decade.

George L. Kline

5. PHILOSOPHY AND RELIGION

I

WHILE AMERICAN SCHOLARS have made important contributions to the exploration and illumination of Russian and Soviet philosophy and religion, several of the basic studies have been written by Europeans. This must be borne in mind not only in reviewing the present state of research, but in considering future needs. It is perfectly true, for example, that no definitive study of Soviet philosophy has yet been produced in this country. However, while a brilliant study in this field would always be welcome, the need does not seem so pressing in the light of the existing works by such European scholars as Bocheński, Wetter, and Acton.

There would seem to be two principal reasons for the preponderance of European scholars among students of Russian and Soviet philosophy. First, most—though not all—of the European students of the subject are of Russian or western Slav origin (Zenkovsky, Lossky, Vysheslavtsev, Weidlé, Koyré; Masaryk, Bocheński). A majority of them received their philosophic training in Russian universities; thus they began with a special knowledge of, and interest in, Russian philosophy, together with a general philosophic competence. Second, institutional support for teaching and research in this area has been stronger in western Europe than in the United States. As an instance, the only chair of the history of Russian philosophy outside the Soviet Union is held by Professor Wetter at the Pontifical Oriental Institute in Rome.

Philosophy and religion have often been regarded as closely linked (e.g., among Russian thinkers of the nineteenth and early twentieth centuries—Leontyev, Solovyov, Berdyaev, Bulgakov, Frank); but they have often been regarded as quite distinct, even opposed (e.g., by contemporary Soviet writers). In any case, for purposes of organizational clarity and convenience, these two fields will be treated separately in the present review.

II

The last decade has seen the publication of a number of solid general works on Russian and Soviet philosophy, supplementing and, to a degree, correcting the still valuable work of Masaryk.[1] Professor Zenkovsky's monumental *History of Russian Philosophy* is the major study.[2] Professor Lossky's shorter work is useful for its exposition and criticism of Russian religious thinkers.[3]

Of recent works devoted to individual thinkers and tendencies in Russian thought, we may note the studies by Hepner, Bowman, Hare, and Haimson.[4] Hepner's book on Bakunin and Revolutionary Pan-Slavism is broader than its title would indicate; it has a good deal to say, for example, about Belinsky, Schelling, Hegel, and "dialectical nihilism." Bowman explores Belinsky's successive attachments to Schelling, Fichte, and Hegel, and his later impassioned repudiation of Hegelian impersonalism. Hare's study focuses upon the historical views of nineteenth-century Russian thinkers, offering relatively little exposition or analysis of their ethical, social, or aesthetic theory. Both Bowman and Hare provide copious and well-translated excerpts from such thinkers as Belinsky, Herzen, Chaadayev, and Leontyev. Haimson's book is an exemplary essay in intellectual-institutional-political history; it deals with philosophy only in passing.

None of the works mentioned thus far treats *Soviet* philosophy in any detail. Of full-length studies devoted exclusively to Soviet dialectical materialism, Professor Wetter's is the most comprehensive.[5] Indeed, its exhaustively detailed exposition makes the book difficult reading for the nonspecialist in philosophy. A more accessible book is the admirably concise critical study by Professor Bocheński.[6] It is to be hoped that the publication of the already completed English translation of this work will not be long delayed.

Marxist-Leninist social and political philosophy is perceptively analyzed in the recent works of Professors Mayo and Maček.[7] Both are models of vigorous criticism, although Mayo addresses himself to a somewhat more sophisticated audience than does Maček, who is concerned with the ways in which Marx, Engels, and Lenin were interpreted and exploited by their political offspring. Both studies are well organized and crisply written.

A work by a younger American scholar, quite different in intention from these two, is Stanley W. Moore's recent volume.[8] Unlike Mayo and Maček, Moore concentrates upon exposition, rather than upon analysis and criticism. But he offers a connected account, often with a real gain in clarity, of what Marx, Engels, and Lenin actually asserted on various economic, social, and political questions.

Of broader philosophic scope, and written from a firm foundation in general philosophy, is Professor Acton's annihilating critical study.[9] Strictly speaking, this work does not fall within the scope of a review of Russian studies, since Acton, who does not read Russian, bases himself upon non-Russian or translated Russian sources. However, it is too important a work to omit upon such slender grounds. And Acton's professional competence and perspective more than make up for his lack of familiarity with the

Russian originals. Such studies by non-Slavicists are not only to be welcomed, but invited.

An excellent brief critique of Marxist-Leninist ontology, epistemology, and social philosophy—as yet available only in Russian —is *The Philosophic Poverty of Marxism* by the late Professor Boris Vysheslavtsev, published under the pseudonym "Petrov."[10]

American scholars have published several other books and a number of articles dealing with Soviet philosophy. Professor Meyer's volume on Leninism,[11] a companion to his earlier study of non-Russian Marxism, represents a solid critical contribution. Like the studies by Moore and Maček, it is concerned primarily with social and political philosophy, but it throws fresh light on a number of questions of Marxist-Leninist doctrine in these areas.

Professor Marcuse's recently published study offers a useful and perceptive, though rather technical, historical-cultural analysis and critique of Soviet philosophy.[12] It focuses upon political, social, and ethical theory, but touches upon questions of logic and dialectic. In general, this work represents a valuable supplement to the primarily analytical studies of Vysheslavtsev, Mayo, Acton, and others. Professor Robinson has made a careful analysis of an important phase of Stalinist social and political philosophy.[13] The interesting studies of Leites are not discussed here since they fall within the scope of the review of political science and ideology.[14]

Kline has published three articles of a general nature; a brief survey of the history of Russian (including Soviet) philosophy; a more detailed review of Soviet philosophy since the death of Stalin; and a concise study of Soviet ethical and social theory.[15] He has also contributed a study of the place and influence of Spinoza in Russian and Soviet philosophy, which includes translations of representative samples of Soviet scholarship on Spinoza.[16]

In the field of logic and the philosophy of science, no major study has yet appeared. Alexander Philipov has published a brief monograph on formal logic and dialectic and the ways in which both have been exploited for political ends in the Soviet Union.[17] Questions of logic and philosophy of science are treated in passing by Bocheński, Wetter, Mayo, and Acton.

A detailed historical examination of the development of the Soviet philosophy of the natural sciences during the formative (and relatively uninhibited) years 1922-29 is provided by David Joravsky in an unpublished doctoral dissertation.[18] Joravsky is a historian and his study falls under the category of intellectual and institutional history rather than philosophy; but it touches competently upon philosophic questions at many points. Joravsky has also published articles and reviews dealing with Soviet histories of science and bibliographies of logic.

A certain amount of material on the philosophy of the biological sciences is included in Kline's study of Darwinism and the Russian Orthodox Church.[19] Professor Wetter has completed a monograph on Soviet philosophy of the biological sciences, *Der dialektische Materialismus und das Problem der Entstehung des Lebens: Zur Theorie von A. I. Oparin* (Munich-Salzburg-Cologne, 1958).

There have, as yet, been no substantive studies of Russian or Soviet aesthetic theory, although a brief monograph on this subject by Philipov has been edited for possible publication in English.

In the field of religion and the church, American scholars, including those of Russian origin, have produced a number of valuable studies. Professor Curtiss has written two comprehensive and thoroughly documented historical accounts.[20] Professor Timasheff has contributed an illuminating short book on the subject, and offers many perceptive remarks in his later, more general study.[21] Professor Spinka's history of the Church and its Patriarchs under the Soviet regime, though less exhaustive than the works of Curtiss, has the advantage of being up-to-date and extremely concise.[22]

A limitation of these studies is their exclusive consideration of the Russian Orthodox Church, to the neglect of schismatic (Old Believer), Roman Catholic, Protestant, Jewish, and Mohammedan groups. This is also true of most articles in the field, e.g., Professor Inkeles' excellent brief survey of family and church in the postwar U.S.S.R.[23]

In the field of Russian religious beliefs, attitudes, and values, less work has been done.[24] Both Zenkovsky and Masaryk, especially the former, offer copious material on Russian philosophy of religion and philosophical theology. In addition to the late Professor G. P. Fedotov's study of *The Russian Religious Mind*, there have been valuable anthologies: e.g., the anthology of Solovyov's writings edited by S. L. Frank (London, 1950), and the recent German-language anthology edited by Bubnoff.[25]

III

Philosophy is a discipline in which it is always helpful, and sometimes essential, to know one's intellectual antecedents. This is particularly true of the relation between Soviet and nineteenth-century Russian social and political philosophy. For example, it is difficult, if not impossible, to understand the Bolshevism of Lenin, Trotsky, and Stalin without a knowledge of the radical nihilism of Bakunin and Chernyshevsky, Nechayev and Tkachov. For this reason, among others, most of the following suggestions will be aimed at deepening and broadening our knowledge of nineteenth- and early twentieth-century Russian philosophic thought.

A preliminary point requires clarification. Would it not be desirable, someone might urge, to set up as a major project the production of a "definitive" history of Russian philosophy? Upon reflection, such a task seems less than essential; the works of Zenkovsky, Masaryk, *et al.*, whatever their minor shortcomings, are adequate. And our far from limitless scholarly energies should be channeled into studies which would involve less duplication of effort and at the same time promise a richer intellectual harvest.

In sum, it does not seem worth while to probe exhaustively into the history of Russian metaphysics, epistemology, or philosophy of science. This conclusion flows from the very nature of Russian (and, to a considerable degree, Soviet) philosophizing. From the late eighteenth century to the present day, Russian philosophers have been primarily concerned with questions of ethics, social and political philosophy, and philosophy of history. Compared to their German, French, and English counterparts, they have devoted much less attention to logic, theory of knowledge, and metaphysics. The relation of the individual to society, the problem of good and evil in individual and social life, the meaning and direction of historical development, the relation of national to universal culture—rather than the nature of being and knowledge, or the presuppositions of science—have been the major foci of their philosophic interest.

It thus seems obvious that at least two kinds of comprehensive study are called for: one focusing upon Russian (including Soviet) ethical and social theory,[26] a second upon Russian (including Soviet) philosophy of history. No one has yet undertaken a full-scale study of Russian philosophy (or philosophies) of history. Such questions receive peripheral consideration in recent works by Riasanovsky and MacMaster, and somewhat fuller treatment in Hare's book, as well as in the earlier study by Chyzhevsky.[27] Isaiah Berlin has written a stimulating essay on Tolstoy's philosophy of history.[28] But a major gap remains in the exploration of Russian philosophies of history, which might profitably be filled, either by one comprehensive study, or by a series of short monographs—e.g., on the Slavophile philosophy of history, on Chaadayev, on Kareyev.[29]

There is an urgent need for a series of monographs devoted to the philosophic views of Herzen, Pisarev, Lavrov, Mikhailovsky, Lunacharsky, Bogdanov, Struve, and many other thinkers. James Billington's monograph, *Mikhailovsky and Russian Populism* (Oxford, 1958), is a substantial and conscientious study, but its chief emphasis falls upon personal and institutional history rather than upon the history of ideas.[30]

As indicated above, the field of Russian and Soviet aesthetics and philosophy of art has been little studied. There is room for a good critical monograph, or perhaps two or three of them, in this area.[31] Here again, nineteenth-century doctrine (Chernyshevsky, Dobrolyubov, Pisarev, Tolstoy) illuminates and sets in perspective recent Soviet developments.

It would also be useful to have several additional studies of particular Western philosophers as they have influenced, and been interpreted by, Russian and Soviet thinkers. A study of Hegel in Soviet philosophy, for example, would be a valuable supplement to Chyzhevsky's book, which deals only with pre- and non-Soviet thinkers (see note 27). This might also be done for Kant, Schopenhauer, Feuerbach, Nietzsche, and perhaps Herder and Schelling. Among political and social philosophers, one thinks of de Maistre (whose doctrinal similarities to Tolstoy are emphasized in Berlin's study), St.-Simon, Fourier, and Proudhon. Studies of Kant, de Maistre, Herder, Schelling, Schopenhauer, and Nietzsche would naturally focus upon the nineteenth century. Those devoted to Hegel, Feuerbach, St.-Simon, Fourier, and Proudhon might profitably include both pre- and post-revolutionary developments.

As a logical extension of such analyses, there is need for a series of comparative studies of Western and Russian thinkers.[32] A number of interesting combinations come readily to mind: e.g., Leontyev and Nietzsche, Lavrov and Mill, Mikhailovsky and Spencer. Due regard should, of course, be paid to contrasts and oppositions, as well as to similarities.

More ambitious comparative studies—of entire philosophic schools or of general constellations of cultural values and beliefs —might eventually be carried out, but only by investigators whose linguistic, philosophic, and historical equipment was truly exceptional. A pioneer study along these lines is Dr. Sarkisyanz's work on messianic and chiliastic ideas and attitudes in Russia and the Moslem, Hindu, and Buddhist East.[33] Even a linguist as accomplished as Sarkisyanz, who commands Russian and Persian, in addition to German, French, and English, has had to rely heavily on translated sources.

Of more restricted scope, but of at least equal promise, is a suggestion put forward by Professor Alfred Meyer concerning the exploration of particular concepts, or groups of related concepts, in Russian philosophic thought. He has himself made the beginnings of such an exploration of the concept of culture.[34] Concepts like "progress," "duty," "consciousness," "conscience," "truth-justice" [pravda], could be similarly analyzed. Such a series of limited studies might eventually be brought together in a general dictionary or encyclopedia of Russian and Soviet philosophy.

With respect to the recent Soviet period, philosophy has been a sterile field. However, some of the younger Soviet philosophers (men in their early and middle twenties) have recently turned with enthusiasm and competence to the more technical branches of logic, logistic, and philosophy of science: viz., mathematical logic, axiomatization, proof theory, formalized languages, information theory, "thinking machines." As yet these men have published almost nothing; but when their work begins to appear, it should be carefully studied.

Finally, there is need for a series of good English translations of some of the important works of nineteenth-century Russian thought, e.g., Lavrov's Historical Letters. Even more pressing from the viewpoint of pedagogy and popularization is the need for a series of anthologies drawn from the works of Herzen, Pisarev, Lavrov, Mikhailovsky, and others.[35]

The most obvious lacunae in research on religion in Russia (both before and after 1917) result from the lack of attention paid to religious groups and institutions other than the Russian Orthodox Church—schismatic Old Believers, Roman Catholics,

Protestants, Jews, Armenians, Moslems, Buddhists. This is understandable in view of the historically privileged position of the Orthodox Church, under both Soviet and Tsarist regimes, and the fact that more than two-thirds of the churched population has always been Orthodox. But substantial monographs could profitably be devoted to each of the major non-Orthodox faiths. There may be difficulties with sources, particularly in the case of the Lutherans (in Soviet Latvia and Estonia), the Armenians, and the various sects of Old Believers. But—as an example— with regard to current Protestant (Baptist) groups, there are the files of the journal *Bratskii Vestnik*. And the possibility may develop of on-the-spot observation and interviewing of leaders and ordinary churchgoers of all sects.

A topic of great current interest is the degree and kind of religious conviction among Soviet young people, especially young intellectuals. Such an investigation verges upon the domain of sociology, social psychology, and perhaps cultural anthropology; and it would involve extensive field work. But neither of these considerations seems a sufficient reason for refusing to undertake such a study. Unsystematic observations and inquiries among young Soviet intellectuals in 1956 and 1957 on the part of several scholars suggest that the results might be most illuminating.

In the field of philosophical theology and philosophy of religion, monographs on men like Solovyov, Leontyev, Rozanov, Bulgakov, Frank, and Shestov are needed. It would be valuable, too, to have anthologies from the writings of these and other religious thinkers, on the model of the Solovyov anthology edited by Frank, or general source books bringing together selections from several writers, like that of Bubnoff referred to above (note 25).[36]

IV

The present situation and future prospects for research in Russian philosophy and religion give no cause for discouragement or dismay. Solid and informative works have been published during the past decade; there is every reason to expect that even better ones will be published during the next. But a word of warning and suggestion is in order. The number of scholars working in these fields is extremely small, and many of them are already advanced in years. The assuring of a *Nachwuchs,* a scholarly "younger generation," is an urgent problem, and one made difficult by the paucity of universities offering graduate courses in Russian philosophy or religion.

Many of the works referred to in this report were produced either by members of history departments or by persons without academic affiliation. This is not in itself alarming; but it indicates a need for closer cooperation between departments of philosophy (and religion) and Russian area programs. Courses in various aspects of Russian intellectual history are offered at Brandeis, California, Chicago, Columbia, Cornell, Harvard, Michigan State, and Wellesley, with students drawn from a variety of disciplines. But these are, for the most part, *lecture* courses. Competent young scholars dedicated to a study of Russian philosophy or religion are much more likely to emerge from an advanced *seminar* on an appropriate topic. And thus far, such seminars are disquietingly few and far between.

Arthur S. Barron

6. SOCIAL RELATIONS

I

THE ACHIEVEMENTS of American behavioral scientists in the field of Russian studies have been noteworthy.[1] They have made significant progress in at least four major areas. The basic institutions of Soviet society have been described with special reference to their structure and functioning. Salient features of Soviet national character have been identified and related to the social structure. Sharp insights have been gained into Soviet demography. A preliminary methodology for the study of totalitarian systems has been developed, and both the special and the general aspects of Soviet totalitarianism have been examined. Almost no work, however, has been done on Russian society before 1917 or on the prerevolutionary origins of such continuing problems as urbanization, industrialization, and the changing composition of the elite.

This accomplishment is the work of a very few people. There are probably no more than thirty sociologists in this country with professional training in Russian studies. In the behavioral sciences as a whole, there are perhaps no more than a hundred with such training. There are several reasons for this: limited opportunities for field work or experiment in Soviet studies, the unavailability of many primary source materials, the difficulty of Russian language training, the lack of opportunities for academic employment, and the failure of some behavioral science departments in universities to recognize Russian studies as a legitimate field of specialization.

In addition, Soviet studies, by their very nature, are removed from the main currents of the behavioral sciences in the United States. They represent, in fact, a dramatic departure from traditional American sociology. That tradition has stressed empirical techniques—questionnaires, IBM tabulation, content analysis, interviewing, the whole paraphernalia of survey research. But American sociologists working on the Soviet Union have relied mainly on the techniques which have dominated European sociology—library research, the use of historical documents, the construction of ideal types and theoretical models. Moreover, traditional American sociology has been largely concerned with "small" problems, with rigorously delimited phenomena, with issues of such scope that they could be explored in the laboratory. It has not generally dealt with society as a whole. Students of Soviet society, on the other hand, have been very much concerned with the vast problems of social structure, with exploring society as a totality. Finally, traditional American sociology has not much emphasized the study of ideology, the functioning of political institutions, or the problem of social change. In Soviet studies these issues have predominated.

In very general terms, the behavioral sciences in this country have used four broad approaches in their study of the Soviet Union.* These have followed each other in roughly chronological order, though there is naturally much overlap.

First on the scene was what might be termed the *partisan* school of Soviet studies. The work done in this early period was

---

* What Daniel Bell refers to as the "Kremlinology" approach is not included. This approach seeks to explain Soviet society primarily in terms of the political jockeying for power that takes place among the men in the Kremlin.

less scientific than propagandist. Its purpose seems to have been less to understand the workings of Soviet society than to demonstrate either its superiority or its inferiority to Western society.[2] Monographs and articles produced in this period were marked by naïveté and special pleading.

Next there emerged the *institutional* or *cultural* school. Here the emphasis was placed on an accurate description of Soviet institutions. Some attempt was made to outline their functions and interrelations, but, on the whole, the main concern was with structure.[3]

A preoccupation with *social psychological* factors and with the Soviet Union as a *social system* characterized a third stage in the development of sociological studies of the U.S.S.R. Here the emphasis has clearly been on interrelations, not only of institutions, but of personality and social structure. In the tradition of structural functional analysis, this approach attempts to study the Soviet Union as a going concern, to determine the functional and dysfunctional interrelations which characterize Soviet social structure, personality, and culture.[4]

Finally, an approach has developed which attempts to view the Soviet Union in the broader context of *totalitarianism* generally. This school moves in the direction of a genuine comparative sociology. The emphasis is on distinguishing between those factors of Soviet society which reflect totalitarianism as it has been known elsewhere, those which reflect unique Bolshevik contributions to totalitarianism, and those which merely reflect changes in social structure characteristic of a rapidly industrialized society in the twentieth century. Scholars of this school are less concerned with the Soviet Union as such than they are with Soviet phenomena as representing more universal trends in social change and social structure.[5]

A review of the literature follows.* Before moving to a dis-

* Because of security considerations, government works were not generally available. This is unfortunate since government research, particularly in the realm of strategic intelligence, is sophisticated and relevant to behavioral

cussion of specific works, however, three general observations will be made. First, it should be noted that the great bulk of these studies are remarkably free from ideological bias. High standards of scholarship have prevailed: Soviet sources are used for facts; quotations are accurate; full attention is given to context. On the other hand, the authors cannot help being ideologically engaged. For one thing, their results are frequently used in a cold war context by journalists, government officials, and action agencies. For another thing, research problems are often defined in terms of their political connotations. No matter how objectively conducted, for example, study of the Soviet system supported by the Air Force tends to have distinct ideological implications.

Second, while these studies have not produced many general propositions useful in the study of human society as a whole, they have nevertheless made some contributions to the theory and methodology of behavioral science. For example, the work of Margaret Mead and Rhoda Métraux at the American Museum of Natural History on studying a culture at a distance represented a significant innovation, and the two-volume study of Soviet communications compiled under the direction of Margaret Mead at the M.I.T. Center for International Studies revealed new methodological techniques.[6] Similarly, Nathan Leites' utilization of Soviet texts (writings, speeches, and pronouncements) as source materials and Barrington Moore's study of the role of social classes in industrialization reflected novel approaches of some significance.[7] At the same time, practical contributions have clearly been made to our understanding of various aspects of Soviet society and to comparative social science, particularly in the substantive areas of social change, stratification, and totalitarianism. Subsequent work and further refinements and interpretation of the data already collected promise to yield additional basic insights.

---

science. On the other hand, it is probably safe to say that much of it is tied directly to the daily twists and turns of the cold war.

Finally, these studies have sometimes tended to neglect problems which relate most clearly to the central and distinctive features of Soviet society. Several such problems come immediately to mind: the nature and implications of Soviet planning, the sociology of occupations in the Soviet Union, the objectives and chief features of the Soviet educational system (including the position of science and technology), and the Soviet Union as a special case of the change from peasant to industrial society. Such gaps undoubtedly reflect in part the inaccessibility of data. In part, however, they may also stem from an overattachment to the theoretical and methodological preoccupations of American behavioral science.

II

Demography. At one time Soviet social statistics were excellent. Precise data on population, the labor force, the social composition of the Party, abortion, divorce, and other topics were readily available to Western scholars. As long ago as the late twenties, however, the Soviet government began to withdraw such information. Soon Soviet social statistics became almost impossible to obtain. Accurate census data, for example, have not been available since 1939.

Considering the obstacles, American research has done an excellent job in throwing light on Soviet population trends. Basic data have been compiled.[8] The dynamics of Soviet population growth have been analyzed. Long-range projections of population growth, especially of the labor force, have been charted.[9] For the early period of Soviet development, excellent sources are available on migration, urbanization, and work force.[10] The validity of certain inferential techniques of demographic analysis has been established. It has been demonstrated, for example, that Soviet literacy rates can be used to arrive at population data.[11] An excellent study of Soviet professional manpower has been made.[12] This study is especially valuable because it relates population data to social structure. It provides genuine insight into Soviet techniques of mobilizing segments of the population for the attainment of the regime's goals. Finally, attention has been given to the special role of women in the Soviet work force.[13]

National Character.[14] Research on national character has typically sought to answer three questions: What are the modal personality patterns in a given society? What are the determinants of these patterns? What role do these patterns play in culture and social structure? Recent work in the United States in the field of Russian national character has, however, been mainly concerned with a delineation of modal personality patterns. Much less attention has been paid to determinants, or to the interaction of personality and social structure.

Utilizing the techniques and concepts of anthropology, sociology, clinical psychology, and psychoanalysis, various students have sought to delineate the personality patterns comprised in Russian national character.[15] Despite some inconsistency in the findings, the results tend to converge.[16] This would seem to provide an indirect measure of validity.

Attempts have also been made to explore the personality characteristics of the Soviet elite. Leites views the Bolshevik's behavior as essentially a "reaction-formation" against the behavior of the nineteenth-century intelligentsia. According to Leites, two principal drives explain Bolshevik character: preoccupation with death and latent passive homosexual impulses. The working out of these impulses is traced by Leites in his analysis of Bolshevik behavior. Submergence in the Party, for example, is viewed as a defense against fear of death; hostility toward the external world is seen as a reaction to the fear of being passive.

In addition to attempting a delineation of modal Russian personality patterns, Soviet specialists have also sought to describe the norms of Soviet behavior as they are defined by the regime. Specifically, an attempt has been made to identify what constitutes "socially required' behavior in the Soviet Union. For example, Bauer has successfully traced the changes in the image of man and his behavior which have characterized Soviet psychology at various stages in its development.[17] These changes are seen as a reflection of basic transformations in Soviet ideology and social structure. According to Bauer, the Soviets have shifted from an image of man as "a creature of the forces of environment," to one of man as being controlled neither by heredity nor by environment, but "an activist, the source of his own error and evil, capable of self-initiation." In the process of this shift the concept of consciousness has been given new emphasis and prominence.

Mead has sought to define what is expected of Soviet citizens in response to authority. She and her associates carefully document the regime's insistence on discipline, purposeful behavior, and seriousness. A major contribution of her study is a demonstration that the regime has different expectations of behavior for persons occupying different statuses in Soviet society.

Several writers have pointed out that there does not seem to be a very good "fit" between the personality structure of the Russian, on the one hand, and the structure and expectations of the regime, on the other. Inkeles suggests that there is a "fairly massive degree of incongruence" between the modal personality patterns of Soviet citizens and the regime, and specifies at least five major areas of incongruence.[18] In much the same vein, Dicks sees a "salient divergence" between the Soviet system and Russian personality. The coercions and deprivations of the regime are interpreted by the Russian as "withdrawal of love and nurtuance." This creates unconscious rage and also inner guilts. The end result is an increase in the atmosphere of "persecutory anxiety and diffuse fear."

Bauer has attempted to explain the phenomenon of disaffection in terms of a lack of congruence between personality and the requirements of the regime.[19] He sets himself the problem of explaining why certain external conditions influence some individuals to disaffection, but not others. According to Bauer, different personality types tend to play different political roles. When the external situation is such that one cannot play a political role which is "congenial" to one's personality, disaffection results.

Several criticisms can be leveled against these studies of Russian national character. An insufficient attempt, it would seem, has been made to relate findings in Russian national character studies to other work done in academic psychology. Though the continuities seem obvious, little effort has been made, for example, to analyze Bolshevik behavior in terms of the authoritarian personality concept.[20] Sufficient attention has not been paid to areas of congruence between Russian personality and Soviet social structure. The development of Russian character—its roots in child-rearing practices, education, and history—has scarcely been examined.[21] Sociocultural factors have received little emphasis in the analysis of Russian character: the literature has been overbalanced in the direction of psychoanalysis.

Theories about Russian national character are too often static and descriptive; little attention has been paid to the problem of change. The notion of variability in Russian national character has been seriously neglected. Because a standard analytic scheme for the delineation of personality patterns is lacking, several crucial dimensions of personality have been unexplored. Nowhere in the literature, for example, is the Russian's concept of self dealt with; extremely little attention has been paid to his typical forms of expressive behavior, his methods for resolving conflict, and so forth.

Public Opinion and Mass Communications. For obvious reasons, American scholars have been unable to conduct surveys of opinion among Soviet citizens. On the other hand, extensive and systematic research has been conducted on the attitudes of *former* Soviet citizens (i.e., defectors) as part of the Harvard Project on the Soviet Social System.[22]

A major attempt has been made to evaluate popular reaction to the Soviet system as it now stands.[23] Perhaps the most significant finding to emerge is that the Soviet citizen approves many of the basic institutional forms of Soviet society. By and large, he sanctions the welfare aspects of the Soviet system, government ownership and control of the economy (except agriculture), and accomplishments in the military and technological realm.

Hostility is focused on police terror and absolutism. A desire for more personal autonomy is particularly intense in the areas of career and family life. No feature of Soviet life seems to be more detested than the collective-farm system, except, perhaps, the secret police.

Attitudes of Soviet citizens toward the West reflect the extensive program of anti-Western propaganda conducted by the Soviet government. The intensity and vituperativeness of this campaign have been well documented.[24] Apparently, the campaign has had a great deal of success in shaping the attitudes of Soviet citizens toward the West, and toward the United States in particular.[25]

No academic study of the impact of American propaganda on the attitudes of Soviet citizens has been made.[26] An assessment has been made of the regime's response to Voice of America broadcasts, but no measure is available of how our message gets through to the public.[27]

The formal structure of the Soviet mass communications system and the Bolshevik theory of public opinion and mass communications have been definitely described by Inkeles.[28] Attention is directed in this study to the special role played by "personal oral agitation" and radio nets in the Soviet communication process. Inkeles concludes that the Soviets have vast and effective resources for the mobilization of public opinion.

Perhaps the chief feature of Soviet mass communications is the degree to which they are controlled by the regime. Various aspects of the Soviet system of control have been studied.[29] The mechanics of Soviet press censorship have been described in detail.[30] Soviet concern for ideological "purity" in science has resulted in the censorship of scientific papers.[31] The ability of the regime to blunt hostility through control of "Letters to the Editor" columns in the press has been analyzed.[32]

Understandably, little work has been done on informal communication patterns in the Soviet Union, though two notable exceptions come to mind. An analysis of word-of-mouth communication has been made.[33] This system serves as a substitute for formal communication among the lower classes; it supplements formal communication for the upper class. Word-of-mouth serves the latent function of releasing tension. Participation in it cannot be regarded as a measure of disaffection, however. That exposure to Soviet media reflects the system of stratification has also been demonstrated.[34] Four channels of communication exist: mass official, aesthetic official, personalized official, and covert. An individual's class position determines his degree of participation in each. High involvement in the system (not necessarily support) leads to high participation in covert channels.

This brief review of the research accomplished in the field of Soviet public opinion and mass communications reveals certain gaps. The effectiveness of content analysis in the study of Soviet communication has been demonstrated,[35] yet little use of the technique has been made. More attention might be paid to the comparison of Soviet media. It would be fruitful, for example, to compare the provincial press with the metropolitan press on specific issues; to compare what the Soviet government tells its own people with what it tells foreigners; or to compare the differences in the Soviet "line" aimed at various foreign countries.

More needs to be done on the structure and functioning of informal communication channels. An analysis of the Soviet humor magazine *Krokodil* might reveal a great deal about current strains and tensions in Soviet society.

Virtually no assessment has been made of Soviet television. The implications of the continued popularity of the Russian nineteenth-century literary classics in Soviet society have not been sufficiently explored, though good initial work has been done on this.[36] Finally, no systematic attempt has been made to ascertain the extent to which the Communist Party has to take public opinion into account in its policy decisions.

Methodology. A most ambitious and complex methodological guide to the study of totalitarian societies as social systems has been prepared.[37] Within the framework of structural functional analysis, this guide attempts to chart the basic setting, components, and operations of a totalitarian social system. Its purpose in doing this is to arrive at a theoretical scheme suitable for the analysis of complex totalitarian systems. In this connection, two major contributions are made. First, the student is provided with an inclusive set of factors which must be encompassed in any thorough analysis of a totalitarian social system. Second, he is alerted to crucial areas of interrelatedness. His ability to interpret and predict behavior is increased.

This study represents a valuable tool in the study of totalitarian systems. Its major drawback would seem to be too much concern with the institutional framework, with structure. Others (e.g., Inkeles) have demonstrated the usefulness of analyzing Soviet society in terms of a series of operating characteristics or "themes." Such themes (e.g., "creating and maintaining myths," "planning and controlling," "rigidity-flexibility," "terror") cut across institutional lines and give stability or continuity of form and structure. Use of these themes as an organizing principle enables the student to deal with the dynamics of Soviet society more successfully than when institutions are used as the focus.

Soviet specialists have also developed useful special techniques for the study of Soviet society. A persuasive theoretical justification for the use of Soviet literature as primary data in developing sociological insights into Soviet society has been made by Simmons.[38] Excellent illustrations of the use of this technique have been given.[39] Profound insights into the mechanics of the Soviet system of class stratification have been derived from a careful study of Soviet novels.[40] A sensitive understanding of the career patterns of local Party secretaries has been obtained through an analysis of postwar Soviet literature.[41]

Analysis of both nineteenth-century Russian literature and official literature, accompanied by the application of psychoanalytic techniques, has produced an assessment of Bolshevik character, structure, and personality by Leites, who has also made an attempt to isolate a code of Soviet behavior which will be useful in prediction.[42]

A critical review has been made of methodological techniques and theoretical approaches to Soviet society.[43] This review defines the major problems which exist in the analysis and prediction of Soviet behavior and evaluates the attempts made to solve them. It emphasizes the ideological and national character approaches, but does not deal effectively with the social system approach. It also gives scant attention to the problem of social change.

A brilliant paper has been written on the difficulties in distinguishing "within-system" changes in the Soviet Union from changes in the system itself.[44] In spite of a few errors in historical facts, this paper is a genuine contribution to an understanding of the nature of social change in the Soviet Union.

Finally, several methodological and control studies based on the Harvard Project contribute to general methodological sophistication regarding such matters as control for sampling bias, distortion of response as a measure of hostility, comparison of interviews and questionnaires, the reliability of coding techniques, and validity.[45]

Much additional work remains to be done, of course. Additional indirect techniques for getting at phenomena inaccessible to ordinary techniques should be devised. The study of career lines, for example, might be developed to an extent which would enable us to arrive at a solid understanding of the social composition of various classes and occupations in the Soviet Union.

A critical review of the broad assumptions about society in general which have a direct impact on how Soviet behavior is interpreted seems in order. Considerable attention, for example, should be devoted to an assessment of the validity of the general assumption that increased education produces a tendency toward greater freedom in a society, toward "mellowing" of totalitarian regimes. A review of Communist semantics is needed. What do the Communists really mean when they speak of "freedom," "class," "peace," etc.? A refinement of techniques for the isolation of areas of strain and tension in Soviet society is needed. A study of conflicts in various Soviet professions may provide valuable insights here. This technique has already proved useful in an analysis of conflict within the Soviet medical profession.[46] Techniques for isolating what is specifically *Soviet* about Soviet society, as opposed to that which is Russian or merely a response to rapid industrialization, must be developed.

Social Problems. Marxist doctrine maintains that social problems flow from capitalism. Since the Soviet Union is a "classless," "socialist" society, social problems are not supposed to exist. The truth is, of course, that they do exist. Even the regime's strict censorship of information cannot hide this fact. Still, because of the regime's suppression of the facts, there have been extremely few studies of Soviet social problems. There are, of course, many journalistic exposés of such problems, but very little serious sociological work.

Definition is a problem in itself. What should be considered a "social problem" in the Soviet Union? Should slave labor camps, for example, be viewed as a form of social disorganization—or rather as a special form of totalitarian control? There is an ambiguity here of definition and frame of reference which clouds the sociological study of such issues.

Hazard has documented the trend of Soviet criminal law toward increasing severity and support of the concept of individual responsibility during the prewar period. Field has reviewed and evaluated reports in the Soviet press of juvenile delinquency and drunkenness.[47] When forced to admit the existence of such problems, the Communists have offered two explanations, both of which leave Marxist theory intact. Such issues are explained either in terms of "capitalist encirclement" or of "remnants of capitalism" in the minds of individual backsliders. As Field points out, however, the more likely explanation lies in a reaction to the boredom, scarcity, and unflagging tempo which characterize Soviet society.

Much more information, obviously, is needed on Soviet social problems. A careful content analysis of crime stories in the Soviet press would help fill in the details. A similar analysis should be made of Soviet criminal cases as reported in legal sources. From the standpoint of the sociology of knowledge, it would be helpful if the changing images of crime, guilt, and law which have characterized Soviet legal thought over the years were carefully traced and related to the social structure.[48]

Considerable attention should be devoted to an analysis of the nature, extent, and causes of social disorganization in the Soviet Union. A concern with social problems, as such, will not suffice. These must be related to structural factors in Soviet society which make for disorganization. The focus should be, not on individual problems, but rather on the broader sociological factors which cause them. Of course, an attempt should be made to determine which aspects of social disorganization are similar in Soviet and Western societies, which are uniquely Soviet, which reflect totalitarianism generally. Naturally, this kind of approach requires that the examination of Soviet social problems be taken out of a purely political context and placed in a more genuinely sociological framework.

Nationality. Much evidence has been collected on the deliberate destruction of national cultures in the U.S.S.R. by the Soviet regime. Russification of national arts and culture has been demonstrated.[49] Russian control of the Party bureaucracy and government in districts where minority groups predominate has been documented.[50] The dynamics of Sovietization of nationality groups, the actual liquidation of national minorities, the Soviet view of "two world camps" as an especially intense and virulent form of Russian nationalism have been explored in detail.[51]

There is disagreement concerning the effect of Russification on the stability and cohesiveness of Soviet society. Some regard the problem of non-Russian national consciousness as a secondary one.[52] They concede that such national consciousness still exists in the Soviet Union but do not view it as a major source of tension or strain. Through the use of survey research techniques in some instances, they demonstrate that social class, rather than nationality, plays the central role in determining attitudes toward the regime. Their view seems to be that such nationalistic feeling as remains is insufficient to motivate revolt, passive resistance, or sabotage, and that time is on the side of the regime since younger members of nationality groups seem far more reconciled to it than do older members, and since there is considerable intermarriage.

Others, however, regard national consciousness as a major source of strain and tension in the Soviet system[53] and as a serious threat to the cohesiveness and stability of the Soviet regime.

Obviously, further research is needed to clarify the issue. Two major gaps in our knowledge need to be filled. First, information on the process of acculturation is almost totally lacking. Second, insufficient examination has been made of Soviet nationalism in the sphere of international politics. Study of the organizational structure of Communist Parties, for example, might well reveal sources of strain between the Communist Party of the Soviet Union and national Communist Parties.

The Family. Soviet policy toward the family has gone through two major stages. Up to the thirties, the regime sought to smash the family as a social institution. Since the thirties, it has sought to stabilize and strengthen it. This has been well documented.[54] Various explanations have been offered for this shift in policy: (1) a desire to compensate for population losses, (2) a desire to have the family act as a "transmission belt" of authoritarian norms, (3) an attempt to control and restrict vertical social mobility, (4) a desire to restore stability to Soviet society, to place social relations on a stable basis adequate to the demands of a large-scale industrialized, stratified, and authoritarian society, (5) pragmatic recognition of the inherent resistance of family relations to planned social change, and of the indispensability of the family in social organization. Unfortunately, little attempt has been made to determine the relative importance of these explanations.

Still less attention has been paid to description of the Soviet family as a functioning social institution. Geiger has made a major study, however,[55] based on interviews and questionnaires of Soviet defectors. This study develops a number of findings concerning the relations between the value and behavior patterns of the urban Slavic family and the larger social system and concerning the functional or dysfunctional significance of these relations for the regime.

According to Geiger, the Soviet family places very great emphasis on education and occupational mobility. Parents in *all* social classes have high aspirations for their children. Adverse material living conditions have a corrosive effect on family solidarity, but experience with political terror enhances solidarity. The family provides a center for anti-regime sentiment, a haven in an atmosphere of distrust, unless directly attacked by the regime. But by and large, Slavic parents are likely to bring up children who are loyal to the existing social order.

Inkeles in his study of the Soviet family has sought to modify those theories of child-rearing which maintain that parents are unable to transmit new value orientations during periods of rapid social change, but instead transmit the old values or surrender this function to others.[56] On the basis of the Russian experience, Inkeles argues that parents can transmit the values of the emerging social order to their children, even if these values conflict with their own. They are motivated in this by a desire to insure the "happiness" or "adjustment" of their children in the social system.

Differences in attitudes between generations have been dealt with by Rossi.[57] According to her, young people are better adjusted to the regime than their elders. The young tend to blame *aspects* of the system, rather than the system itself, for any sources of dissatisfaction. They lay more stress on Soviet achievements, and give greater support to the regime, than do older persons. But, being more involved in the regime, they also expect more from it.

Gaps in research on the Soviet family are a lack of information on peasant and minority families, child-rearing techniques and values, images of romance in Soviet values and literature, divorce, authority patterns in the family, and the impact of state boarding schools on personality and family solidarity.

Stratification. The concept of stratification has been heavily emphasized in the study of Soviet society. It would be fair to say that the Harvard Project, for example, viewed social class as a major integrating concept. Most other Soviet specialists have also stressed its importance in explaining the functioning of Soviet society and the attitudes and behavior of Soviet citizens. The fact that Soviet society has a well differentiated class system* marked by extreme differences in income, status, power, and style of life has been demonstrated.[58] Special attention has been paid

---

* Though there is disagreement in the listing of the various social classes, most specialists would probably agree that any list should differentiate the Party elite, the intelligentsia, the middle bureaucracy, skilled workers, unskilled workers, peasants, and slave labor.

to the privileged position of the Soviet elite.[59] Interesting comparisons have been made between the style of life, privileges, and outlook of the Soviet intelligentsia and the bourgeoisie of nineteenth-century Europe.

Most specialists point to an increasing rigidity in the Soviet stratification system. Vertical social mobility in the Soviet Union, they feel, is on the decline. Such factors as the changing social composition of the Party and managerial group, tuition fees, the Labor Reserves, a declining rate of economic expansion, the introduction of uniforms for the various ranks in many Soviet occupations, the exercise of parental influence in obtaining special privileges for children in education and jobs, and the regime's announced intention to create special boarding schools for the children of the Soviet elite are cited as evidence of a brake on social mobility.

In addition, a very careful statistical study by Feldmesser has demonstrated that, despite the announced intention of the regime, advantages due to status have persisted in the Soviet Union: "the occupational chances of persons of toiler origin improved under the Soviets, but *not* at the expense of those of nonmanual origin."[60]

In the realm of values it has been shown that "organized inequality" has constituted a part of official ideology since 1934. At the same time, there has been an attempt to preserve the official myth of the "classless society." This has created a certain degree of strain and tension. It has been argued by Moore, however, that the emergence of a well differentiated class system was inevitable in the Soviet Union, since social inequality is a "functional prerequisite" of any industrialized society.[61]

Interesting comparisons can be drawn between the Soviet and American systems of stratification. Inkeles finds the Soviet system "open," "universalistic," and characterized by an emphasis on "achieved status."[62] These criteria also accurately describe the American system.

In both societies class position serves as a determinant of educational opportunity. On the other hand, considerable evidence is offered by Feldmesser to indicate that "status privilege in access to higher education is *more* pronounced in the United States than in the Soviet Union."[63] According to Feldmesser, children of manual background in the U.S.S.R. have roughly twice as good a chance of attending college as children of similar background in America.

No studies have been made of comparative social mobility, though Feldmesser argues that mobility is, and will probably remain, higher in America.[64] He maintains that private business offers a channel for talent not found in Russia, and that American emphasis on "social justice" ensures the continuance of such opportunity.

Finally, prestige ratings of various occupations are found to be highly similar in the United States and the U.S.S.R.[65] This reflects universal features of the occupational structure in industrialized societies. Some variability does exist, however, in the ratings of agricultural and service occupations.

Broadly speaking, it seems clear that the American and Soviet systems of stratification show great similarities. In most essentials they are alike. The major differences, of course, relate to the greater significance of political criteria in the U.S.S.R.

In addition to analyzing the objective features of the Soviet class system, Soviet specialists have also studied salient subjective factors. By and large, these studies indicate a lack of "class consciousness" among Soviet citizens.[66] This does not mean that cleavages do not exist. Lower classes feel somewhat more deprived than other classes and verbalize more hostility. The intelligentsia evidence some feeling of "guilt" about special privileges and advantages. On the whole, however, inter-class feelings are "amicable."

Three explanations are offered for this lack of class consciousness: (1) Because of the rapid vertical mobility which has characterized Soviet society, the membership of the various classes is still heterogeneous. As the classes become more homogeneous, more of a class point of view should emerge. (2) The totalitarian controls of the regime prevent any kind of political coalescence along class lines. (3) The various classes focus all their hostility on the Party, thus reducing the chances for class cleavages.

The last explanation, however, seems to beg the question. It fails to take account of the fact that the Party may constitute a social class in is own right, a point of view recently and persuasively set forth by Milovan Djilas, for example.[67] Failure to examine the Party in these terms is a major failing of previous studies of the Soviet stratification system.

Another major gap is the failure of American sociologists to spell out the implications of the Soviet experience for the values which characterize the American class system. Though considerably less free than American society, Soviet society may prove to have more equality in several respects. This seems to be the case with access to higher education, for example. How compatible is equality with freedom? Does political freedom necessarily imply inequality? These are questions which would bear further examination.[68]

Other topics which suggest themselves for further research are the role played by Soviet purges in the stratification system, the degree of success achieved in giving manual labor special status and prestige in the U.S.S.R., the techniques used to resolve the ideological and social contradictions inherent in an ideology embracing both "classlessness" and "organized inequality," the emergence of a managerial elite in the Soviet Union, and the impact of this group on Soviet values and on the regime itself.

Industrial Sociology. Industrial sociology is a much neglected field in Soviet studies. Data are difficult to collect. Problems of the kind that are customarily studied in this country—human relations, communications, absenteeism, turnover, labor strife—have not been as important in the Soviet Union.

A major theme in the work accomplished thus far by American specialists has been the degree of autonomy enjoyed by Soviet managers. In his study of management in the Soviet industrial firm, Granick has indicated that a "considerable independence of decision-making" is left to the manager of the Soviet enterprise.[69] Among Soviet managers, Granick argues, much "entrepreneurial-type" ideology survives. Employing Weber's definition of bureaucracy, Granick also maintains that less bureaucracy exists in large Soviet firms than in comparable firms in the United States. Obviously, there is some evidence to the contrary. The Soviet press itself stresses the need to make inroads on "crippling bureaucracy" in industry. The recent steps toward decentralization in industrial planning and administration in the U.S.S.R. probably reflects in part a genuine concern with bureaucracy. Finally, in comparison with managers in the United States, Soviet managers have so little say in such fundamental matters as pricing, wages, capitalization, and quantity of output that greater bureaucracy would seem inevitable in the Soviet system.

Some scholars, of course, do emphasize the formal bureaucratic features of the Soviet enterprise.[70] Perhaps there has been an overemphasis on such features. If so, Granick's contribution is a welcome corrective.

After studying the formal structure and functioning of the Soviet firm, Berliner has also stressed the entrepreneurial activities of the manager.[71] These activities are numerous and significant. Faced with a rigid Plan, with scarcities, and with severe punishment for failure (or very generous rewards for success), the Soviet manager is forced to live by his wits. His activity in deceiving the Party, in using "*blat*" or "pull," and generally in evading the formal requirements of the regime is persuasively detailed.

The tensions which characterize the relations between Party representatives and the Soviet plant manager have been excellently discussed in the collective work by Bienstock, Schwarz, and Yugow.[72] This study makes it plain that the workers have long since been left out of the power equation in the Soviet enterprise. It is especially valuable for its treatment of the role of the collective farm manager and of the functioning of the collective farm enterprise. These are both subjects which have received extremely little attention.

The role of forced labor as a "massive social and economic fact" in Soviet society has been well documented.[73] Such studies have dealt satisfactorily with the extent of forced labor and its contribution as a form of terror and as a source of cheap labor for special tasks of capital construction. Although data are scarce, these topics and the latest attitude of the regime toward forced labor deserve further investigation.

Several important gaps remain to be filled. The nature and effectiveness of incentives, as opposed to coercions, have scarcely been touched in an analysis of the motivations and accomplishments of the Soviet labor force. The emergence of a managerial elite, its values, and its impact on Soviet society have not been carefully examined, though there has been a great deal of journalistic speculation on this. The effect on the Soviet regime of increased material well-being and further economic advancement has not been studied, though these factors may well have profound consequences.[74]

Soviet experience, if any, with testing, training, human relations and the like has not been evaluated. Finally, shifts in the modes of legitimization of industrial authority in the U.S.S.R. have not been analyzed.

Social System. Analysis of social systems seeks to identify the operating parts of a society, to determine the functional interdependence of the parts, and to determine the repercussions produced in the total system by a change in any of its parts. Assuming that the general relationships between the parts have been determined, it should be possible to predict roughly the nature and extent of change in the system.

Three themes have predominated in the analysis of the Soviet Union as a social system: the structure and functioning of Soviet institutions viewed as an interrelated whole, the Soviet Union as a special type of totalitarian social system, and the potentialities for change in the Soviet system.

The most ambitious attempt to describe the structure and functioning of Soviet society as an interrelated whole is the Harvard Project on the Soviet Social System.[75] A study has been published which sets forth the major findings of the Harvard Project in nontechnical terms.[76] In addition to identifying the major operating characteristics of the system, this study attempts to calculate the impact of these characteristics on the individual Soviet citizen and on specific Soviet groups. A summary evaluation of the strengths and weaknesses of the system is made.

The Harvard approach seems, however, to lack a unifying concept, a basic organizing principle.[77] Several "operating characteristics," "formal institutions," and "adjustive mechanisms" are identified. But no attempt is made to gauge relative weights, importance, or significance. No priorities are established. From the Harvard analysis, it is difficult to determine which aspects of the system are likely to act more as independent than as dependent variables, which are likely to have the greatest impact on other parts of the system, and which serve as the "motor force" of the system. The dynamics of the system as a going concern are spelled out, but little insight is given into the sources and potentialities of change. Moreover, it is difficult to assess the regime's capacity for survival, since the Harvard Project does not provide a measure of those characteristics that are essential to its maintenance or of those that can be modified without a change in the nature of the system itself.

Paradoxically, this deficiency stems from the Project's major strength—its emphasis on social psychological factors. Most previous studies have stressed the political aspects of the Soviet system. The Harvard study strikes out in a fresh direction. Yet in view of the dominance of the political factor in Soviet society (i.e., the centralized control which the regime exerts over all aspects of life), the Project fails to explore this factor adequately.[78]

A more general and less sociologically penetrating study of the Soviet social system has been produced at the M.I.T. Center for International Studies.[79] This study focuses on conventional institutions. It leans heavily on historical and purely descriptive materials and makes little effort to demonstrate interrelationships or to include social psychological data. It does, however, demonstrate an appreciation for the central role of power and command in Soviet society.[80]

Several studies have been written of aspects of the Soviet Union as a special type of totalitarian social system. A careful analysis has been made of the role of the purge in the Soviet system.[81] Both the functional and dysfunctional consequences of the purge for the system as a whole are described.

As a corrective to theories which perhaps overemphasize raw power factors in explaining Soviet behavior, a study has been made of the "totalitarian mystique" as a factor in the motivation of Soviet leaders.[82] The concept of mystique goes beyond formal ideology in the sense that it is common to *all* totalitarian societies. The substantive content of the mystique is described.

The role of individual indoctrination and training in the development of the totalitarian elite in Soviet society has been described.[83] A solid analysis of the Soviet Union's ability to mobilize its educational institutions along totalitarian lines has been made.[84]

The attempts of the regime to stamp out religion have been discussed, and the fundamental incompatibilities of religion and totalitarianism have been explored.[85] Soviet specialists have not, however, assessed the potentialities of Communist ideology to meet "religious" needs of individuals and groups. A major question is the extent to which "totalitarian mystique" can serve some of the basic psychological functions of religion.

Many of these studies of Soviet totalitarianism suffer, incidentally, by not specifying which aspects of Soviet totalitarianism are unique and which are found in other totalitarian societies. This is definitely a problem for further research.

Several studies of the potentialities for social change in the Soviet system have been made. Wolfe maintains that Soviet totalitarianism exerts such pervasive and crushing control over its population that no essential change in the system is possible from within.[86]

An effort has been made to differentiate between the various levels on which change can occur, and has occurred, in the Soviet Union.[87] Five levels of change are identified, but little attempt is made to determine at which level a given change is operating.

After defining three basic modes of power in any society (i.e., traditional, rational-technical, political), Moore attempts to determine which mode the Soviet Union will come to emphasize most in the future.[88] He shows that the predominance of any one mode limits the range of workable alternatives for the solution of other problems. Moore views the Soviets as ultimately striking a new balance between rational and traditionalist elements. In another study, he discusses the limitations of directed social change in Soviet society.[89]

Two major studies have attempted to describe patterns of change in the Soviet Union since the founding of the regime. Timasheff views all social changes in the Soviet Union as the working out of conflict between the new institutions and national Russian traditions.[90] Inkeles sees three major phases of change: the heroic phase (up to 1924), the phase of building new institutions (up to 1934), the phase of stabilization of the new society (since 1934).[91] According to Inkeles, the major determinant of the tempo and direction of social change has been "the differential adaptability of social organization to consciously directed change." This factor has produced different rates of change in different areas of the society. Far from reflecting consciously planned direction, Soviet social changes reflect such factors as unanticipated consequences of planned change, reaction to external threats, and the resistance of basic institutions to change.

In terms of gaps, studies of social change in the Soviet Union have failed to take sufficiently into account irrational factors, the impact of events in other countries (particularly in the Soviet orbit) on Soviet affairs, and the role played by ideology in the behavior of the Soviet elite.

III

It is hoped that in the years ahead continued progress in American sociological study of the Soviet system can be achieved and that more American sociologists will be attracted to this field. Basing themselves on the solid foundations that have been laid, American behavioral scientists should be able increasingly to concentrate on problems that relate to what is most central and distinctive in the Soviet system. Most attention should be paid to matters that reflect the new modes of organizing life, governing people, and administering institutions that are at the heart of Soviet society. Emphasis on how the Soviet system is functioning in its key features, and with what consequences, is also likely to yield in the long run the most useful knowledge for sociology as a whole. In this regard, the selection of problems for study should be guided less by the methodological and theoretical concerns of contemporary American sociology than by a desire to undertake an accurate and realistic accounting of what is taking place in Soviet society.

John Turkevich

7. SCIENCE

I

IT MUST BE ACKNOWLEDGED from the outset that scholarly investigation of the progress of science in Russia has been very limited. This is due to a variety of causes. At universities and research centers, fields such as history, art, literature, politics, and economics are well established. Scholarly work in these fields is assured by an organization of professorships, graduate studies, extensive library collections, publications, and recognition for the successful scholar. By contrast, the history of science is a relatively new field and until recently has not enjoyed comparable support.

As for the scientist himself, he finds little of the time or atmosphere necessary for delving into a description, philosophy, or history of scientific achievements. The ever-pressing demand on the scholar in the sciences to take an active part in the unfolding of the physical and biological world circumscribes his interest in the past. His primary interest in earlier accomplishments is to find a basis for his own scientific explorations. The individual successes of his scientific predecessors have been for the most part consolidated, and their personalities and national environments have faded out in this process. Only here and there in the structure of the sciences do traces remain of the great personalities, when laws and theories have come to be known by their names; and of the national environment, when chemical elements are named after the country of their discoverer. Certainly the historical sequence of discoveries is but dimly recognized in a science. The increasing amount of factual knowledge required of the student of science has resulted in the gradual disappearance of courses in the history of individual sciences. This has been followed by the omission of historical questions in examinations for advanced degrees.

Most scientists lack knowledge of the historical threads which led to the development of their science and of the personalities that contributed to its growth. Aside from a small group of historians of science, few professional scientists are interested in scholarly work on the history of their science. Moreover, historians of science are more often concerned with static science, such as classical Greek science, or the scientific knowledge of the Chinese or Arabs, or of the French during the Revolution. General histories of science usually end with the opening of the twentieth century.

In view of the fact that American and Soviet science came to fruition during the twentieth century, it is not surprising that there has been little formal scholarly work in their histories. Similarly, our universities have paid little attention to the relation between government and science. It must be recognized, however, that the number of people qualified for work in the study of Soviet science is limited by rather special requirements. The scholar must have a command of the Russian language, and there are relatively few scholars who can use Russian. In addition, the specialist in this field must have sound knowledge in more than one branch of science. Finally, he must find moral and financial support for what is still a rather exotic branch of scholarship. In these days when universities and research institutes find it difficult to finance studies in such established fields as Soviet literature, language, politics, and economics, it is small wonder that scholarship in the history and sociology of Soviet science hardly exists in the formal traditional sense, but is carried on in large measure by amateurs like the present writer, who work on the subject in their spare time and cherish it as a hobby. The limited amount of formal scholarship is supplemented by a surprisingly large number of studies by such amateurs. Their productivity reflects in part the general interest on the part of the American people in the Soviet scene.

II

Americans began to take an interest in Russian science half a century ago. An article was written on Pavlov's studies in physiology as early as 1909.[1] This interest has had its ups and downs. The plight of the Russian intellectual during the civil war and the early years of the Soviet regime evoked sympathetic interest from the American scientist. This resulted in a number of articles on Russian science.[2]

In the late twenties and during the thirties relations were established between Soviet science and that of the West. Scientific information flowed, through the medium of journals, between this country and the Soviet Union. Tables of contents and abstracts of individual articles were given in a Western language in all important Russian journals. Three prestige journals, the *Comptes rendus* of the Academy of Sciences of the U.S.S.R., the Soviet *Journal of Physics*, and the *Physiocochemica Acta*, were published in the languages of western Europe. Organizations like VOKS in the Soviet Union and American-Russian committees encouraged contacts between scientists of the two countries and aided in the exchange of scientific literature. A number of American scientists undertook studies in Soviet research centers, and individual Soviet postdoctoral students studied in the United States. With the establishment of these normal relations and in the absence of startling discoveries in the Soviet Union, little was published in this period on Soviet science.

World War II again aroused sympathy in American scientific

circles for the Soviet scholar, working in a country half conquered and widely devastated by the Germans. The various committees for cultural and scientific relationships with the U.S.S.R. carried on as best they could under war conditions. These activities soon came to an end when the Soviet government dropped an Iron Curtain and made "anti-cosmopolitanism" the order of the day. The flow of journals was impeded. A language barrier was set up when the Soviet journals discontinued the use of Western languages in their tables of contents and abstracts, and the Academy of Sciences of the U.S.S.R. suspended the publication of the three prestige journals in Western langauges. Few American scholars visited Soviet laboratories, and there were no Soviet scientific visitors in this country. In the meantime, interest in the U.S.S.R. and matters Russian was unfortunately sometimes viewed in the United States with suspicion, as symptomatic of sympathy for the Communist cause.

The genetics controversy in the Soviet Union, raising as it did the fundamental issue of government control of scientific inquiry, again turned the attention of the general public to the Russian scientific scene. A number of studies were published on the subject of Stalinism and freedom of scientific research.[3] Some of our scientific and educational leaders concluded that a country that indulged in such an inquisition of science as in the Lysenko case could not have an effective science. The public readily accepted the verdict that all science was dead in the Soviet Union. With this acceptance, interest in the technological achievements of the Russians again decreased. However, the steady advance of Soviet achievement in military fields—atom bombs, hydrogen weapons, missiles, and ultimately the visible evidence of this progress in the *sputniks*—all this revived an interest which was less sympathetic to than apprehensive of the accomplishments of Soviet science. This interest was coupled with an awareness both of the strong emphasis on science and mathematics in the Soviet schools and of the large number of technically trained graduates being produced by the Soviet educational system. The American public now became eager to know answers to a number of questions concerning Soviet science and education.

What is the record of accomplishment of the U.S.S.R. in the various individual fields of science? What is the prognosis for the future development of science in the Soviet Union? What are the elements that assured the Soviets success in space science, where their distinction is indisputable? Is this due to better organization, more effective exploitation of their scientists, stronger motivation, or smoother liaison with the military? Does their educational system have unusual features? Will they be able to continue to turn out a large number of scientists and engineers? How good are their scientists and engineers? Partial answers to these questions may be found in scholarly work published in the U.S.S.R., but American scholars have not yet answered them.

Scholarly activity in this country has not produced a history of Russian or Soviet science. This is not surprising, for there is no systematic or complete history of Russian science in the Russian language. On the other hand, there are abundant secondary sources for such a history.[4] Furthermore, in 1947, to mark the thirtieth anniversary of Soviet rule, a number of studies were published on the progress of individual fields of science in the Soviet Union,[5] and on January 5-11, 1949, a special session of the Academy of Sciences of the U.S.S.R. was devoted to reports on "The History of the Natural Sciences." These and other materials could serve as sources for a general history of this subject; yet only a handful of studies have appeared in this country on the history of Russian science.[6]

Several biographies of Russian scientists, and one autobiography, have been published in the United States. An authoritative Soviet biography of M. V. Lomonosov (1711-65) has been translated under the auspices of the Russian Translation Project of the American Council of Learned Societies.[7] Lomonosov, the great scientist, poet, teacher, grammarian, and founder of the University of Moscow, is certainly a towering figure in the development of Russian science. Professor Posin has written a fictionalized biography of D. I. Mendeleev (1834-1907), and there is a life of Pavlov (1849-1936) by Babkin.[8] There has also appeared in the United States an interesting autobiography by V. N. Ipatieff (1867-1953), one of the leading chemists of the last decades of the Empire and of the early Soviet regime, who not only carried out important work on high pressure catalysis but after the October Revolution was active in organizing chemical research and industry in the newly established Soviet state. He later emigrated from Russia to the United States and became a leader in American chemistry and the petroleum industry. His autobiography is a valuable contribution to our knowledge of Russian and Soviet science of the twentieth century.[9]

The organizational aspect of Soviet science is of particular interest.[10] To some, the unusual strength the Soviet Union has shown in the missile field and the conquest of space has seemed to reflect the excellent organization of these projects, effective liaison between pure science and industry, and a clear understanding of the role of scientific research on the part of government leaders. This understanding is surprising in view of the genetics controversy. The organization of the Soviet Academy of Sciences has been the subject of recent research,[11] and attention has been called to the important statement by Academician Kapitsa on the problems associated with the organization of basic research in modern society.[12] Work has also been done on the position of Soviet scientists and on scientific training in the U.S.S.R.[13]

Russian publications contain a good deal of material on the nature of the planning carried out by Soviet administrators. Obviously some of the planning was badly conceived, and there have been some crude efforts to impose Marxist or Stalinist dogmas on the development of science. As a result, such disciplines as genetics and theoretical chemistry have all but vanished from the Soviet scientific scene. On the other hand, planning must have been well carried out in the nuclear energy and missile fields. Students of the relation of government to science might well study this aspect of Soviet science.[14] In recent years the present writer has conducted an undergraduate seminar on "Government and Science" at the Woodrow Wilson School of Public and International Affairs at Princeton University, and he has become convinced of the value of such studies and of the need to extend them to Soviet science.[15] The relationship between science, on the one hand, and Marxism-Leninism-Stalinism, on the other, has begun to engage the attention of Russian specialists and will be a fruitful field of work for many years to come.[16] The issues involved transcend the Soviet scene. In the genetics controversy and the subsequent repercussions in other fields, the whole question of the freedom of the individual to pursue scientific work came into focus. Professor Zirkle has contributed a valuable volume to the literature of this subject.[17]

Soviet accomplishments in natural science have attracted general interest in recent years. Typical of this interest was the symposium on "Soviet Science" held at the Philadelphia meeting of the American Association for the Advancement of Science on November 27, 1951.[18] General appraisals of Soviet science have appeared, both in the published proceedings of this symposium and in more recent publications.[19] Brief accounts are available of Soviet work in several disciplines in the natural sciences, and in mathematics.[20] There have also been several studies of Soviet medicine.[21] Needless to say, scholars in many specialized fields draw on the results of Soviet research, which may be followed in the abstracting publications of the various branches of science.

Closely related to the problem of studying Soviet science is that of translation. Scholars acquainted with the Russian language now have the aid of dictionaries specializing in several technical fields. There is also a textbook for specialists in science interested

in learning the Russian language.[22] Interest in Russian science
has far outstripped the linguistic knowledge of American scientists, however, and the translation of current Soviet materials has
become a major undertaking.

In the late thirties a group of American petroleum companies
privately circulated translated tables of contents, abstracts, and
complete translations of certain select articles in Soviet journals
dealing with hydrocarbon and petroleum chemistry. This enterprise lasted for about eight years under the direction of Dr. J. C.
Tolpin. After World War II, John and Ludmilla Turkevich
organized and edited a *Guide to Russian Scientific Periodical
Literature*. It was published for the Atomic Energy Commission
by the Brookhaven National Laboratory. The guide came out as
a monthly for five years, 1948-52, when its support was with-
drawn by the Atomic Energy Commission in Washington. The
functions of the guide were taken over in a more extensive but
somewhat diffuse way by the *Monthly Index of Russian Accessions,* published by the Library of Congress at Washington.[23] At
the present time there is increasing activity in the complete translation of certain scientific journals. In the United States 54 Soviet
scientific and technical journals are now being translated into English and 128 are being abstracted.[24] Similar translation programs,
although on a smaller scale, are being undertaken in Australia,
Canada, Great Britain, and India. In these countries, as in the
United States, the government plays a major role in this enterprise.[25] Important Soviet articles relating to the ideology and
organization of the natural sciences also appear in translation in
the *Current Digest of the Soviet Press*.

No review of this subject would be complete without mention
of the very considerable attention that has been devoted to Soviet
science in Great Britain and western Europe. British scientists
have been interested in this subject for many years, and have
produced a number of important studies.[26] In recent years German
scholarship has also turned to this field of study, with the publi-

cation of at least two outstanding works on the relationship between ideology and the natural sciences in the U.S.S.R.[27] At the
same time a semiannual journal, *Osteuropa-Naturwissenschaft,*
was established in Stuttgart in 1955 under the editorship of
Arnold Buchholz with the purpose of following current Soviet
scientific trends. A similar function is performed in the field of
medicine by the *Review of Eastern Medical Sciences,* published
in Munich under the editorship of H. Schulz. Finally, it should
be noted that a number of general descriptive works by Soviet
scientists have been translated into English by the Foreign Languages Publishing House in Moscow.[28] While there is a strong
element of propaganda in these publications, an informed and
discriminating reader can learn much from them.

III

From what has been said, it is clear that in this, as in so many
other fields relating to Russia, there are many opportunities for
new research. A single general volume on Russian science both
before and since the October Revolution would be most useful.
Authoritative biographies remain to be written of those outstanding Russian scholars who have won a permanent place in
the history of science. Interesting studies could be made of the
lives and contributions of the many Russian-born scientists who,
like Ipatieff, emigrated to the United States and western Europe.
Included in such a list would be the mathematicians Tamarkin
and Lefschetz, the physicists Gamow and Zworikin, the chemist
Kistiakowski, the biologist Dobzhanski, the microbiologist Waks-
man, the airplane designers Sikorsky and Seversky, the engineer
Timoshenko, and many others.

It would be well, also, to encourage the study of developments
in the individual disciplines of the natural sciences, as well as
the related fields of mathematics, medicine, and technology. Such
studies would depend in some degree on finding scholars who
combine scientific training with knowledge of Russian. In at least

one instance, however, two scholars with complementary skills have joined forces with great success to produce a study of this sort,[29] and this pattern may well be applicable to other cases. Similar results might also be achieved through conferences and symposia.[30]

The study of the role of science in the Soviet Union also provides a challenging new approach to certain general problems in which the social scientist needs the help of the scientist. To what extent, for example, does Marxism in the abstract, as well as the more specific doctrines of Leninism and Stalinism, and perhaps later formulations, form a part of Soviet scientific thought? Why has one discipline been very largely dominated by ideology, while others appear to be as free from ideological restraints as they are in the West? Are those that appear to be free, really free? Is it possible that in certain disciplines, vital to military strength, national interest has won out over ideology? To what extent have the disciplines that are relatively free from ideological controls provided a place of refuge for those who might have preferred to work in such persecuted fields of study as biology, psychology, and philosophy? What can the organization of science teach us about the relationship between scholarship and politics in the Soviet Union? Many other questions of this character come to mind as one contemplates the problems posed by Russian science, and it is hoped that this challenge will be taken up by political scientists and sociologists, as well as by those scholars trained in the natural sciences who are concerned with the social role of their discipline.

W. A. Douglas Jackson

8. GEOGRAPHY

I

UNTIL WORLD WAR II, the attention of American geographers, if measured in terms of their output, was focused primarily on the United States. The advantages for research afforded by the great wealth of material available, both in libraries and in the field, attracted them to study their own geographical milieu. Yet, in spite of the difficulties associated with research on foreign areas, due either to lack of data in this country or to the financial burden imposed by field study abroad, some parts of the world did receive firsthand investigation by American geographers. Latin America, relatively close at hand, provided a fertile field, and geographers from the United States made substantial contributions to our knowledge of the lands and peoples south of the Rio Grande. Japan and China, to some extent, also came in for study by American geographers. On the other hand, Europe and its colonies were for the most part left to competent European geographers. Little attention was directed toward the Soviet Union and the geographical impact of the revolutionary changes that were occurring in that vast territory. In fact, in the prewar period only two American geographers devoted any significant amount of time to study of the Soviet Union.[1]

World War II stimulated the interest of geographers in the Soviet Union, as well as in other areas to which they had previously paid little attention. Foundation support, which has grown steadily since 1948, has done much to encourage and facilitate this development by enabling geographers to increase their familiarity with foreign languages and cultures, thus giving rise to an expanding number of young specialists capable of undertaking competent research on foreign areas. Yet, however rapid the growth of interest in the rest of the world, American geography in Russian studies remains essentially an underdeveloped discipline. In view of the Soviet Union's prominence in world affairs, the lack of attention given Soviet geography is altogether regrettable. Too few geographers are writing about the largest and most complex political unit in the world, and their numbers are increasing at much too slow a rate. There is not, therefore, a large body of geographical literature upon which a balanced discussion of past development in the field can be based.

II

Practically all of the writing on the geography of the Soviet Union belongs to the postwar period. It consists of several general works and a small collection of articles, published mainly in the two major professional geographical journals, the *Geographical Review* and the *Annals* of the Association of American Geographers. Monographs are lacking. A review of the literature should also include, however, a brief reference to the major works of persons in closely related fields; while they are not geographers, their work does in part reflect geographical techniques or method in presentation.

The general works, without exception, are descriptive in nature and traditional in organization and treatment. *The Basis of Soviet Strength* by Cressey, an expansion of the relevant chapters in his general study on Asia, is designed primarily for college use. It has the distinction of being the first general study written by an

American on the geography of the Soviet Union. In a popular vein is his later publication entitled *How Strong is Russia?*[2]

In a somewhat different category is Shabad's *Geography of the USSR: A Regional Survey*. Organized regionally, as its title implies, the book relies heavily on Soviet sources for descriptions of economic and political changes. This survey, which is primarily factual, constitutes a valuable handbook for reference use. Shabad's special contribution, included in the earlier part of the book, is his use of electoral districts, as published in *Pravda*, to arrive at generalized postwar population figures.[3]

Unlike Shabad, Mirov deals almost exclusively with the elements of the natural environment in his *Geography of Russia*.[4] The summaries of the regional associations of climate, topography, soils, and vegetation are good though brief, lacking the detail found in Berg's monumental study of natural regions. These four works, then, constitute the general literature on the geography of the Soviet Union.

American geographers have also been active in making available to the profession translations of several of the better Soviet studies. Under the editorial guidance of Morrison and Nikiforoff, Berg's work has been translated and published in the United States. A companion volume, the prewar economic geography of the U.S.S.R. by Balzak, Vasyutin, and Feigin, was edited by Harris. Though Marxist in interpretation and now considerably out of date, it was the most detailed, systematic economic geography available at that time and has constituted a valuable addition to the literature in English on the economic-geographic changes in the Soviet Union up to 1939.[5] Currently, Suslov's detailed study of the physical geography of the Asiatic part of the Soviet Union is being prepared for publication in English.[6]

It is natural that American geographers should want translations of the better Soviet works; in a sense, these studies represent source materials for both student and teacher alike. American geographers have also turned to western Europe for assistance.

Perhaps the best general survey of the geography of the Soviet Union is by the German geographer, Leimbach, now in the process of being translated and revised at the University of Maryland for use in its overseas geography teaching program. Thiel's descriptive regional study of the Soviet Far East has already been revised and translated.[7] Of the French works, Jorré's text, although less thorough than Leimbach's, has been used rather extensively in the translated edition in American universities where courses on the geography of the Soviet Union have been offered. George's work, still untranslated, has less merit because of a lack of objectivity. Two British books, by Gregory and Shave, and by Gray, are marred by serious factual errors.[8] Since most of the general studies are now somewhat out of date, a need exists for one or more new American texts on the geography of the Soviet Union. John A. Morrison has such a book in preparation.

A review of the entire periodical literature, limited in extent though it may be, cannot be attempted here. However, because some articles tend to focus upon a small number of related topics of an economic-geographic nature and thus reveal the special interests of current American writers, they deserve special comment.

The studies on regionalization and regional development by Morrison, Shabad, and Shimkin not only are basic but constitute a significant contribution to our knowledge of the geographical spread of Soviet development.[9] Morrison, examining territorially the conflict of economic principle with the nationality principle in the prewar Soviet attempts to redraw internal boundaries, detected a trend toward realism in the establishment of administrative areas based on the practical requirements of administration. Shabad, on the other hand, concerned with the Soviet concept of economic regionalization, found that Soviet ideology and economics were major factors in bringing about the existing regional structure. Somewhat different, too, is Shimkin's study, which deals solely with the impact of industrialization from 1926 to 1950 on the pattern of regional development; he attempts to assess the possible effects of Soviet plans and of the greater utilization of underdeveloped human and physical resources on the future economic geography of the country.

Harris's urban study reflects an awareness of the impact of industrialization under prewar Five-Year Plans on the growth and function of cities. His method of analysis illustrates how techniques used to study phenomena in the United States might effectively be applied to similar phenomena in the Soviet Union, given the necessary data.[10] Selecting cities of over 100,000 in population according to the 1939 census, and using the 1935 per capita value of industrial production for those cities in terms of 1925-27 prices, Harris arrived at a four-type functional classification of cities which brought rather favorable comment from Soviet geographers.[11]

The lack of postwar data on agricultural land use, such as were available before the war by minor civil divisions, has tended to limit the scope of agricultural geographic research. From time to time geographers have participated in symposia dealing with Soviet agriculture, and while they have contributed to an over-all understanding of the problems under consideration, their papers have, nevertheless, been of a survey type, reflecting the frustration that arises from the necessity of having to use only the limited materials available.[12] On the other hand, where more information has generally been available, as with some of the major projects undertaken by the Soviet government to increase agricultural production by altering the traditional patterns of land use, geographers have been able to arrive at definite conclusions as to their geographical feasibility. Jackson's studies of agricultural conditions in the dry steppe are critical of Soviet efforts to expand widely the basis of dry farming, although he sees a possibility of limited success for the current virgin and idle land scheme through the extensive sowing of drought-resistant durum wheat.[13] Attempts to expand irrigation in central Asia through further use of the not-too-abundant waters of the Amu Darya, and the need for and problems associated with irrigation in southeast Russia, have been critically analyzed by Field.[14] Rodgers has applied standard geographic techniques to the study of land use in the non-chernozem (non-black earth) between Moscow and Leningrad.[15]

Other topics which have been studied by geographers vary considerably. The theory of the "urge to the sea" has been effectively refuted by Morrison.[16] Taskin has examined the economic implications of the falling level of the Caspian Sea, due to evaporation and the diversion of Volga River water;[17] and Rodgers has mapped and analyzed changing patterns in the Soviet pulp and paper industry.[18]

Of studies in related fields which employ in part a geographical approach, only those more widely used by geographers need be mentioned. Shimkin's study of Soviet minerals is exhaustive, reflecting a careful job of recording and analyzing Soviet resources, production, and consumption. Volin's monograph on agriculture offers an especially valuable discussion of crop geography, and his dot maps of distributions in 1938 are extremely useful. Somewhat different in scope are the agro-climatological studies by Nuttonson, published by the American Institute of Crop Ecology. These incorporate systematized data on temperature, precipitation, and length of growing season for selected stations in the Soviet Union as well as their North American analogues. Lorimer's population study, in both text and maps, provides valuable information on growth and changes.[19]

This is not the place to attempt a thorough inquiry into the reasons why geography represents an underdeveloped discipline in Russian studies. However, some of the factors responsible for retarding its growth must be recognized if a path to future progress is to be found.

Most of the current writers bring to their study a solid grounding in geography, as well as a certain degree of familiarity with the language and culture of the Russian area. Much of the writing which appears in the professional journals, therefore, is based on primary or Soviet source materials, and clearly reveals the efforts of American geographers to rise above a mere recording of facts concerning Soviet geographical development. But, as indicated previously, there are too few trained geographers attempting the study of Soviet growth and change.

The question that immediately arises, then, is a simple one. Why are so few geographers attracted to pursuing advanced work on the Russian area? Perhaps the answer lies in the fact that they are overwhelmed and repelled by the considerable amount of time and energy they must expend in order to gain familiarity with the language and culture of the area, over and above that required to gain competence in their own discipline. It is not likely, therefore, that the geographer who has himself specialized in the Russian area will find at any one time that he has more than a handful of students studying under his guidance. The mortality rate, too, is high.

Young geographers who wish to build a sound foundation in the geography of the Soviet Union must have access to the training afforded by an area program, which provides valuable opportunity for interrelated study in several disciplines. It is possible, at present, to combine training at the graduate level in both geography and the Russian area at only a few institutions. The alternative compels the geographer to undertake at some point in his graduate work an intensive program of area and language training at one of the major centers of Russian study away from his home university. Neither of the two major eastern centers for Russian studies, Harvard and Columbia, has participating geographers, supported by solidly established geography departments. These centers attract the greatest number of students interested in the Soviet Union, but there can be no contact with the geographical approach, a contact which might stimulate some students to develop, simultaneously with their area specialization, a sound foundation in this discipline. Such centers, therefore, should be encouraged to broaden their programs to include training in geography.

Field work has always been an important method of geographical research, but during the last twenty years it has been impossible to undertake field work in the Soviet Union, although brief travel is now permitted. Inability to travel extensively and to study at first hand the area of interest cannot but have a dampening effect on the morale and work of the geographer. At the same time, the lack of readily available quantitative data, necessary to meaningful geographical analysis, has resulted in a spotty literature on the Soviet area. Geographers have worked, it could be said, where they have been permitted to work.

It would be quite inaccurate, however, to paint an altogether gloomy picture for geographical research on Russia. Data have been scarce, it is true, but geographers have also suffered, to some extent, from unfamiliarity with the source materials that are available in the libraries of this country or elsewhere. The publication by the Library of Congress in 1951 of a two-volume bibliography on the geography of the Soviet Union was an important step in the right direction.[20] Periodic revision of the bibliography would be beneficial, too, in view of the significant increase in the volume of material published in the Soviet Union and now available in the United States. The appearance within recent years of up-to-date, detailed atlases of the Soviet Union, as well as *oblast* maps showing *raion* subdivision, and the issuing once again of statistical handbooks augur well for future geographical research and writing.

III

Any program aiming at the establishment of a more significant place for geography in Russian studies must recognize, first of all, that the basic need is to train more students. Interest in the geography of the Soviet Union among American students might be stimulated if the stronger departments of geography throughout the country gave more attention to the Soviet Union as a region. On the other hand, the major centers for Russian study should make every effort possible to expose their students to geography.

Not to be ignored is the need to stimulate contacts between American and Soviet geographers; such contacts might lead to opportunities for travel and research inside the Soviet Union, although it is doubtful that extensive field study there will become possible in the near future.

As was noted, geographical research in the past has been spotty and fragmentary. Therefore, more broadly conceived studies, both regional and topical, are required if the contribution of the geographer to the Russian area is to grow substantially. Particularly needed is the development of a conceptual frame of reference, or a philosophy of Soviet geographical change and growth, within which American geographers might work. The latter, in this connection, might do well to explore more fully, however unrewarding they may seem to be, the theories which Soviet geographers have advanced concerning their own work. Certainly, the frequent and insistent attempts in the Soviet Union to create rational, functional regions, whether administrative, economic, industrial management, or agricultural, warrant closer scrutiny in order to assess the existing stage of development, as well as to gain some insight into the ultimate goal and patterns to be achieved.

Systematic topical studies also hold great promise, not only in terms of the study of specific phenomena, but also as related to other phenomena and to the geographic whole. American geographers, as a rule, have tended to give more attention to the economic aspects of Soviet geography, for the most part ignoring the physical. Perhaps this is as it should be, since the work of Soviet physical geographers is in general useful, while economic geography has been largely neglected by Soviet scholars. American geographers might then direct their efforts to any number of economic topics and related problems. What, for example, are the relationships among resources, which constantly need re-evaluating in the light of new discoveries and changing technology, manpower, population, and industrial growth and location? What is the role and function of the city?—a subject which increasingly is attracting the attention of the Soviet geographer. Is there a hierarchy of places and how are these linked by expanding Soviet transportation facilities? Can Soviet agriculture meet the demands of a rapidly growing population, which is becoming increasingly urbanized? In what manner is the city affecting the utilization of the lands of the neighboring *kolkhozes* and *sovkhozes*?

At the same time, political and administrative geography represents a field much neglected by both Soviet and American geographers. Careful examination of pertinent geographic, political, and economic materials and data may yield fruitful studies. How and to what extent does the Soviet political-administrative map reflect Soviet political, economic, and geographic reality? What territorial functions do the subordinate administrative units perform? How closely do the national territories reflect national groupings and how significant is the political-administrative boundary?

Soviet cartographic techniques, exemplified in the newer Soviet atlases, have made important progress within recent years, and open up a large and complex field of study, which also demands attention.

If any of the foregoing suggestions have validity, there should be realized over the next five or ten years a greater volume and range of geographical writing in the United States on the Soviet Union. Indeed, the serious deficiencies in the literature must be overcome if geography is to play a significant role in any program of concentrated Russian studies, and if it is to demonstrate that it does truly have a point of view and an approach capable of making a major contribution when brought to bear full force on the Soviet area. The challenge exists, and there is much to be done.

Edward J. Brown

9. LITERATURE

I

THE PURPOSE of the present review is to assess the value of research in literature since 1945 as a contribution to our understanding of Russia, and to indicate its gaps and shortcomings and the most profitable lines of development for the future. We have not, of course, confined our attention to Soviet literature alone, but have considered also the most important research on Russian literature of the nineteenth century and even earlier; indeed, Soviet literature can hardly be understood, nor can research in it be properly evaluated, without constant reference to its roots in the past.

Much has been accomplished in the years since the first Russian area program was set up at Cornell University in 1943. Academic training in Russian, the training of specialists for teaching and research, and integrated area programs had received little attention up to that time; and Russian literature, both old and new, offered a rich field for American scholars. Since 1945 major studies on all aspects of Soviet life have been added to the excellent but limited material which existed at that time. In the field of Russian and Soviet literature the performance of the last ten

years is impressive: the number of monographs and essays, both
published and unpublished, is striking and their general quality
is high. Moreover, the major institutions during this time have
trained many new people in the techniques of research and
writing. For example, at Columbia University twenty-one Ph.D.
degrees and over eighty M.A. degrees have been awarded in the
field of Slavic languages and more than half of these were in
Russian and Soviet literature. Such figures hold promise of a great
increase in research activity and publication in the near future.

The main purpose of our review has not been to outline accomplishments in the field of literature, but rather to locate
lacunae and to emphasize shortcomings—in short, to point out
not so much what has been done as what has not. In everything
that follows, it is assumed that the reader is aware of the great
progress in this field since 1945.

II

A number of general works on the history and criticism of
Russian literature have been made available to the teacher and
student, among them Whitfield's one-volume abridgment of
Prince Mirsky's *History of Russian Literature*,[1] a new edition
of an old book. Except for a very brief section on Soviet literature, this edition does not claim to add anything to the original
work of Mirsky, which was completed in 1926. In addition to
Mirsky, we have Marc Slonim's extensive two-volume history of
Russian literature from the earliest times.[2] In either of these works
the student will find a treatment of the main facts and even of
subsidiary facts and personalities in Russian and Soviet literature.
Yet neither book is completely satisfactory as a reference work for
the scholar or as an introduction to the field for the sophisticated
American student. Mirsky's book is extremely valuable for its
original and stimulating, though at times highly personal, critical
interpretations of certain authors and periods; but Mirsky is not
always adequate in his treatment of intellectual and ideological

backgrounds, and without this, much of Russian literature remains unilluminated. Figures of great moment for literature such as Stankevich, Belinsky, Herzen, Mikhailovsky, and many others are given only a few scant pages in this otherwise fine work.

There is wide agreement on the need for a general work in literary history and criticism. But what is the condition of the field with regard to specialized works on particular topics and individual figures? And have we at our disposal the scholarly monographs and dissertations upon which general studies must be based? As a matter of fact, many works on individual writers of the pre-Soviet period have appeared during the last ten years, works which vary widely in their approach and scholarly purposes and which range from Simmons' lengthy and definitive biography of Tolstoy[3]—a work that made available to the American reader much new material on the writer's life and thought—to a number of brief but interesting and thoroughly readable biographies and critical studies that have appeared recently in book form—most of them, it is true, not by Americans. For example, in Britain David Magarshack has brought out two books on Chekhov as well as biographical studies of Turgenev and Gogol, along with his growing list of translations of the Russian classics;[4] Janko Lavrin has published a series of useful introductory works on Pushkin, Gogol, Tolstoy, Goncharov, and other writers;[5] and W. H. Bruford[6] and Ronald Hingley[7] have each published a book-length study of Chekhov. A book on Belinsky has already appeared,[8] an older work on Dostoyevsky has been reissued in a revised edition,[9] and books on several other writers are in the making.

It should be mentioned that some extremely important research on the earliest period of Russian literature has been accomplished in the United States. An outstanding example of cooperative, interdisciplinary scholarship is *La Geste du Prince Igor'*,[10] to which the principal contributors were Roman Jakobson, Henri Grégoire, Marc Szeftel, and George Vernadsky. Another work which should be mentioned, also a cooperative enterprise, is *Russian Epic Studies*,[11] edited by Roman Jakobson and Ernest J. Simmons. Articles on literature of the seventeenth century have frequently appeared in our journals, William E. Harkins of Columbia being one of the chief contributors of work on this period. Horace W. Dewey of the University of Michigan has worked in the medieval field on linguistic, legal, and literary problems.

We are not well supplied, however, with detailed, systematic, original and primary research on particular periods in the history of Russian literature; on many important nineteenth-century authors; on successive trends, both intellectual and stylistic; or on the important literary works themselves. It is true that our literary journals have carried excellent original articles on rather special and limited topics: the style of Bunin; certain types of symbolism in Dostoyevsky; various urges within him, including the matricidal and the parricidal; the technique of the "interior monologue" in Tolstoy; the interpretation of Gogol's story "The Nose," to mention only a few. These studies constitute a valuable body of research. Still, there is at present no major study of Tolstoy's *War and Peace* by an American scholar, though this lack will soon be corrected by the forthcoming appearance at Columbia of a dissertation on this topic.[12] A brief study of Dostoyevsky's novelistic technique in *The Brothers Karamazov* was published in 1957,[13] and a larger work on the novel is now in preparation at Columbia as a doctoral dissertation.[14] Two interesting articles on *Oblomov* have recently been published; but Goncharov's peculiar world as reflected in his fiction has lain fallow for many years, and Mazon's monumental work, which appeared in 1914, settled nothing finally.[15] The student of Russian literature and the teacher have been waiting for investigation and original discussion of the great literary works of the nineteenth century, the books which bulk so large in the intellectual experience of Russians, both Soviet and pre-Soviet.

We are not better off with regard to particular periods, trends, and schools of thought in Russian literature. Apart from Chyzhevsky's provocative book *On Romanticism in Slavic Literature*,[16] the study of Russian romanticism has not yet passed beyond the stage of annotated stereotypes. The "natural school" must be discussed in lectures on Russian literature, but we do not yet know exactly what it was and are learning only gradually;[17] the idealistic philosophers of the thirties are barely visible to us through a haze of established and impenetrable generalizations. The "men of the sixties" and their great antagonist Dostoyevsky offer opportunities that are still far from being exhausted.[18]

It has frequently been pointed out that the field suffers from an absence of comparative studies that would throw light on the interrelationships of Russian thought and writing with western European cultural and intellectual movements. Despite the contributions in this area of such productive scholars as Waclaw Lednicki[19] and of younger men like George Gibian,[20] there is still no work for the period since Pushkin that is comparable to Ernest J. Simmons' *English Literature and Culture in Russia* for the period up to Pushkin.[21] Many rich fields in pre-Soviet literature are yet to be exploited by American scholarship.

Perhaps we should remind ourselves that there is no need to look for new and remote areas of research, to study figures of secondary importance, or to discover unexpected or recondite topics in the work of the major figures. With us, hardly anything has already been done. The relatively few works so far made available—excellent though they are—have not settled anything for all time, and all signs indicate that our younger scholars are prepared and eager to do a job of reinterpretation on many topics, figures, and periods. We need not look far afield for problems to investigate concerning any Russian author; we can begin almost anywhere.

It should be emphasized again that much research is in progress at the moment this is written, and that this work will in the near future result in filling some of the gaps noted here. A number of works on Russian literature of the nineteenth century have recently appeared: Seduro's *Dostoyevsky in Russian Literary Criticism;*[22] Poggioli's *The Phoenix and the Spider,*[23] a collection of interesting critical essays; and the *Letters of Gorky and Andreev,* edited by Peter Yershov.[24] Among recently completed dissertations one should mention the study of Mayakovsky's early poetry by Lawrence Stahlberger (Harvard); "Sterne's Influence on the Early Tolstoy," by Peter Rudy (Columbia); "Symbolists' Criticism of Gogol," by Zoya Yurieff (Radcliffe); "Between Image and Idea: the Poetry of Blok," by Franklin Reeve (Columbia); "Viazemsky's Literary Criticism," by G. Ivask (Harvard); "Dostoyevsky's Underground Man," by Robert Jackson (California); and two studies of Herzen, by Allen McConnell (Columbia) and Martin Malia (Harvard). Dissertations are now in progress on the *Znanie* group of writers (Lydia Weston Kesich, Columbia), on Tyutchev (Richard Gregg, Columbia), and on Karamzin (Henry M. Nevel, Columbia); and postdoctoral research is now well advanced on a study of Gogol by Leon Stilman of Columbia, a study of Dostoyevsky's influence in France by Rufus Mathewson of Columbia, a work on Stankevich and his circle by Edward J. Brown of Brown University, a study of the Natural School of the 1840's by Kenneth Harper of the University of California at Los Angeles, a study of Leskov's literary technique by Hugh McLean of Harvard, and a biographical study of Leskov by William B. Edgerton of Indiana University.

In turning to research in literature of the Soviet period, we find that we are well served with works of both a general and a particular nature. There are two general histories dealing with the Soviet period: Marc Slonim's *Modern Russian Literature,*[25] and Gleb Struve's *Soviet Russian Literature, 1917-1950,*[26] books which provide information on all aspects of Soviet literature. A number of valuable insights on relations between Russian literature of the past and of the Soviet period are provided in *Con-*

tinuity and Change in Russian and Soviet Thought, edited by
Ernest J. Simmons, a collaborative effort not devoted specifically
to literature which seeks constants in the intellectual history
of Russia, both old and new.[27] A similar effort to bridge the past
and present is found in Rufus Mathewson's recently published
dissertation, *The Russian Positive Hero: An Inquiry into the
Aesthetics of Radicalism* (New York, 1958).

Research on specific topics in the field may be conveniently
treated under three classifications: (1) studies of Soviet-Marxist
literary policy, theory, and criticism; (2) studies of literature as
social documentation; and (3) literary-critical studies. Under the
first heading we should mention a number of works published by
the Columbia University Press, among them *The Proletarian
Episode in Russian Literature,*[28] which examines the period from
1928 to 1932, when the Stalinist authorities finally eliminated
all trace of independence from Party doctrine in Soviet literature,
being forced in the end to liquidate their own proletarian organization as a hotbed of dissidence. Luckyj's *Literary Politics in the
Soviet Ukraine*[29] is an excellent study of the struggle for an independent national literature which makes use not only of all
pertinent published materials but also of the unpublished diaries
and letters of one of the leading participants in the events of that
day. Both of these works were originally written as dissertations at
Columbia University. Another book that is concerned with literary politics and policies, among other things, is *Through the
Glass of Soviet Literature,*[30] edited by Ernest J. Simmons, an
interesting and sometimes very able series of research papers in
which the emphasis is on the use of Soviet literature and literary
criticism as valid documentation of Soviet life. A large number
of excellent Master's essays on kindred topics have been produced
in past years at Columbia, some of which have already been
published as articles in scholarly journals; another series will
soon appear in book form.

Among studies of Soviet-Marxist criticism we might mention

Deming Brown's dissertation—soon to be published—on Soviet criticism of American literature, and Burton Rubin's dissertation —now in progress—on Plekhanov and Russian Marxist literary criticism. These studies will greatly enrich our resources in this field, since they give much indispensable background and historical information on current Soviet attitudes and ideas about the nature and function of literature.

We have been weakest in the production of genuine literary and critical studies. Victor Erlich's excellent *Russian Formalism*,[31] a study of literary criticism in the early twenties, is a fine exception. Ernest J. Simmons has just published a study of the works of Fedin, Leonov, and Sholokhov, which shows, by detailed analysis of their major novels, how these writers created works of enduring literary merit within the framework of Party dictation.[32] The four volumes so far published in the series, Harvard Slavic Studies,[33] have presented a number of interesting articles on Soviet literature.

There is no doubt among those who know the field that American research on Soviet literature represents a solid accomplishment. In the course of investigating literature, literary life in the Soviet Union, Marxist literary theory, and Soviet literary practice, our scholars have been able to throw light on all aspects of Soviet life, and their work on literature is regarded as useful by scholars in other disciplines. However, since it is our policy not to dwell overlong on positive accomplishments, we shall proceed immediately to point out some faults, defects, and shortcomings.

One sweeping criticism of research in this field over the last ten years is that a great deal of time and talent has been invested in the painstaking and detailed study of a stunted growth: Soviet literature. Even if one grants the assumptions that underlie such a criticism, we must still reply that basic research had to be done in order to establish certain facts that could not be taken for granted. If today Soviet literature is not as much of an "enigma wrapped in a mystery" as it was ten years ago, if today we know much more than we once did about the real meaning of such terms as "proletarian literature," "socialist realism," "the positive hero," it is largely because so much work has been done in the interval that we can, on some things, speak with knowledge. We have taken great pains to document thoroughly the now known and admitted fact that the Communist authorities, after a brief literary revival in the twenties, deliberately and consciously inhibited the production of literature, replacing it as far as possible with propaganda and educational materials in the forms usually employed by literature: the novel, the play, the poem. Once this was convincingly demonstrated, we studied in meticulous detail the methods and processes of control: we have investigated VAPP, RAPP, VAPLITE;[34] we have studied the Writers' Union; and we have examined the careers of Soviet literary men in order to discover not so much what they wrote as why they had to write it. We have studied Soviet criticism less as criticism than for its political motivation and content. And we now know in great detail how conformity to political directives was imposed on Soviet literature. An indispensable labor was performed and the ground was cleared of many misconceptions that were widespread in 1945.

This approach to Soviet literature has been criticized on the ground that, owing partly to the severe limitations of Soviet literature itself, much research effort has been concentrated not on literary production but on literary theory, literary organization, and literature as social documentation. The charge has been made that literary scholarship has impinged unduly on other disciplines and at times has been almost indistinguishable in its approach and purpose from the work of the historian or the political scientist.

In the absence of poems, plays, and novels giving honest, direct, and immediate literary formulation to the raw material of Soviet life, American scholarship has often been reduced to political and social analysis of the voluminous product which has gone under the name of Soviet literature. The use of Soviet literature as social documentation has yielded some good results, but these results have always to be evaluated with the greatest care, since the literature we study is perhaps the one literature in Europe least likely, except by accident, to reflect the real experience of actual people.

In defense of the political and sociological analysis of Soviet literature it has been said that since the "area" approach to Russian studies involves integration and cross-fertilization of the disciplines, the research in literature of an area program ought to grow out of and contribute to the whole study of a given area. In the Columbia Russian Institute area program and in other such programs, for instance, literature of the Soviet period has been emphasized. Problems have been studied, the solution of which would be of value to the social and political historian as well as to the historian of literature in general. It has been pointed out that this "sociological" approach to literary research is a widely accepted one, that it has yielded much of value, and that it is entirely valid if it is not allowed to obstruct or obscure other possible avenues of research, which might not so readily enter into an area program.

Perhaps the issues involved here should be defined more closely. It would seem that there are at least two possible approaches to the study of literature in its relation to a given society: (1) the study of literature as a source of information about the society which produces it; and (2) the study of social conditions as factors which influence the form and content of literature. Either approach is a valid one for Soviet literature, but it may be well to keep the distinction in mind. The first approach—the use of literature as social documentation—has only a limited usefulness when applied to Soviet literature, since that literature was reduced during the Stalin period to the status of a government-controlled educational and propaganda tool. The study of this controlled literature tells us very little about actual social conditions in the Soviet Union, though it does give us much information about the state of mind of the Soviet government, and its programs and policies at any given moment. The second approach makes use of information already at hand concerning social conditions in order to understand and interpret the literature. It is obvious that this approach is necessary and inevitable in the study of Soviet literature, and that we cannot begin to understand the latter without using information gleaned from the work of social scientists, or literary scholars engaged in similar investigations.

Perhaps this distinction should also be kept in mind when we consider the place of literature in an area program. However, the sociological approach obviously does not exhaust the possibilities of literary study, even in an area program. One might very well question whether there is really any conflict between the study of literature for its purely aesthetic and literary values, and the use of that literature in the total, integrated study of a given area from the viewpoint of several disciplines. Is it not the purpose of an integrated area program that *all* points of view should be represented, including that of the literary specialist? Might not studies of literary form and content, the critical analysis of aesthetic standards as revealed in the literature of a nation, contribute an ingredient to area programs that those programs sometimes lack? The study of literature—not only as social documentation but for its own sake—is a source of direct and immediate contact with the most sensitive, conscious, and articulate section of any society, and only a literary specialist can make this contribution.

At the same time, the peculiar nature of Soviet society demands from the literary scholar a historical perspective and a political sophistication that can scarcely be compared to the equipment that is considered necessary for the study of the literatures of western Europe. The research of the last ten years on the relation of Soviet literature to Soviet society has been indispensable as a part of the groundwork for a study of Soviet literature as literature. Moreover, the sociological or political approach to Soviet literature must continue to play its part in our future research, for we must keep ourselves informed about the changing nature of the political controls that are imposed upon the creative impulse of Soviet artists. Equipped with this growing knowledge about the place of the writer in Soviet society, the American literary scholar will find great and exciting opportunities awaiting him in the field of Soviet literature.

Perhaps the most immediate need is for monographs on key figures and leading schools of thought in Soviet literary history. Studies are called for on LEF, the Perevaltsy, the Constructivists, and the Serapion Brothers. Even the Proletcult has yet to be studied as a literary movement. The list of writers whose works must be examined more closely before we can generalize about the Soviet period is a long one, and includes most of the leading figures in Soviet literature. Curiously enough, since Kaun's biography, published in 1931, there has been almost no serious work by American scholars on so important a figure in Soviet literature and politics as Maxim Gorky.[35]

We know from the research of the past ten years how seriously the development of Soviet literature has been stunted by political regimentation, but the glimpses we have gotten since 1955 into literary life below the surface of the officially printed page make it clear that, even in Soviet society, literature continues to serve in some measure as a vehicle for the transmission of human values that resist the corrosive force of totalitarianism. Such symptomatic books as Dudintsev's *Not by Bread Alone,* the works in the two volumes of *Literaturnaya Moskva,* and Pasternak's *Doctor Zhivago* open to the student new vistas of study on the interaction between the Soviet literary artist and the society in which he lives. This challenge will call forth all the ingenuity of the scholar experienced in studying the social content of

Soviet literature and all the literary insight of the scholar who is trained in formal criticism. Together they can make a contribution of unusual significance.

III

No attempt has been made to spell out in detailed terms the research needs of our field, though some specific suggestions have been made. There seems to be wide agreement that a general work of literary analysis and criticism is sorely needed for Russian literature. Such a work would not replace, but supplement, the histories we now have, with greater emphasis on actual literary production as a revelation of Russian intellectual life of the nineteenth and twentieth centuries. The intimate connection of literature in Russia with ideas and ideology makes such a work indispensable.

Before such a work can be written, much preliminary work remains to be done on individual writers and critics and on certain periods in Russian intellectual history. The just completed Jubilee Edition of Tolstoy in ninety volumes is ground waiting to be tilled; the complete works of Belinsky, recently published, offer new and interesting material that ought to be investigated; the work of Chekhov has been neglected by American scholarship, although Chekhov not only was an important innovator and influence in European literature generally, but offers a free commentary on Russian intellectual and social life at the turn of the century. There is a long list of topics awaiting our interest and our scholarly labor.

We have remarked on the lack of comparative studies and on the importance they hold for us. Men now at work in the field recognize the futility of studying Russian literature in isolation from its sources and close relatives in western Europe. An interesting and fruitful line of endeavor would be the study of Russian culture—even in its most particularist and Slavophile moments—as a significant peripheral branch of European culture.

Russian writers are placed in clearer perspective when understood as part of a larger cultural and intellectual pattern. The idea now has gained wide acceptance that every specialist in Russian literature must to some extent also be a comparativist.

What has already been said about research in Soviet literature indicates one direction in which we ought to move. A more general suggestion, applicable to Russian literature before the Revolution as well as since, arises out of the nature of Soviet scholarship. The quantity of literary research that has appeared in the Soviet Union is enormous. One of its most commendable achievements has been the publication of such series of literary archival materials as *Literaturnoye Nasledstvo, Zvenya,* and the *Letopisi* of the State Literary Museum; and the publication of scholarly editions of such writers as Belinsky, Chekhov, Chernyshevsky, Dobrolyubov, Gogol, Gorky, Herzen, Nekrasov, A. N. Ostrovsky, Pushkin, Saltykov-Shchedrin, and Leo Tolstoy. All this material has been a boon to specialists on Russian literature everywhere. Along with this documentary material Soviet scholars have likewise published a great deal of original research, some of which is of very high quality. The requirements of Soviet Marxist orthodoxy, however, have so influenced the bulk of Soviet literary scholarship that the resultant interpretation of Russian literature suffers from an imbalance unacceptable to most scholars who do not share the Soviet Marxist faith. This situation presents two basic challenges to students living beyond the confines in which this faith is imposed: to help restore the balance by working on topics that are neglected by Soviet scholars, and to strive to correct misinterpretations wherever the requirements of Soviet orthodoxy lead Soviet scholars to conclusions that are open to question.

Quantitative examples of this imbalance can be seen in Matsuev's recent bibliography of literature and literary scholarship published in the Soviet Union from 1938 to 1945. Works written by and about Gorky fill thirty-nine pages of this book, and the list for Mayakovsky fills twenty-one pages, while Turgenev gets only four and a half pages and Goncharov only one. In the whole period from 1938 to 1945 Matsuev lists only two articles published in the Soviet Union on S. T. Aksakov, four on Fet, nine on Tyutchev, three on A. K. Tolstoy, three on Apollon Maikov, eight on Pisemsky, six on Stankevich, and none at all on Alexander Blok, Balmont, Vyacheslav Ivanov, Merezhkovsky, the Slavophiles, and a host of Soviet writers whose names disappeared from the Soviet press in the 1930's. Among critics the bibliography on Chernyshevsky fills seven pages; while Apollon Grigoryev gets two articles; Druzhinin, one; and Annenkov, Leontyev, and N. K. Mikhailovsky, none at all.[36]

These merely quantitative comparisons give only a partial indication of the gaps in published Soviet scholarship and the wealth of opportunities for significant research on Russian literature that await the American scholar. Some of the gaps have already attracted American specialists, as shown by references made above to research in progress or recently completed, and likewise by such books as Oleg Maslennikov's study of Bely and the Symbolist poets[37] and Zavalishin's recent work on early Soviet writers.[38] Among the numerous possibilities for group research it has been suggested that a seminar might be held on "Continuity and Change in Russian and Soviet Literature," from which there might emerge a series of research papers that would establish the modality of literary succession or invention in the old and the new. Studies of the element of dissent in the works of nearly all the prominent Soviet writers might yield information on the pattern of "inner revolt" in the total development of Soviet literature. Despite the relaxation of controls since the death of Stalin and the rehabilitation of many Soviet writers whose names could not previously be mentioned in print, there are still numerous figures and aspects of Soviet literature that can be discussed in print only outside the Soviet Union, among them such significant writers as Remizov, Pilnyak, and Zamyatin.

The Frenchman studying English literature or the Englishman studying French literature must overcome great handicaps of language and cultural experience before he can hope to match the research of native scholars. Naturally, the Englishman, Frenchman, or American studying Russian literature must overcome the same handicaps; but their freedom from the subtle network of controls over scholarly research in the Soviet Union gives their work a potential importance far greater than that of any research the English and French may produce on each other's literature. As long as this situation lasts, foreign scholars must continue their effort to fill the gaps and correct the imbalances wherever they can in the structure of literary scholarship on Russia. But as they work they can hope that the unnatural importance of their own research on Russian literature will eventually disappear, along with present-day barriers in the Soviet Union to full freedom of inquiry and communication.

Francis J. Whitfield

10. LINGUISTICS

I

A MOST IMPORTANT ASPECT of American study of Russian linguistics since World War II has been the increase in opportunities for scholars in the field to maintain contact with each other and to carry on a profitable exchange of ideas. Near the beginning of the period, for example, at the Stanford meeting of the Modern Language Association in 1949, the first meeting of the Slavic and East European "Group II," devoted specifically to linguistics of the area, took place. Neither of the papers delivered at that meeting was concerned primarily with Russian linguistics—or, indeed, with linguistics in the narrow sense.[1] The topics discussed were the original homelands of the Balts and of the Slavs—problems in which linguistics assumes the function of an auxiliary science. But it was made clear at the meeting that the choice of these general subjects reflected the intention of the organizers and participants to inaugurate the new discussion group with emphasis on the broad implications of linguistic research, the interrelations of such research within the Slavic and East European field, and its relations with other disciplines. Subsequent developments—not merely within the Modern Language Association—have confirmed this setting, even extending the frames of research in the field.

This catholic approach is one of the valuable traditions of American Slavistics, inherited from the pioneers of Russian studies in this country. In spite of every practical reason for confining their attention to the Russian field, interpreted narrowly, and in spite of no little pressure to do so, these early workers succeeded in clearing the ground for the broad developments in Slavic studies that followed the end of the last war. The importance of this inheritance cannot be overstressed. Professor George Y. Shevelov of Columbia, in reviewing this report, has commented:

There may be no deep insight into either the structure of Modern Russian or its history without knowledge of the other Slavic languages. This is the only guarantee against one-sidedness, naive exaggerations based on insufficient knowledge, and premature generalizations by amateurs. Neither adequate research nor high-level teaching of Russian is thinkable without mastering the data on at least some of the other Slavic languages. Concentration on Russian linguistic studies alone would not only be shortsighted from the point of view of orientation in the entangled inter-Slavic relations, but would mean a depreciation of Russian studies themselves. . . . The emphasis on Russian, very much in vogue now under the influence of *sputniks,* but always basically sound, would turn out to be unfortunate if it led to a neglect of other Slavic languages, at least as an auxiliary means for better understanding of Russian. These considerations, of course, do not imply that the study of Russian should be comparative. What is important is knowledge of the other Slavic languages, not necessarily their explicit use in any particular piece of research.

To such a broad conception of its responsibilities, the Modern Language Association group has been attached from its very beginnings, and, together with other organizations of a related character, it has provided much needed forums for linguists working in the Slavic and East European area. Thus, gradually, one of the first prerequisites for rapid, efficient exchange of information concerning research in Russian linguistics has been attained. In this connection, particular mention should be made of such a meeting as the Conference of American and Canadian Slavicists, held at Ann Arbor, June 27-29, 1953. This congress, with one session devoted entirely to Russian linguistics and another to Slavic linguistics in general, offered special advantages that cannot be duplicated in meetings where non-Slavic studies occupy the greater part of the available time. The desirability of establishing a regular schedule of such Slavic congresses should be given serious attention in any program for strengthening the position of Russian linguistics in this country.

Two years after the Stanford meeting, and two years before the Ann Arbor Conference, "in view of the rapid development of Slavic studies in America," as the masthead explained, an entire number of the linguistics journal *Word* (Volume 7, Number 2) was devoted primarily to articles and reviews in the field of Slavic linguistics. It is pertinent, in such an essay as this, to note that this important event was made possible by a generous grant from the Committee for the Promotion of Advanced Slavic Studies, n.c. In the following year, the same Committee supported the founding of a special journal, *Slavic Word*, appearing annually as a fourth number of *Word* and serving as a central organ for American studies in Slavic linguistics and— in the small measure possible—as a place where Slavicists abroad could present their work to an American audience. The editors' introduction may be quoted to illustrate their conception of the activity to be reflected in, and encouraged by, the new journal, and to emphasize once again the lively contacts with other parts of the field and with other disciplines that have characterized the healthy growth of Russian linguistics in this country over the past dozen years:

In the principal American centers of Slavic studies, scholars are actively engaged in a systematic description of contemporary Slavic languages, making full use of the recent methodological achievements in structural linguistics and such cognate fields as cultural anthropology, theory of social interaction, symbolic logic, communication theory, sound analysis, etc. This synchronic approach· is being supplemented by a more profound enquiry into the historical phonology and grammar of different Slavic languages, their genetic interrelations, and their affinities with adjacent tongues. Here again, the rich accumulation of experience gained in structural analysis, areal studies, and contiguous historical disciplines will be put to full use.

The robust optimism of this manifesto would, of course, have sufficiently identified its principal composer and the leading spirit behind the journal, even if Roman Jakobson's pervasive influence had not been evident throughout this and the following issues. There have been, and will be, other occasions for appreciating the extent and the quality of his exceptional contribution to the development of American Slavistics, but even in a brief report of this kind it should not go unmentioned.

In all, four numbers of *Slavic Word* appeared—all with the aid of the Committee for the Promotion of Advanced Slavic Studies, n.c. In addition, the same Committee supported the separate publication of two significant monographs in the field, issued as supplements to *Word* in 1951 and 1953: Karl Menges's *Oriental Elements in the Vocabulary of the Oldest Russian Epos, The Igor' Tale*—continuing the new phase of *Igor'* studies inaugurated by the great collective volume of text, translations, and commentary that was published in New York shortly after the war[2]—and Yury Šerech [—Shevelov]'s *Problems in the Formation of Belorussian.*

The demise of *Slavic Word,* after its fourth issue (1955), involved serious consequences for the well-being of Russian studies in this country. Neither general linguistic reviews nor the growing number of journals, series, and yearbooks devoted to Slavic studies as a whole and involving many disciplines can fill the gap. These other outlets have, indeed, in varying degrees, tended to reflect the generally increased activity in Slavic linguistics, both in the quantity and in the quality of the research they have published in the field.[3] At the same time they cannot, by their nature, fulfill the functions of a journal devoted exclusively to Slavic linguistics.

II

The picture of research opportunities in Russian linguistics over the past decade is, in general, a cheering one. Conditions have improved for fruitful cooperation of scholars in the field and for exchange of information on the results of their work. Long-term projects, reflecting some of the most advanced positions in contemporary American and European linguistics, have attracted able Ph.D. candidates and young postdoctoral scholars and furnished an important part of their training. The gradual spread of Russian studies over the country has involved an increasing number of university centers in the promotion of Slavic linguistic research. If it has been necessary to record an occasional disappointment and setback, still a heartening example has been given of what can be accomplished with the timely application of appropriate stimuli.

The use that has been made of improved research conditions and the exploitation of new areas of research and new methods have, on the whole, well justified the efforts and hopes of those who took the lead in these developments. Inevitably, given the extraordinarily rapid growth of the field during the period under consideration, and given the very ambitious and all-embracing program under which the work has been planned, many of the expected results are observable only in part. Theoretical mappings of extensive areas of inquiry, preliminary methodological discussions, progress reports, and studies of sample problems selected from a larger nexus constitute a good proportion of the evidence that Russian linguistic studies are advancing with ever greater momentum.

Lest this report be taken to overemphasize certain newer aspects of linguistic research, it should be stated clearly that there is no intention to minimize more conservative approaches. Projects which apply new methods and try to pave new ways deserve particular support, but in any branch of science no single approach can guarantee an absolutely adequate and complete cognition of reality. Every method, by its own nature, disregards certain aspects of reality. It is very important, therefore, not to rely on one method alone in any scholarly investigations, Slavic linguistics included.

A conspicuous example of the application of modern techniques to questions of basic theoretical importance is to be found in the collective research project supported by the Rockefeller Foundation and dealing with intensive X-ray and sound-spectrographic study of Russian speech sounds, making possible the calculation of relations between their motor and acoustic aspects. The results of these studies that have so far appeared, and the refined distinctive-feature analysis that they have helped to make possible, have already had far-reaching effects, not merely on Russian and on Slavic linguistics, but on general linguistic theory.[4]

Work is in progress using similar techniques of statistical communication theory on Russian phonemic complexes, vocabulary, and connected text. In this connection might also be mentioned the ground-breaking *Russian Word Count and Frequency Analysis of Grammatical Categories of Standard Literary Russian,* prepared by Harry H. Josselson (Detroit, 1953), which, beyond its immediate results, suggests further statistical work that will be required from other premises and other points of view.

Structural studies of Russian radical, derivational, and inflexional morphemes, of morphophonemic alternations, and of devices of word-composition are being undertaken and are already represented by a number of exploratory articles that promise a fresh contribution to the analysis of Russian sign-structure in its expression aspect. Content-analysis of morphological categories, sign-classes, and constructions in Russian, cutting across traditional and often theoretically indefensible boundaries of morphology, syntax, and semantics, hold similar promise of having basic implications for linguistics, extending far beyond the Russian field. Work on the semantic spectra of such categories as aspect and tense in Russian, for example, again illustrates the function that Russian studies have assumed of bringing into the core of linguistic research phenomena that have in the past tended to receive only marginal attention in this country.

At the meeting ground of linguistic and literary studies, where are located such subjects as the formation of literary languages and their peculiar characteristics in relation to other usages, the devices of poetic language, and the many other problems of stylistics, research plans in our field again warrant the expectation that, with proper encouragement, American Slavic linguistics will stake out territories still relatively unfamiliar to general linguistic research in this country. This expectation is strengthened by the friendly collaboration of scholars representing different traditions and by their generous contribution to the training of a new generation of American research workers and teachers. Various possible lines of such research, making use of sophisticated synchronic and diachronic techniques, are indicated in programmatic articles like Jakobson's "Kernel of Comparative Slavic Literature"[5] or Šerech [—Shevelov]'s "Toward a Historical Dialectology: Its Delimitation of the History of Literary Language."[6]

Significant also is the readiness of workers in Russian linguistics—perhaps in part because of the very newness of the discipline in this country—to establish contact with other disciplines that must be called on for aid in any vigorous program of linguistic investigation. Already noted in connection with phonetic and phonemic studies, this characteristic is equally evident in such current research as that on machine translation from Russian (which also has basic theoretical implications of great importance) and is well exemplified by the already mentioned collective volume on the *Igor' Tale,* along with the several supplementary studies that it has inspired. Comparative work involving connections between the Slavic and Baltic languages, particularly associated with long-range research projects at the University of Pennsylvania, is another instance of this "open" aspect of our studies, further exemplified by current research on contacts between Russian and languages that are in neither the Slavic nor the Baltic family.

It may, then, fairly be claimed that, within the general expansion of Russian studies in the last decade, linguistics has had a significant share in the training of able young scholars and teachers, the development and application of new research methods, and the awakening of interest in an increasing number of universities. Here, as in other aspects of Russian studies, progress was largely made possible through the farsighted planning and effective cooperation of the universities and the foundations and through the devotion and skilled leadership of the senior scholars in the field. Moreover, Russian linguistic studies have benefited, not only from the rapidly growing concern with Russian studies as a whole, but also from lively contemporary developments in American linguistics.

The picture is gratifying on the whole. But it must be added that our linguistic studies are still only in the beginning of their healthy growth. A number of important and challenging projects lie ahead. For example, there have been no studies at all of a comprehensive nature in Slavic historical phonology and grammar; almost no studies in dialectology; no important studies on etymology and onomastics; no studies in synchronic comparative phonology and grammar of the Slavic languages (except H. Rubenstein's *A Comparative Study of Morphophonemic Alternations in Standard Serbo-Croatian, Czech and Russian* [Ann Arbor, 1950]); and very few on the history of the Slavic literary languages. We have been promised numerous and ground-breaking studies in the structure of Modern Standard Russian, but so far almost nothing in this field has come out.[7]

If the potentialities of the field are to be realized, intelligent planning, efficient use of the resources accumulated, and continued cooperation of institutions and individual scholars are all badly needed. Specifically, lines of effective communication among scholars in the field must be assured. Among other problems, mention has been made of the need for a central outlet for the publication of research and the review of current Slavic linguistic work both here and abroad. It also devolves on those concerned with maintaining favorable conditions of research to investigate means of providing regularly scheduled congresses for specialists in the field.

III

In considering future research needs and the encouragement of specific lines of research, wisdom dictates that we be guided by the successful beginnings that can now be recorded. The organic growth of Russian linguistic studies in America over the last decade reflects in large part the precept and example of scholars committed to the belief that only basic research over a broad field of inquiry can make a healthy climate for work of permanent significance. The most important investigations of the Russian language have accordingly been carried on in the vanguard of present-day linguistic studies and have run parallel with analyses of closely related languages. An understanding of the need for such a setting for research, and an appreciation of its long-term value, are prerequisites for the proper encouragement of Russian linguistics, just as they are for the encouragement of any other area of linguistic studies.

In common with those other areas, the Russian field shares, by its very nature, certain general conditions of development. Common sense and a reasonable concern for the efficient use of limited personnel will require that priority be given to research that can be better done here than elsewhere. Put the other way, caution should be exercised in the planning of work for which indispensable firsthand materials are available mainly in the Soviet Union, at least until opportunities are afforded for prolonged study and field work abroad. Mere restatements of well-worked problems in modern Russian grammar, for instance, so far as they are based on no particularly new or "American" methodology and rely primarily on secondary sources or, in studies of the spoken language, on a limited number of accidentally available informants, would represent unsound and wasteful use of our resources. Other important limitations to be considered are those imposed when the investigator's native language is not Russian.

On the other hand, American scholars enjoy peculiarly rich opportunities for research in areas that are ignored or underdeveloped in the Slavic countries. The application of new techniques of linguistic analysis to the Russian language has already been cited several times as an example. Many problems of a politically sensitive nature in the Soviet Union, like the influence of jargons on modern Russian, the influence of Russian on the other languages of the U.S.S.R. and vice versa, peculiarities of propaganda language, or Western influences in Russian, require the unbiased treatment of free scholarship and promise rich returns both for their own sake and for their obvious implications outside the field of linguistics.

Ten years ago, a national conference on the study of world areas, held under the sponsorship of the Committee on World Area Research of the Social Science Research Council, observed the need for an improved Russian-English dictionary. It may not be inappropriate to suggest here that a study should be made of the resources available for a large-scale, cooperative project, exploiting modern techniques of bilingual lexicography, to provide a dictionary fitted to the needs of American scholars.

As in other fields of Russian studies, there has been some tendency in linguistics, with notable exceptions, to weigh the balance heavily on the side of contemporary subject matter. Despite an awareness of the largely unexplored comparative and historical fields and despite some outstanding achievements in attacking them, scholars in linguistics have oriented much of their work toward synchronic description. Yet both diachronic and synchronic comparative studies, which have suffered from considerable shortcomings in the Soviet Union, offer opportunities for American-trained scholars to make important contributions. Structural interpretation of linguistic developments and historical dialectology have already been cited as examples of promising research fields where investigators who are unhampered by political bias or pressure and are armed with modern methods of analysis may expect to find rewarding topics and may help significantly in deepening our knowledge of Russian civilization and history.

In commenting on this report, Professor Shevelov has pointed out that the development of Slavic studies in general and Slavic linguistics in particular under present world conditions is important to assure American contributions to this branch of science, to strengthen the prestige of the United States in the cultural field, and to ensure a solid basis for the vitally important spread of a knowledge of the Russian language. In addition, achievements in Slavic linguistic studies may easily become a matter of cultural export to countries of Asia, Africa, and Latin America. These countries are beginning to teach Slavic languages and literatures. Assistance in providing teaching staff, textbooks, and other aids is or will soon be wanted. Naturally, first glances are turned to Russia. But American Slavic linguistics may have some advantages in comparison with Russia. It can supply these countries with Slavicists and Slavistics with no political implications; it can offer more modern methods and better technical equipment; the English language is familiar in many of these countries. And the only real advantage of Russia, the unlimited number of native speakers, can be partly countered by the fact that America also has many persons with both English and a Slavic language as native languages.

Consolidation of the gains achieved during the period under

review, maintenance and improvement of the conditions that
have made those gains possible, increased attention to the relatively neglected portions of the comprehensive program lying
behind Russian linguistic studies in America from their inception,
and increased awareness of where American research can render
best and most efficient service—these would seem to be desiderata
on which all responsible workers in the field find themselves in
agreement. A candid view of the foundations that have been
laid and a no more than moderately optimistic appreciation of
future opportunities give good reason for hope in the increased
prestige and importance of Russian linguistics in America in the
years ahead.

Robert M. Slusser

11. MUSIC

I

As USED IN THIS ESSAY, the term "Russian music" refers primarily to music composed in pre- and post-1917 Russia. In a historical sense, however, "Russian music" includes the work of *all* those composers who received their training and spent their formative years in Russia, regardless of whether they left Russia after the 1917 revolutions. Thus, Rachmaninoff and Stravinsky, who lived abroad after 1917, must be considered "Russian" composers, as well as Prokofiev, who emigrated but returned, and Miaskovsky, who never left Russia. Music in the Soviet Union today is still under the strong influence of the work of the pre-revolutionary generation of composers, the émigrés as well as those in Russia. For example, music written by Stravinsky since 1930, despite the official ban on its performance or reproduction in the Soviet Union, is the subject of avid study among Soviet composers, and thus forms one of the basic influences helping to determine the future direction of "Russian music." Moreover, the work of the émigré composers is rooted to a considerable extent in the specifically Russian cultural and musical milieu in which they were trained. The term "Russian music" is therefore used in a historical and organic, as well as a political and geographic, sense. "Soviet music," on the other hand, refers specifically to music composed in post-1917 Russia.

While this essay deals primarily with work done in the United States, musicology is an international discipline, with its oldest and best established centers outside the United States; it has therefore been necessary to take into account not only studies completed in the United States but also publications in English from other countries, as well as those in European languages.

This is a survey of writing about music, not a survey of the music itself. The story of the popularization of Russian music in the United States is a long and extremely interesting one, but no attempt has been made to tell it here, except as it finds partial reflection in books and articles.

In the field of Russian area studies, Russian music has so far figured only as a small and obscure frontier province, seldom visited and imperfectly explored, whereas in the world of music it is an important and strategically located territory. Inevitably, therefore, the major share of the task of studying Russian music has been carried out by critics, commentators, scholars, and professional writers whose primary concern is with music. In evaluating the work done, this fact must be kept in mind.

II

In the final analysis, most of the writing about music, from journalistic criticism to scholarly studies, reflects and is based on the standard repertoire. Furthermore, a firsthand knowledge of the music itself is a prerequisite to any serious study of the subject. A consideration of what Russian music is performed and recorded is therefore a necessary preliminary to our inquiry.

Russian music has long formed an essential part of the standard repertoire. Works by most of the major composers of nineteenth- and early twentieth-century Russia are performed almost as frequently in New York, Paris, and Rome as in Leningrad and

Moscow. In their treatment of post-1917 composers, however, the Soviet Union and the West diverge sharply; whereas in the West works written under the Soviet regime gain acceptance only after overcoming the double obstacle of unfamiliarity and ideological strangeness, in the Soviet Union it is precisely these works which constitute the major part of the repertoire.

Consequently, the student dependent on concert performances alone for his knowledge of Russian music would inevitably miss the greater part of the music currently being composed in the Soviet Union. To some extent this situation can be remedied by the use of recordings. Thanks to the technological revolution wrought by the invention of the long-playing record, not only is most of the standard repertoire available on records,[1] but many Soviet works seldom or never played in the West can be heard.[2] Although the coverage is by no means complete, it seems likely that in the course of time most works of major importance will become available in recorded form.

It remains true, nevertheless, that music is a field in which direct observation and study are of primary importance. It is therefore to be hoped that among the American students who will be visiting and studying in the Soviet Union in coming years will be some with an interest and training in music.

Published works on music include both general and scholarly studies. The subjects represented in both categories closely conform to the prevailing taste in performance—with few exceptions, the composers dealt with are those whose works are most popular.

The books on Russian music which have been published in English over the past forty years present few novelties. There are a number of surveys and historical studies, biographies of a relatively few composers or performers, and a considerable body of criticism and appreciation.[3] From the standpoint of the Russian area specialist, most of these works leave much to be desired. An adequate knowledge of the Russian background is often lacking, and when scholarly standards are met, they tend naturally to be those of the musician rather than of the area specialist. Most of the more solid works are by a handful of writers who for many years have specialized in the study of various aspects of Russian music.

Some of the most valuable publications from the standpoint of scholarship reflect the tastes and initiative of a few individual publishers rather than any broad popular interest. Since books in this category usually represent a financial risk, their number is limited and what has been published is only a small fraction of what would be desirable from the standpoint of Russian area studies. We are given Tchaikovsky's *Diaries,* but not his extensive and valuable correspondence; Stravinsky's *Autobiography* and *Poetics of Music,* but almost nothing on his talented contemporary, Scriabin; Rimsky-Korsakoff's autobiography, but none of César Cui's critical writings; an excellent documentary biography of Musorgsky, but nothing on such seminal figures as Glinka and Dargomyzhsky.[4] In view of the limited sales such works can be expected to have, however, Russian area specialists should no doubt be grateful for what has been vouchsafed, rather than complain about what is withheld. It must be recognized, nevertheless, that the documentary and scholarly materials on Russian music published commercially, despite their value, do not in themselves provide an adequate basis for serious musicological or area-study analysis of Russian music. Moreover, such analysis presupposes both a technical preparation in music and the ability to use source materials in Russian or other Slavic languages.

There are only a few works which deal with the relationship between music and the system of political controls in the Soviet Union, mainly written by journalists who specialize in Soviet topics.[5] A few books in this category represent defenses of the policies of the Communist Party.[6] Such works, useful as *prima facie* evidence, must be treated with due caution as contributions to scholarship.

Russian music has a definite place in all standard works of musical reference. Whether the place is adequate and whether the treatment is sound are questions, however, which the Russian area specialist will wish to raise.

It is encouraging, therefore, to be able to report that the basic work of musical reference in the English language—*Grove's Dictionary of Music and Musicians,* now in its fifth edition—presents an admirable example of professional musical scholarship judiciously but unobtrusively aware of the major factors which have determined the evolution of Russian music. In smaller musical reference handbooks, one finds varying degrees of comprehension of the special problems of Russian music.[7] With *Grove's* available as a standard, however, the Russian area specialist need experience no great alarm concerning the basic reference data being used by musical scholars.

At the same time, this is not to say that Russian area specialists can rest satisfied with what has been provided by the editors of works of musical reference. Such editors necessarily treat Russian music as a component of music as a whole and only to the extent they consider justified by its intrinsic importance. While this approach produces reasonably good results for the pre-Soviet period, it is less satisfactory for post-1917 Russian music. It is the Soviet period of Russian music which most urgently requires documentation and elucidation, since here Russian music diverges most significantly from the practices and standards of the West. It is exactly the music of this period, however, which engages the attention of Western scholars least, whether because it is not felt to be of value as music or because professional writers on music tend to regard with distrust any subject involving political considerations. Thus the complex phenomena of Soviet music, especially those related to its enforced subordination to the political goals of the Communist Party, are not treated adequately in any standard Western reference handbook on music. A real need for Russian area specialists, therefore, is the compilation of accurate reference data on the major aspects of contemporary

Russian music—its educational institutions, its composers and performers, its theoretical postulates, and the major stages of its evolution.

Students of contemporary Russian music will find much useful information on their subject in the musical journals of the West In the United States and Great Britain there are more than a dozen such journals, ranging from small news bulletins to scholarly and specialized musicological publications. If one adds journals published in western Europe, one has an extensive and varied group upon which to draw.

While reserving for separate treatment the strictly musicological journals, it can be said that the information provided in the specialized music press consists generally of three types of material, occurring singly or in combination: (a) reviews of performances of new compositions, (b) reports and reviews of performances by Soviet musicians in the West or by Western musicians in the Soviet Union, and (c) general articles and editorials on the state of Soviet music, the relation between Communist Party controls and music, and similar topics.[8]

Writers in the British and western European journals tend to stress purely musical considerations, with a corresponding neglect or underestimation of political factors, while writers in the American journals often show a greater awareness of the latter element, but with only a vague conception of the actual techniques and purposes of the system of political controls. Used with caution, however, and interpreted against the background of a fuller knowledge of Soviet political factors than is usually available to professional writers of music, the articles and reviews in musical journals are an invaluable aid to research.

A relative newcomer to the field of social and humanistic studies, musicology is now firmly established in the United States and other Western countries.[9] It is legitimate, therefore, to survey its achievements in the field of Russian music and to measure them against the potential significance of the subject.

Available evidence points to the conclusion that musicology, not only in the United States but in the West generally, does not consider Russian music, whether pre- or post-Soviet, to be a major field of inquiry. Articles on problems of Russian music, particularly of the post-1917 period, seldom appear in musicological journals,[10] while graduate dissertations in musicology on any aspect of Russian music have been few and far between.[11]

That this situation is not peculiar to the United States is suggested by a recent survey of musicological activities in West Germany since 1945,[12] and by the announced schedule of the Seventh Congress of the International Musicological Society,[13] both of which lack any indication of concern with Russian music.

Several possible explanations for this situation come to mind. In the first place, the professional world of music has evidently lost interest to a considerable extent in the music currently being composed in the Soviet Union, perhaps believing that it possesses neither the untrammeled experimentalism of earlier Russian music nor a healthy organic relation to the central current of Western music. Lacking such interest, Western musicologists apparently feel little stimulus to investigate the current Soviet musical scene, despite its significance as a battleground of art and politics, nor do they feel the need to study Russian music of earlier periods, even though it forms one of the major sources of contemporary Western music.

Secondly, the science of musicology appears to be predominantly concerned with studying the evolution and characterization of the Germanic component of Western music. The majority of American graduate dissertations in musicology, for example, deal with some aspect of Germanic music.

Thirdly, the language barrier undoubtedly contributes to the neglect of Russian music by Western musicologists. With few exceptions, articles and books on the subject are by men linked to Russian studies by some personal connection. There appears to be little realization in the professional schools of music of the need to train young scholars to work in Slavic language sources.

Finally, it seems evident that the inescapable presence of political considerations in the very center of modern Russian music has led some Western musicologists to view the field as somehow less "scholarly" than other branches of musicology in which political considerations are either entirely absent or are at a safe historical distance.

Whatever the reasons, the fact remains that professional musicology in the West, including the United States, has hardly begun to devote serious attention to the study of Russian music. It is furthermore clear that there has been little effective collaboration between professional scholars and departments of music and Russian area specialists.

During the last decade the field of Russian studies has grown up about the musicologist and the professional writer on music without their noticing it. Conversely, the specialist in Russian affairs has paid little attention to developments in Russian music.

An exception to this general picture is a study on Soviet music and musicians now being conducted by Stanley D. Krebs, a Ph.D. candidate at the University of Washington. His project includes "investigation, analysis and reporting of Soviet music, Soviet literature and criticism on music, and the phenomenon of the identification of creative activity with the Soviet state," to quote from Mr. Krebs' own definition of his study.

A full-length study of Soviet music by a refugee scholar—*Music under the Soviets*, by Andrei Olkhovsky, a former professor at the Kiev Conservatory—reflects firsthand knowledge of the subject in many of its aspects.[14] Including an extensive bibliography and an index of composers and compositions, it is the most comprehensive treatment of the subject now available in English.

Special mention should be made of the excellent work being done by the *Current Digest of the Soviet Press* in publishing translations of important articles on Communist Party policy in the field of music. With few exceptions, however, the *Current Digest* does not publish translations of articles on purely musical subjects.

An attempt to correlate data from the two chief fields involved in any study of Soviet music—art and politics—was made in a recent article by the author of the present report.[15] The inclusion of this article in a symposium surveying developments in the Soviet Union since the death of Stalin was in itself a noteworthy sign of an awakening interest in the subject among Russian area specialists.

III

The general picture which emerges from our survey is as follows: first, Russian music of the period before 1917 has established a strong place in the musical consciousness of the Western world. It is widely and frequently performed, and enjoys broad popularity. In regard to post-1917 Russian music, it is necessary to distinguish between the two channels into which it has split. With few exceptions, the music now being composed in the Soviet Union has ceased to be a subject of concern or a creative stimulus to the musicians and composers of the West. The work of the émigré composers, however, continues to exert a major influence, not only in the West but also in the Soviet Union.

Second, there is a considerable volume of writing and publishing on certain aspects of Russian music. General as well as scholarly books and articles are numerous on those composers whose works are most frequently performed. Much of what is published is useful for the purposes of scholarship, although it does not fully serve those purposes, either as to the depth of penetration of particular topics or the range of subjects covered.

Third, professional American and Western musicology has

so far hesitated to come to grips with the special problems of Russian music—its relation to the music of other areas and periods, its contemporary milieu, and its significance for the West.

Fourth, Russian area specialists have up to now devoted little attention to Russian music, despite its intrinsic importance as a major component of Russian culture, a seminal force in Western intellectual life, and a crucial area of the interaction of art and politics in the Soviet system. There are signs, however, of an awakening interest in the subject and a realization of its potential significance on the part of Russian area specialists.

IV

If the contention is granted that Russian music is a subject worthy of scholarly investigation, one may well ask who is to be considered responsible for its study. Is it desirable to add another to the already extensive list of subjects with which the Russian area specialist is concerned? Would it not be possible to leave music in the hands of the professional musicians, critics, and musicologists?

For reasons already discussed, it seems probable that, for at least the near future, musicologists and writers on music in general will not fully meet the need of area specialists for scholarly study in the field of Russian music, particularly of the Soviet period. Even if the musicologists and their associates should increase the degree of their attention to Russian music—a development greatly to be desired—there are still many problems in the field which can be adequately explored and illuminated only by the Russian area specialist, who is trained to evaluate the elements of Russian and Soviet intellectual and cultural life and who has the necessary background of language and area experience.

What are some of these problems? The following list is intended to be suggestive rather than exhaustive.

(1) *Historical subjects.* From the viewpoint of the Russian area specialist, the major historical problems relating to music

center around its role as a significant component of Russian cultural and intellectual life. In this regard, a number of important specific subjects await examination: the origins of Russian opera and its relationship to the institution of serfdom, the close tie between music and literature in the operas of Serov, the influence on the evolution of mid-nineteenth-century Russian music of the concepts of the *Narodniki,* to name only a few. In addition, a most useful general study would be a survey of the evolution of Russian music from the reign of Catherine II to the Bolshevik Revolution. Such a survey would be immensely helpful in illuminating many aspects of the development of Russian culture.

In addition, biographical and critical studies of most of the key figures in Russian music are urgently needed. While satisfactory studies exist of some of the most popular composers—Tchaikovsky, Musorgsky, Rachmaninoff—there is nothing, or next to nothing, on such men as Balakirev and Borodin, Scriabin and Taneev, Miaskovsky and Khachaturian. Particularly valuable would be critical studies of the life and work of composers whose activity spans the transition from pre- to postrevolutionary Russia, such as Prokofiev and Glière. In the works of such men it is possible to trace the direct impact of politics on music, and in the degree to which politics has influenced their work, one can read the auguries for the future of music in the Communist system.

(2) *Subjects in political science.* An analysis of the evolution of political controls over Soviet music could be expected to shed fresh light on the general problem of the nature and purpose of such controls in Soviet cultural life. Moreover, since music has proved singularly resistant to Communist Party dominance—thereby forcing the Party to develop new techniques and concepts in attempting to control it—such an analysis would have special significance. A comparative study of the system of controls in music and painting should have value for a fuller understanding of the parallel system in literature, which has so far received the major share of attention from Russian area specialists.

A critical study of the concepts and practices of the Soviet Union's most influential musicologist and theorist, B. V. Asafiev, would contribute greatly to our knowledge of the interrelation between the Soviet intellectual elite and the Communist Party. In his life and writings Asafiev spanned the wide gamut from the experimentalism of the 1920's (when he enthusiastically welcomed Stravinsky's most radical innovations) to the "socialist realism" of the 1940's (when he lent the weight of his authority to the Party's dictates in the field of music). The stages in Asafiev's intellectual evolution present an epitome of the forced marriage between aesthetics and political imperatives in Soviet culture.

A highly significant process, to which comparatively little attention has been paid in the West, is the extension of Soviet controls and conceptions in music (and other artistic fields) to the vassal nations of eastern Europe. These countries, each with its own more or less well established musical tradition, are now being forcibly assimilated into the Soviet cultural pattern. Studies of the transition taking place would sharpen our understanding of the Communist dynamic and the interaction of cultural and political factors in the Communist system.

(3) *Subjects in aesthetics and philosophy.* A historical study of the development of genres in Russian music—the symphony, the opera, the song—would help to distinguish those evolutionary processes organic to music itself (e.g., the emergence of a specifically Russian symphonic tradition) from those which have their origin in political considerations (e.g., the decline of chamber music in the Soviet Union and the concomitant rise of the "mass song").

One of the most creative periods in Russian music is that covering approximately the years 1895-1925. The close relation between the musical aesthetics developed during these years and other branches of Russian culture is generally recognized (for example, the relation between the music of Scriabin and symbolist poetry). What may not be as fully realized, however, is the extent to which the artistic impetus generated in Russia during this period still constitutes one of the major creative forces in modern Western culture. In choreography, for example, a field which is most intimately related to music, the strongest single influence in America today is that of George Balanchine, an émigré artist whose outlook and aesthetic system were developed in late nineteenth- and early twentieth-century Russia. The debt modern American music owes to this generation of Russian musicians will be apparent if one adds the names of Koussevitsky, Horowitz, Pyatigorsky, and Milstein, to mention only a few. A full study of this key problem in contemporary aesthetics would require the collaboration of scholars in a number of fields, but Russian area specialists have a special opportunity and responsibility to explore the origins and first stages of a movement which is now of significance throughout the Western world.

Successfully to carry out the study of problems such as these, it is clear, will require closer collaboration between musicologists and Russian area specialists. Bridges must be built, in the construction of which both sides will have their assigned task—a greater degree of attention to the role and significance of music on the part of Russian area specialists, and among musicians and musicologists, a greater degree of awareness of the special problems and opportunities presented by the study of Russian music as part of Western cultural and intellectual life.

Paul Willen

12. ARCHITECTURE AND
MINOR ARTS

I

IT MAY BE safely stated at the outset that of all the images by which we commonly identify the basic character of a civilization the most powerful single image is probably the one created by architecture—in which both the aesthetic and the functional genius of a people are embodied. The Parthenon of ancient Greece, the Colosseum of imperial Rome, the Gothic cathedral of medieval Europe, and our own glass-enclosed skyscrapers are familiar examples of this type of identification.

Curiously enough, the Soviet—or Communist—civilization has not as yet produced a striking visual image of this kind, and its present leaders have repudiated the monumental Palace of Soviets by which Stalin had once hoped to fix a place for himself, and the civilization he wrought, in architectural history. The complete failure of the Soviet society to produce an indigenous style may be taken, incidentally, as one indication of their continuing dependence on western Europe for the fundamental ideas by which their allegedly independent civilization is being built.

The absence of a single architectural image for Soviet Communism does not, however, mean that the study of Soviet architecture is useless to us in our efforts to determine the essential character of its culture. In their effort to appear independent of western Europe, the Soviet architects have evolved a rather stuffy and eclectic architecture based on a variety of styles popular in Europe between the fourteenth and nineteenth centuries. The neo-classic façades which have resulted—in so sharp a contrast with the gleaming concrete structures of the postrevolutionary era—unquestionably bear some relationship to the authoritarian character of the Soviet regime; and, likewise, the rigid and formal planning concepts adopted by the Soviet architects in the mid-1930's surely are not unrelated to the fixed and hierarchal concepts of social structure which are held by the Soviet political theorists.

At the same time the limits of this type of symbolic analysis should be recognized. In our modern technological age styles are transplanted and reproduced with such ease that adoption of a given style can disguise (deliberately or otherwise) as much as it can reveal. Soviet architectural style, for example, rejects modern technology as an influence; yet it would be wrong to conclude from this that the Soviet leaders, who determined this style, are averse to modern technology. We find Yugoslav architects employing the same concepts of modern design now prevalent in most of western Europe; and yet it would be equally hazardous to conclude from this that the "inner feeling" of Yugoslav Communism is therefore radically different from the "inner feeling" of Soviet Communism. These variations in architectural style are certainly of importance—as significant perhaps as the bold stand made by modern architecture in both Poland and Hungary in the period of Communist "take-over" following World War II, when Polish and Hungarian architects fought, with some success, the introduction of Stalinist-style extravagance—but they must be handled with caution.

At the same time these complexities should not paralyze the

student in his attempts to utilize architecture as a barometer of Soviet civilization. Certainly the striking contrast between the avant-garde architecture of early postrevolutionary Russia and the heavy neoclassical architecture of Stalinist Russia is of more than passing historical significance; and certainly the slight modification of this overbearing monumentalism in the post-Stalin era deserves close observation. The deep surprise felt by many American visitors to the Soviet Union, on discovering the ornate Soviet style, underlines the pertinence of studying these reflections of changing Soviet attitudes.

American (and Western) scholarship in Russian architecture has thus far been extremely limited. Several excellent studies of prerevolutionary art have appeared in English, most notably George Heard Hamilton's *The Art and Architecture of Russia*, published in 1954.[1] This book has been well received, and it is regrettable that nothing of comparable stature has appeared for the period since 1917.

The reason for this lack of interest in Soviet art and architecture is not difficult to find. The field is a very specialized one, demanding the skills of a trained architect or art historian—few of whom have, for aesthetic reasons, deemed Soviet works of sufficient interest to merit close inspection, to say nothing of extended study.

In the 1920's, when Russian architects were lurching boldly ahead toward new artistic horizons, this was not true; and American specialists, such as Alfred Barr, now the director of collections for the Museum of Modern Art, made special trips to Russia to see Soviet architecture at first hand.[2] Several English architects also kept a close watch on Soviet developments, as well as one or two Frenchmen.[3] Frank Lloyd Wright went to Russia in 1937, and wrote extensively of his impressions.[4] Talbot Hamlin of Columbia University also wrote on the subject, describing the philosophy and prospects of Soviet architecture.[5] Many German

architects worked closely with the Russians, participating directly
in their planning.

But in the late 1930's, with the virtual extinction of modern
architecture in the U.S.S.R., this interest on the part of Westerners largely disappeared. Articles appeared in architectural
journals, sadly or indignantly describing the mounting extravagance and tastelessness of Soviet architecture,[6] but there were no
firsthand reports, and very little detailed study. Soviet architecture
had, for all practical purposes, isolated itself from the main stream
of modern aesthetic thought, and the lack of genuine curiosity
which Western architects felt (and still feel) about their Russian
colleagues was as natural as the intense curiosity (to which there
is much testimony) which Soviet architects feel about Western
developments.

Perhaps the decline in professional interest in Russia helps to
explain the relatively small amount of scholarly attention paid to
Soviet architecture since 1946. Scholarship (in the strict sense
of the word) has been limited to the work of three Americans,
none of whom has produced a first-rate and complete study. These
are Arthur Voyce, who published *Russian Architecture* (New
York, 1948), Maurice Frank Parkins, *City Planning in Soviet
Russia* (Chicago, 1953), and the present writer, whose study,
"Soviet Architecture in Transformation, a Study in Ideological
Manipulation," was completed as a Master's essay at the Russian
Institute of Columbia University in 1953.[7]

The books by Voyce and Parkins both contain interesting material, but neither volume comes to grips with the major issues
posed by the aesthetic changes which occurred in Soviet architecture. In accepting the return to classicism in the thirties as a
natural reaction to the intense modernism of the earlier period,
Voyce oversimplifies what was a very complex historical process.
Parkins, for his part, assumes a degree of continuity in the Soviet
approach which the material he has assembled tends to belie.
Voyce's book lacks some of the necessary scholarly apparatus.

Parkins' volume, on the other hand, is well documented, and contains an excellent annotated bibliography.

Indeed, in some respects city planning is of greater importance than architecture, since the problems are practical rather than aesthetic and Soviet policy could not so easily indulge itself in the fantasies which seized architecture in the 1930's. Furthermore, here the problems are primarily organizational, and in this field the Soviets have shown themselves considerably more adroit than in the humanities.

The Master's essay by the present writer attempts to deal with the broad questions of long-range change which are not treated by Voyce and Parkins. It traces the major developments, describes the different architectural organizations, summarizes crucial debates, notes important personalities, delineates different styles, and assembles the key governmental decrees and decisions. But it is handicapped by its heavy concentration on purely ideological considerations, in accord with the general goals set for the work, as well as by the author's insufficient knowledge of the complex history of twentieth-century architecture. Much has happened since it was written which would lead the author to modify some of his early conclusions.

Thus there is today no single reliable and thorough study of Soviet architecture; this subject remains a gap in the growing body of American scholarship on Russia.[8] The importance of the subject should not be exaggerated. Soviet architecture conceals as much as, if not more than, it reveals; and the very dearth of interesting or original architecture (as well as of painting, interior design, landscape architecture, graphic design—indeed, all the visual arts) reflects its relative insignificance in the total Soviet picture. Genuinely aesthetic discussions have not been heard in almost a generation; even Khrushchev's 1955 criticism of Stalinist architecture was phrased entirely in economic terms. But insofar as the almost complete destruction of creativity in architecture—

replaced by a mediocre and monotonous monumentality—is itself significant, it does deserve at least one serious full-length study, or at the very least, continuing observation by an experienced scholar. The materials for such a study exist in abundance, and Soviet architects themselves are now accessible, many of whom lived through the years of the greatest aesthetic storms (there have been no architectural purges to speak of).

Such a study could be undertaken in one of two ways: either by encouraging a student with an artistic bent, who is now engaged in Russian area training, to specialize in this field, or by offering a grant to a recognized art historian to make a full-scale study. There are six different realms into which research might profitably be directed:

(1) The great outburst of talent in Russian architecture in the 1920's—associated with the term "constructivism"—is not unknown to Western students. However, its real place in the history of the Russian arts has not yet been documented and assessed. Frequently these early achievements are attributed to the strange and chaotic atmosphere of the immediate postrevolutionary years; however, there are some students who feel that this creative surge was primarily Russian, rather than Soviet, in character and that, as in literature, the theater, and the plastic arts, many of its origins can be traced to prerevolutionary times. Hamilton closes his fine book with the following comment:

That the future [post-World War I] held promise of Russia's increasing participation with Western Europe in the foundation of modern art as we have come to know it and in the development of a particularly Russian revision of that art, there can be no doubt.[9]

An account of the partial fulfillment, in the 1920's, of this promise, and of the subsequent destruction of the "magnificent talents" (Hamilton's term) which Russia exhibited in the first three decades of this century has still to be written. Such an account would conclude an important chapter in the history of Russian art and aesthetics, a chapter for which 1917 was not the decisive year, but which spanned the whole brilliant period from 1900 to 1930.

(2) The crucial years in Soviet architecture, as in so many other fields, were 1928-33. Those were the years in which fundamental decisions were made, in which the Soviet leaders apparently sensed (with amazing intuitive grasp, feeling their way from month to month) that there was something incongruous about modern technological architecture in the new totalitarian state—in spite of the fact that this was the very period in which the building of Russia's extraordinary technological apparatus was being so ruthlessly begun. Lunacharsky delivered an astounding speech on this problem; so did a number of other leaders. Behind the scenes, Kaganovich reorganized the architectural cadres, advancing unknown young men over respected veterans, well before these young men had the faintest notion of why the veterans had to fall. Many architects fought back, and never did accept the new doctrines; countless others yielded. A depth-study of these few years might offer new clues. The documentary material is extensive, including many periodicals, pamphlets, decrees, competition awards, and a number of books, including one full-length Soviet study published a year or two ago.[10]

(3) This writer's essay ended with the year 1936, leaving the intervening years virtually untouched by American scholarship. In architecture very little has happened in these years, except for Khrushchev's 1955 denunciation of Stalinist excesses (in the direction of costly ornamentation); but a cursory study should be made, simply to complete the picture. Particular attention might be paid to reports of abortive attempts in 1944-45 by certain Soviet architects to return to a more simple and human style.

(4) Any further study of Soviet architecture should be undertaken by someone who has actually seen the buildings in their natural setting. This is not merely for aesthetic reasons, but to gain some sense of how people live and work in these enormous and overwrought buildings—how they react to them. Neither

Parkins nor Voyce, nor this writer, could say much on this subject, beyond speculation based on their own limited experience. (Voyce was permitted to spend thirty days in the U.S.S.R. in 1958 and received a friendly reception from Soviet officials and in Soviet institutions concerned with architecture, city planning, and related matters.) The gleaming surfaces of modern architecture, their bold geometric forms, their light-weight walls and free forms, their vast expanses of glass and daring use of exposed steel, have become so much a part of the accepted landscape of the non-Soviet world that it is difficult to imagine that fully one-third of the world's population is growing up today in a milieu utterly barren of these effects.

(5) The field of city planning (of such increasing importance in the West) definitely requires further investigation on the part of American students of Soviet Russia. City planning spans a large horizon—from the aesthetic problems of architecture to the administrative problems of municipal government—and thus provides an excellent view of a wide variety of social policies. Parkins' book neither exhausts the available sources nor offers an analytic foundation by which to judge Soviet policy and practice. In the light of the importance of planning in the U.S.S.R., and in the context of increasing American use of city planning principles, this area would seem a logical one for further research.

(6) The most important task, however, is not one of research, but of evaluation and interpretation. Assuming a certain connection between architectural style and the "inner core" of a civilization, what can be honestly and accurately said about the significance of the monumentalism of Soviet architecture? The omnipotence of the state is one easy answer; and yet the problem seems to lie deeper. Why, in spite of Soviet emphasis on technology, has the regime rejected a technologically inspired architecture? Or is it really correct to reduce modern architecture to technology; is there rather something basically ideological in its nature? Is there something inherently democratic about modern

architecture—simple, direct, functional, utterly incapable of pomp and awesomeness—which the Soviet leaders consider of more importance than any technological consideration? Comparisons with the architecture of Nazi Germany and Fascist Italy, as well as with that of Tito's Yugoslavia and Peron's Argentina, might be profitable.

II

The minor visual arts in the Soviet Union have been characterized by the same developments and trends which we noted in our discussion of architecture. Russian achievements prior to the revolution had brought the country into international artistic preeminence, producing such figures as Kandinsky, Tatlin, Gabo, Pevsner, and Chagall, among others. Although many of these individuals left the country soon after the Revolution, their influence was felt, and indeed nurtured, by Russian artists throughout the 1920's. Magazines employed a bold, imaginative layout, with a great use of color, varied types, montage photography, and superimposed drawings and copy; art exhibits reflected every new movement of European art, including the cubism and expressionism then current. The impact of modern art was evident in posters, book jackets, furniture design, and even in the formal insignia of state. In the 1930's a complete reversal occurred. Posters lost their dazzling color; magazine layout became stodgy and formal; and "realism" became the order of the day in art. Specifically, in each field, this is what happened:

Interior decoration: large formal rooms, frequently with high ceilings, separate treatment of architecture and interior design, rejection of the modern concept of flowing space and flexible partition, little attention to the natural properties of materials, heavy use of wallpaper and formal decorative devices such as moldings, little appreciation of sunlight and direct exposure through the use of glass, heavy carpeting, and huge picture frames.

Furniture design: heavy "Victorian" furniture, lavishly up-
holstered and decorated, dark wood stains to add to the massive
effect, tables covered with "elegant" embroidery, symmetrically
arranged flowers, and frequent use of overwrought chandeliers.

Landscaping: formal gardens, axial arrangements, frank imi-
tations of Versailles, Villa d'Este, and other famous seventeenth-
century baroque attempts to force nature into a strong, precise
human pattern on a large scale, and formal and symmetrical
distribution of statues, fountains, walks, and so forth.

Book and magazine layout: again, extremely conservative practices in every field, although with far less lavishness of product;
straightforward, unimaginative typography, avoiding both the
elaborate styles of the nineteenth century and the imaginative innovations of the twentieth; emphasis on easy readability, as in
children's textbooks, rather than on attractiveness of style.

Industrial design: here the Soviets have also taken a conservative approach, either following a completely utilitarian technique
(giving no expression to the functional aesthetic implied in the
manufactured product, an approach which has revolutionized industrial design in the West over the past twenty-five years) or
following a conservative Western precedent—as in the case of
automobiles, TV sets, etc.

The sole possible exception to Soviet conservatism in industrial
design is in advanced scientific and military apparatus—rocketry,
jet aviation, and so forth—where the Russians seem to have followed some of our most daring leads, from the aesthetic as well
as the scientific point of view. This field seems to occupy a special
place in the Soviet aesthetic world. The principles which prevail
in Soviet architecture—notably adherence to the past—could
hardly be transferred to the aesthetic side of the design of a jet
airplane. However, it is interesting to note that the building which
houses Russia's first atomic energy plant was constructed according to the archaic principles of Stalinist architecture. The recon-
ciliation of these two phases of Soviet life—revolutionary science

and a reactionary aesthetic—must pose as many problems to the alert Soviet administrator as they do to Western students.

Western research in this field is virtually non-existent, although there has been much informal reporting on the subject from Western travelers. In regard to source materials, however, there is little need for extended work. The evidence is largely pictorial and exists in such abundance that the student need hardly lift a finger to uncover it. Every recent visitor to the Soviet Union may offer his own comments based on firsthand observation.

This vast material must, however, be organized by a competent student, and each of the tentative summary statements put forward above must be confirmed, disputed, or modified, as the case may be. This job is primarily one of collection and arrangement. The contrast with prevailing Western practices and standards will be so marked and clear-cut that little interpretive analysis will be necessary at the first stage of the proposed study. Where the contrast is not marked, as in the field of advanced scientific apparatus (and there are other such exceptions to the general rule, especially if one includes the east European countries and certain non-Russian areas of the U.S.S.R. itself), special evaluation will be required.

After such a fact-finding survey has been completed, the data should be turned over to a sociologist or a social psychologist for further study. The problems are no longer essentially aesthetic, but sociological. In the visual arts this is even truer than in architecture, where certain pseudo-aesthetic ideas are occasionally presented in Soviet work and discussions. But with regard to interior decoration, for example, the problems are practical, intimate, and between the planner and the individual. The key questions which should be asked are:

(1) What is the way of life fostered by this particular type of visual experience? What might the Soviet planners have in mind?

What is the actual result of their decisions? What are the day-to-day consequences of such a visual atmosphere—so seemingly stifling to Westerners accustomed to the light, airy, free-flowing designs and insignia of our life?

(2) How can modern technological activities be conducted in an atmosphere characterized by these archaic formalities and outdated designs? The delicate lace and embroidery, the stuffed sofas, the small windows, the heavy window frames, the ornate lampshades—how do these fit into a life so full of the sharp precision of modern machinery and space orbiting?

These questions have deep ramifications which concern our total evaluation of Soviet life and culture. It may indeed be discovered—with the aid of sociological and psychological research and insights—that although modern visual design springs from industrial life, many phases of modern design inhibit the most efficient behavior in an industrial state. In other words, the sophisticated modern design of the West, based on the machine, may be inimical to the labor discipline so necessary for efficient utilization of the machines. In any case, it is possible that certain Soviet leaders have reasoned this way, and it would be well worth while to examine critically this and alternative suppositions. The study of Soviet visual design may offer some valuable clues to our discussion of the total Soviet culture—particularly the relative importance of its authoritarian and scientific components.

Harold H. Fisher

13. POSTSCRIPT

As I HAVE READ these reports of what has been done and as I look back over the years during which I have had the privilege of watching the development of Slavic studies in this country, I have been struck by the effects of the changes in the motivation of these studies and in the atmosphere in which and the methods by which they have been carried on. I propose to comment on motivation, atmosphere, and methods and to offer six "theses" for the consideration of those who will be making the new record during the next ten years.

In this field of research, as in every other, scholars hope to add to the store of knowledge. To this end they use the methodology of the discipline in which they have been trained in accordance with the principles of intellectual or, as it is sometimes called, academic freedom. The denial of this freedom by the Communists has, of course, affected Russian research by Soviet scholars. It has also affected Russian research by Americans through the restriction or prohibition of library research and field work by foreigners in the U.S.S.R. Soviet policy with respect to cultural exchange has shifted since the 1920's from en-

couragement to discouragement and back again as the Communist
general line has shifted from soft to hard and hard to soft. Individuals and institutions interested in this field are doing their
best during the present (1959) soft turn in the Party line to develop the exchange of scholars, students, and materials, but it
will not be wise to base our future plans on the belief that the
Communists are being won over to our view of intellectual freedom and that their present policy will continue indefinitely.

In our own country during the first decade after the Second
World War intellectual freedom was under attack. The quality
of Russian research, as the essays in this book show, did not
suffer. This was due to the integrity of those who guided or did
the research and to the support they received from their own institutions and the interested foundations. But no field of research
can be wholly insulated from pressures of this kind whenever
they arise, as they do from time to time in our society. Graduate
and postgraduate research have their roots in the undergraduate
courses which produce young scholars, and all scholars are affected by the general climate of opinion prevailing in the colleges
and universities. In their investigation of the effects of the general tension on social science teaching in colleges and universities
during what they call "the difficult years," Messrs. Lazarsfeld and
Thielens found that the topics most often avoided as dangerously
controversial were Communism, Soviet Russia, and Red China,
and that the teachers interviewed "often complained of problems in obtaining and using materials needed for their writing
and research. Leading the list, of course, are books and pamphlets
dealing with Russia and Communism which cannot be obtained
or are considered too risky to use."[1]

I am not going to discuss the causes of these tensions or of the
changes in the Communist Party line but I should like to make
two points that have a bearing on future Russian research.

(1) The Communists may change their policies regarding
cultural exchanges, as they have in the past, and prohibit or

effectively discourage research by foreign non-Communists in the U.S.S.R. We should take this possibility into account and not allow our collecting of research materials to decline, but on the contrary we should expand collecting especially in those disciplines in which, as these reports show, more research needs to be done.

(2) The academic mind is under less stress now than during "the difficult years," but this is no guarantee that it will remain so. In fact, it seems to me not only possible but likely that tensions may again be generated as competition between different political and social systems intensifies, regardless of how seemingly peaceful coexistence turns out to be. This possibility ought not to be a matter of indifference to those who will be doing research during the next ten or fifteen years. The best, perhaps the only, way to prepare for this possibility is to create among those who teach and do research in this and other similarly exposed areas a sense of common purpose and mutual support in the exercise of the principles of intellectual freedom which, with private initiative and public support, have made possible the splendid achievements of higher education in the United States in the last sixty years.

Russian research is not self-supporting; it must be considered sufficiently worth while to persuade some people to want to do it and others to want to encourage and help them. The number of persons so persuaded and the amount of moral and material help given them have been determined by two influences. One was an appreciation of Russian culture, an interest in the history, literature, and institutions of Russia, and a belief that a knowledge of these matters was rewarding to those who gained it. A second influence has been an awareness of the growing revolutionary power that originated in Russia, its nearness, thanks to the revolution in communications, and its challenge to our way of life.

Russian activities in the North Pacific in the early years of the last century no doubt disturbed others besides John Quincy Adams, but the American academic community seems not to have been much aroused by these remote affairs or by de Tocqueville's famous prophecy about the two great and growing nations "marked out by the will of Heaven to sway the destinies of half the globe," the one whose principal instrument was freedom, the other servitude. And when Commodore Matthew Calbraith Perry warned of the inevitable mighty battle between the "antagonistic exponents of freedom and absolutism" which would decide "whether despotism or rational liberty must be the fate of civilized man," it appears to have made very little impression on the members of the American Geographical and Statistical Society to whom he gave the warning, and it made no impression at all on the *New York Daily Times,* which did not get around to publishing it until a hundred years later on March 6, 1956.

Two men who, at the turn of the present century, used their considerable influence to establish the study of Russia in American universities were moved, it would appear, by a great liking for the Russian land, Russian culture, and certain qualities of Russian national character which have won the warm admiration of many other Americans. Archibald Cary Coolidge and Charles R. Crane may have had a premonition of the role a nation with such a reservoir of talent would be bound to play. They were certainly aware of and may have been influenced by George Kennan's *Siberia and the Exile System* and by the sympathies of the "American Friends of Russian Freedom" for the pre-Marxist revolutionaries. Probably they read Albert J. Beveridge's rather florid appreciation of Russian achievements as an imperial power and his startled interpretation of Pobedonostsev's exclamation, "Russia is no state; Russia is a world!," but it does not appear that Coolidge and Crane encouraged Russian studies as being required in the national interest. They seem to have believed that the study of Russia, and interestingly enough of the Near East and the Far East, was rewarding and important in itself and that young Americans should have the opportunity to discover this.

The fact that the study of Russia, past and present, has been rewarding and seemed important to many suggests that it should be made possible for more young people to find this out, and what is more, that it is necessary to do this if we hope to achieve the larger quantity and higher quality of research recommended by the contributors to this volume. This is particularly true of those fields of specialization in which much less has been done than in history, literature, and political science. If students who are drawn to such disciplines as economics, sociology, anthropology, philosophy, geography, fine arts, education, and the sciences are to contribute to our knowledge of Russia, they must be enabled to find out that the exercise of these disciplines in the Russian field gives rewards that are worth the extra effort required. These young students will not make this discovery if we merely increase the number of courses in Russian history, literature, comparative government, or comparative "isms," though this would help. It would be even more helpful if those who are teaching in the Russian field and especially those who are training future researchers and teachers made a special effort to inform themselves and then to inform their students why these undermanned sections of the Russian field are interesting and why some knowledge of them is valuable not only to the area specialist but to those whose major interest lies in a discipline which does not have an area focus.

The intellectual satisfactions of Russian area study ought never to be lost sight of, but they are by no means the only motive for work in this field. One need not take at face value the resolution of the Twentieth Congress of the Communist Party of the Soviet Union that "the emergence of socialism from within the bounds of a single country and its transformation into a world system is the main feature of our era," but one should not pretend that this transformation, which might well perplex both Marx and Lenin, is a transitory phenomenon of interest only to historians. A system,

as the Communists call it, which in less than fifty years has trans-
formed Russia, has been imposed on a third of the world's population living on a fourth of the earth's surface and commanding
about a third of the world's production, and has made some impressive and ominous advances in science and technology calls for
study on its own account. Such a study must begin with the
Russian area, where the system began and developed, and it
should include all the fields of specialization reviewed in this book
and some that are not. And it must take into account other areas
in which Communists are trying to transplant and adapt an alien
order.

Those who direct or support Russian research in the academic
world and those who do research and transmit its results all help
to form public opinion, but they are also influenced by the prevailing climate of opinion, which is the product of many forces,
among them the international situation, economic conditions,
technological developments, the current line of the Communist
Party, and the policies of the Administration in Washington. The
climate of opinion about Russia has changed several times since
1917, reflecting in part the sharp changes in the Communist line.
Russia has been viewed as the victim of crackpots and criminals
whose cruel depredations were one of the costs of war. Russia has
been regarded as the scene of a national revolution which, because it was long overdue, had gone to extremes from which it
would swing back as radical policies proved unworkable and as
the admirable qualities of the Russian national character prevailed. This happy outcome seemed nearer realization when
Soviet Russia, after some disturbing incidents, was on our side
in the Second World War. Then suddenly when the war was
over and the main trend of Soviet policy became clear, the atmosphere changed again. The urge to diabolize replaced the tempta-
tion to eulogize. "Know the enemy" was added to the traditional
motives for research in fields relating to national security.

And now the climate of opinion is changing once more. Public opinion has been stirred and confused by the unfolding of Khrushchev's policies in the U.S.S.R., in Europe and the Middle East, and in outer space, by the lengthening shadow of Maoist China, by polemics over revisionism, dogmatism, and literary treason, by atomic threats, impressive production figures, and a modest resumption of cultural exchange. This disturbed atmosphere has led to much soul-searching, shrill and often uninformed denunciations of our whole educational system, and demands for crash programs to close the gap.

Two aspects of this agitation are of concern to Russian research. One, which affects other areas equally, is the current tendency to stress the physical sciences to the detriment of the humanities and the social sciences. Another problem is that since the Second World War the government has taken an increasing interest in stimulating research on the Soviet Union. I am concerned lest in recognizing the necessity for government research and more emphasis on science, we assume that the more government research we have, the less private enterprise research we need. I am convinced that the contrary is true. Of course we need government-directed intelligence and scientific research of the highest quality, and our needs will increase during the coming years. At the same time, to maintain the high quality of government research and to meet the increasing need for trained minds, we must enlarge the scope of private training and research untrammeled by the exigencies of pressing issues or shifts in official policy.

A number of thoughtful people have come to the conclusion that what the Communists now call "the socialist world system" should not be looked upon as just a resourceful and wicked conspiracy aimed at world domination, but as a method of organizing society in the age of industrialism. This view stresses the achievements of the Soviet Union in economic development, political power, and technical and social progress. The Communists appear to be accomplishing this by combining a remarkable operational flexibility with an inflexible retention of a power monopoly exercised by the Communist Party through a totalitarian despotism which shows no immediate signs of disintegrating, withering away, or mellowing.[2]

With this view I agree, but I should like to add that events seem to indicate that the further the socialist world system is extended, the more difficult appear to be the problems of rigid, centralized control. It seems to me unlikely that problems of this character can be solved by operational flexibility alone. This suggests that with or even without further extension of the system, these control problems may profoundly modify the relations of the members of the system with each other and inevitably with the rest of the world.

With this proviso, my first thesis is: That the Communist movement should not be regarded merely as a new formula of revolt and a new and efficient method of oppression, which it is, but also as a movement firmly and powerfully established in the Soviet Union and dedicated to the promotion throughout the world of a form of social organization evolved in Russia. This implies due emphasis in teaching and research on both the undeniable accomplishments and the undeniable costs of the Communist system. It implies study both of the relation of some of the features of this system to Russia's past and of Soviet Russia's inheritance from the achievements of Imperial Russia.

Second, that there is need today for more emphasis on interpretive writing on Tsarist and Soviet Russia to supplement the impressive body of monographic studies now available. To the extent that much monographic work has been based on assumptions drawn from west European or American experience, it would be useful to test new interpretations based on the unique factors in Russia's development and on comparative studies of conditions in the non-Western world.

Third, that studies of contemporary Russia cannot be separated from the Communist movement and that since the Communist movement is transnational and interactive, special efforts should be made to have liaison with and, where possible, to cooperate in studies of other areas where Communist rule has been set up or where the achievements of the Communists have great attraction.

Fourth, that the greatest contributions to knowledge and the public interest will be made if the results of research in relevant disciplines are integrated, or at least interrelated. This does not mean the substitution of group research for individual research, for which there is no substitute. The work of the individual scholar will nevertheless be enriched by knowledge of what has been done and of the methods used in other disciplines. This implies "the timely application of appropriate stimuli," as Professor Whitfield puts it, to those fields of specialization in which, as these essays show, more research might well be done. It also implies patient and continued effort to work out ways to maintain interdisciplinary contact and to integrate the contributions of the different disciplines when integration will give a deeper understanding of what is being investigated.

Fifth, that the results of research in the Russian field should be transmitted to the people of this country through general education and the various media of communication in order to provide the basis for informed discussion of issues of great moment to us all. This means more cooperation with teachers and other agents of enlightenment who, because of distance from centers of research or lack of access to the products of research, are sometimes out of touch with work being done in this field.

Sixth, that the advancement of research as well as the public interest are best served by the maximum exchange of views of those doing research and the maximum availability of research materials. This means making the most of inventions that facilitate the communication of materials and ideas. It also means the expansion of exchanges already begun with countries in which Slavic studies have long been established like France, Britain, and Germany, with countries where such studies have been more lately initiated such as Japan, Turkey, and India, and with the countries of the Soviet orbit.

Most of the suggestions made by others and by me in this book are a lot easier to propose than to effect. They are, in fact, aspirations. They demand patience, which most scholars have, time and money, which they have not—at least not enough—and a capacity for cooperation. What is most needed, perhaps, is a realization that the intention to deepen and disseminate knowledge of Russia and the Communist movement during the next decade is more than a worth-while form of academic enterprise; it is a proposal to test the resourcefulness and integrity of scholarship in applying the principles of intellectual freedom to the fateful and controversial issues of our century.

NOTES

2. HISTORY

1. *Peter the Great* (2 vols.; New York, 1884).
2. See especially his address to the American Historical Association in December, 1895, entitled "A Plea for the Study of the History of Northern Europe," *American Historical Review*, II (October, 1896), 34-39.
3. *Slavic Europe: A Selected Bibliography in the Western European Languages* (Cambridge, Mass., 1918).
4. *Russian Expansion on the Pacific, 1641-1850* (Cleveland, 1914).
5. *The Russia I Believe In: The Memoirs of Samuel N. Harper, 1902-1941* (Chicago, 1945).
6. George Kennan, *Siberia and the Exile System* (2 vols.; New York, 1891); Albert J. Beveridge, *The Russian Advance* (New York, 1904).
7. This series was edited by Sir Paul Vinogradoff until his death in 1925, and thereafter by Professor Michael T. Florinsky, who contributed a valuable summary volume: *The End of the Russian Empire* (New Haven, 1931).
8. Frederick S. Rodkey, *The Turco-Egyptian Question in the Relations of England, France, and Russia, 1832-1841* (Urbana, 1924); William L. Langer, *The Franco-Russian Alliance, 1890-1894* (Cambridge, Mass., 1929); B. P. Thomas, *Russo-American Relations, 1815-67* (Baltimore, 1930); Vernon J. Puryear, *England, Russia and the Straits Question, 1844-1856* (Berkeley, 1931); Philip E. Mosely,

*Russian Diplomacy and the Opening of the Eastern Question in 1838
and 1839* (Cambridge, Mass., 1934); A. Lobanov-Rostovsky, *Russia
and Asia* (1st ed., New York, 1933; 2nd ed., Ann Arbor, 1951);
Leonid I. Strakhovsky, *The Origins of American Intervention in
North Russia* (Princeton, 1937), and *Intervention in Archangel*
(Princeton, 1944); Sergius Yakobson, "Russia and Africa," *Slavonic
and East European Review,* XVII (1938-39), 623-37; XIX (1939-
40), 158-74; R. P. Churchill, *The Anglo-Russian Convention of 1907*
(Cedar Rapids, 1939); C. E. Black, *The Establishment of Constitutional Government in Bulgaria* (Princeton, 1943).

9. Geroid T. Robinson, *Rural Russia Under the Old Regime*
(New York, 1932; new ed., 1949); George Stewart, *The White
Armies of Russia: A Chronicle of Counter-Revolution and Allied In-
tervention* (New York, 1933); A. G. Mazour, *The First Russian
Revolution, 1825* (Berkeley, 1937); Douglas K. Reading, *The Anglo-
Russian Commercial Treaty of 1734* (New Haven, 1938); Alfred
Levin, *The Second Duma: A Study of the Social-Democratic Party
and the Russian Constitutional Experiment* (New Haven, 1940);
John S. Curtiss, *Church and State in Russia: The Last Years of the
Empire, 1900-1917* (New York, 1940); Robert J. Kerner, *The Urge
to the Sea: The Course of Russian History* (Berkeley, 1942); Raymond H. Fisher, *The Russian Fur Trade, 1550-1700* (Berkeley,
1943); G. V. Lantzeff, *Siberia in the Seventeenth Century: A Study
in Colonial Administration* (Berkeley, 1943).

10. H. H. Fisher, *The Famine in Soviet Russia, 1919-1923: The
Operation of the American Relief Administration* (New York, 1927);
T. A. Taracouzio, *Soviets in the Arctic: An Historical, Economic,
and Political Study of the Soviet Advance into the Arctic* (New York,
1938); Calvin B. Hoover, *The Economic Life of Soviet Russia* (New
York, 1931); D. Fedotoff White, *The Growth of the Red Army*
(Princeton, 1944); Samuel N. Harper, *Civic Training in Soviet
Russia* (Chicago, 1929), and *Making Bolsheviks* (Chicago, 1931);
W. R. Batsell, *Soviet Rule in Russia* (New York, 1929); Matthew
Spinka, *The Church and the Russian Revolution* (New York, 1927);
Nicholas S. Timasheff, *Religion in Soviet Russia, 1917-1942* (New
York, 1942); Paul B. Anderson, *People, Church, and State in
Modern Russia* (London, 1944); J. Bunyan and H. H. Fisher, *The
Bolshevik Revolution, 1917-1918: Documents and Materials* (Stan-
ford, 1934); Elena Varneck and H. H. Fisher, *The Testimony of
Kolchak and Other Siberian Materials* (Stanford, 1935); James
Bunyan, *Intervention, Civil War, and Communism in Russia, April-*

December, 1918: *Documents and Materials* (Baltimore, 1936); Olga
H. Gankin and H. H. Fisher, *The Bolsheviks and the World War:
The Origin of the Third International* (Stanford, 1940); Kathryn
Davis, *The Soviets at Geneva: The U.S.S.R. and the League of
Nations, 1919-1933* (Geneva, 1934); W. L. Mahaney, Jr., *The
Soviet Union, the League of Nations and Disarmament: 1917-1935*
(Philadelphia, 1940).

11. Anatole G. Mazour, *An Outline of Modern Russian Historiography* (Berkeley, 1939; 2nd ed., Princeton, 1958); F. C. Barghoorn,
"The Russian Radicals of the 1860's and the Problem of the Industrial Proletariat," *Slavonic and East European Review* (American
Series, II), XXI (March, 1943), 57-69; Michael Karpovich, "Klyu-
chevski and Recent Trends in Russian Historiography," *ibid.*, 31-39,
and "A Forerunner of Lenin: P. N. Tkachev," *Review of Politics*,
VI (July, 1944), 336-50.

12. Vernadsky: (New Haven, 1943, 1948, 1953); Florinsky: (2
vols.; New York, 1953).

13. Alexander A. Vasiliev, *The Russian Attack on Constantinople
in 860* (Cambridge, Mass., 1946); Samuel H. Cross, *Slavic Civiliza-
tion through the Ages* (Cambridge, Mass., 1948); William K. Med-
lin, *Moscow and East Rome: A Political Study of the Relations of
Church and State in Muscovite Russia* (Geneva, 1952); Douglas
M. Dunlop, *The History of the Jewish Khazars* (Princeton, 1954);
Francis Dvornik, *The Slavs: Their Early History and Civilization*
(Boston, 1956); and Jerome Blum, "The Beginnings of Large-scale
Private Landownership in Russia," *Speculum*, XXVIII (1953), 781-
790, "The Smerd in Kievan Russia," *American Slavic and East
European Review*, XII (1953), 125-29, and "The Rise of Serfdom in
Eastern Europe," *American Historical Review*, LXII (1957), 807-36.

14. C. B. O'Brien, *Russia under Two Tsars, 1682-1689* (Berkeley,
1952); Peter B. Putnam (ed.), *Seven Britons in Imperial Russia, 1698-
1812* (Princeton, 1952); J. R. Masterson and H. Brower, *Bering's
Successors, 1745-1780* (Seattle, 1948); Marc Raeff, *Siberia and the
Reforms of 1822* (Seattle, 1956); Donald W. Treadgold, *The Great
Siberian Migration* (Princeton, 1957).

15. David Hecht, *Russian Radicals Look to America, 1825-1894*
(Cambridge, Mass., 1947); Bertram D. Wolfe, *Three Who Made a
Revolution* (New York, 1948); Frederick C. Barghoorn, "D. I.
Pisarev: a Representative of Russian Nihilism," *Review of Politics*,
X (April, 1948), 190-211; Nicholas V. Riasanovsky, *Russia and the
West in the Teachings of the Slavophiles* (Cambridge, Mass., 1952);

Hans Kohn, *Panslavism: Its History and Ideology* (Notre Dame, 1953); Leopold H. Haimson, *The Russian Marxists and the Origins of Bolshevism* (Cambridge, Mass., 1955); Donald W. Treadgold, *Lenin and His Rivals: The Struggle for Russia's Future, 1898-1906* (New York, 1955); Michael B. Petrovich, *The Emergence of Russian Panslavism, 1856-1870* (New York, 1956); Alfred G. Meyer, *Leninism* (Cambridge, Mass., 1957); George Fischer, *Russian Liberalism: From Gentry to Intelligentsia* (Cambridge, Mass., 1958); James H. Billington, *Mikhailovsky and Russian Populism* (Oxford, 1958).

The variety of interest in Russian intellectual history is reflected in the essays in Ernest J. Simmons (ed.), *Continuity and Change in Russian and Soviet Thought* (Cambridge, Mass., 1955); and Hugh McLean, Martin E. Malia, and George Fischer (eds.), *Russian Thought and Politics* ("Harvard Slavic Studies," Vol. IV; Cambridge, Mass., 1957), dedicated to Professor Michael Karpovich.

16. Leonid I. Strakhovsky, *Alexander I of Russia* (New York, 1947); Marc Raeff, *Michael Speransky: Statesman of Imperial Russia, 1772-1839* (The Hague, 1957); Samuel Kucherov, *Courts, Lawyers, and Trials under the Last Three Tsars* (New York, 1953); William H. E. Johnson, *Russia's Educational Heritage: Teacher Education in the Russian Empire, 1600-1917* (Pittsburgh, 1950); David M. Lang, *The Last Years of the Georgian Monarchy, 1658-1837* (New York, 1957); Oliver H. Radkey, *The Agrarian Foes of Bolshevism* (New York, 1958).

17. Stuart R. Tompkins, *Alaska: Promyshlennik and Sourdough* (Norman, Okla., 1945); Edward H. Zabriskie, *American-Russian Rivalry in the Far East: A Study in Diplomacy and Power Politics, 1895-1914* (New York, 1946); M. N. Pavlovsky, *Russian-Chinese Relations* (New York, 1949); David Dallin, *The Rise of Russia in Asia* (New Haven, 1949); A. Lobanov-Rostovsky, *Russia and Europe, 1789-1825* (Durham, N. C., 1947), and *Russia and Europe, 1825-1878* (Ann Arbor, 1954); Walther Kirchner, *The Rise of the Baltic Question* (Newark, Del., 1954); George A. Lensen, *Russia's Japan Expedition of 1852 to 1855* (Gainesville, Fla., 1955); C. Jay Smith, Jr., *The Russian Struggle for Power, 1914-1917: A Study of Russian Foreign Policy during the First World War* (New York, 1956); Charles Jelavich, *Tsarist Russia and Balkan Nationalism: Russian Influence in the Internal Affairs of Bulgaria and Serbia, 1879-86* (Berkeley, 1958).

18. Simon Liberman, *Building Lenin's Russia* (Chicago, 1945) and William Reswick, *I Dreamt Revolution* (Chicago, 1952).

19. Nicholas S. Timasheff, *The Great Retreat: The Growth and Decline of Communism in Russia* (New York, 1946); Frederick L. Schuman, *Soviet Politics at Home and Abroad* (New York, 1948), and *Russia Since 1917* (New York, 1957); Barrington Moore, Jr., *Soviet Politics: The Dilemma of Power* (Cambridge, Mass., 1950); David J. Dallin, *The Changing World of Soviet Russia* (New Haven, 1956).

20. Oliver H. Radkey, *The Election to the Russian Constituent Assembly of 1917* (Cambridge, Mass., 1950); Richard Pipes, *The Formation of the Soviet Union: Communism and Nationalism, 1917-1923* (Cambridge, Mass., 1954); George Barr Carson, Jr., *Electoral Practices in the U.S.S.R.* (New York, 1956); Zbigniew Brzezinski, *The Permanent Purge: Politics in Soviet Totalitarianism* (Cambridge, Mass., 1956).

21. John A. Armstrong, *Ukrainian Nationalism, 1939-1945* (New York, 1955); John S. Reshetar, Jr., *The Ukrainian Revolution, 1917-1920* (Princeton, 1952); Basil Dmytryshyn, *Moscow and the Ukraine, 1918-1953* (New York, 1957); A. G. Park, *Bolshevism in Turkestan, 1917-1927* (New York, 1957); F. Kazemzadeh, *The Struggle for Transcaucasia, 1917-1921* (New York, 1951); Nicholas P. Vakar, *Belorussia: The Making of a Nation* (Cambridge, Mass., 1956).

22. R. P. Casey, *Religion in Russia* (New York, 1946); John S. Curtiss, *The Russian Church and the Soviet State* (Boston, 1953); Matthew Spinka, *The Church and Soviet Russia* (New York, 1956); George Fischer, *Soviet Opposition to Stalin* (Cambridge, Mass., 1952); George Barr Carson, Jr., "Changing Perspectives in Soviet Historiography," *South Atlantic Quarterly*, XLVII (April, 1948), 186-95; Sergius Yakobson, "Postwar Historical Research in the Soviet Union," *Annals of the American Academy of Political and Social Science*, CCLXIII (May, 1949), 123-33; Anatole G. Mazour and Herman E. Bateman, "Recent Conflicts in Soviet Historiography," *Journal of Modern History*, XXIV (March, 1952), 56-68; Alfred A. Skerpan, "Modern Russian Historiography," *Kent State University Bulletin (Research Series I)*, XL (October, 1952), 37-60; C. E. Black (ed.), *Rewriting Russian History: Soviet Interpretations of Russia's Past* (New York, 1956).

23. These publications are discussed in other chapters in this volume.

24. John A. White, *The Siberian Intervention* (Princeton, 1950); Robert P. Browder, *The Origins of Soviet-American Diplomacy*

(Princeton, 1953); Robert D. Warth, *The Allies and the Russian Revolution* (Durham, N. C., 1954); Betty Miller Unterberger, *America's Siberian Expedition, 1918-1920* (Durham, N. C., 1956); George F. Kennan, *Russia Leaves the War* (Princeton, 1956), and *The Decision to Intervene* (Princeton, 1958).

25. Pauline Tompkins, *American-Russian Relations in the Far East* (New York, 1949); Max M. Laserson, *The American Impact on Russia: Diplomacy and Ideology, 1784-1917* (New York, 1950); Thomas A. Bailey, *America Faces Russia: Russian-American Relations from Early Times to Our Day* (Ithaca, 1950); William A. Williams, *American-Russian Relations, 1781-1947* (New York, 1952); William H. McNeill, *America, Britain, and Russia: Their Co-operation and Conflict, 1941-1946* (London, 1953); Herbert Feis, *Churchill—Roosevelt—Stalin: The War They Waged and the Peace They Sought* (Princeton, 1957).

26. Harriet L. Moore, *Soviet Far Eastern Relations, 1931-1945* (Princeton, 1945); David J. Dallin, *Soviet Russia and the Far East* (New Haven, 1948), and *Soviet Espionage* (New Haven, 1955); Rodger Swearingen and Paul Langer, *Red Flag in Japan: International Communism in Action, 1919-1951* (Cambridge, Mass., 1952); Robert C. North, *Moscow and Chinese Communists* (Stanford, 1953); Allen S. Whiting, *Soviet Politics in China, 1917-1924* (New York, 1954); John N. Kautsky, *Moscow and the Communist Party of India* (New York, 1956); Henry Wei, *China and Soviet Russia* (Princeton, 1956); David T. Cattell, *Communism and the Spanish Civil War* (Berkeley, 1955), and *Soviet Diplomacy and the Spanish Civil War* (Berkeley, 1957); George Lenczowski, *Russia and the West in Iran, 1918-1948* (Ithaca, 1949); Gerhard L. Weinberg, *Germany and the Soviet Union, 1939-1941* (Leiden, 1954); Alexander Dallin, *German Rule in Russia, 1941-1945* (New York, 1957); Robert J. Alexander, *Communism in Latin America* (New Brunswick, 1957); Xenia J. Eudin and H. H. Fisher, *Soviet Russia and the West, 1920-1927: A Documentary Survey* (Stanford, 1957); Xenia J. Eudin and Robert C. North, *Soviet Russia and the East, 1920-1927: A Documentary Survey* (Stanford, 1957); Gerald Freund, *Unholy Alliance* (New York, 1957); Clarence J. Smith, *Finland and the Russian Revolution, 1917-1923* (Athens, Ga., 1956); Anatole G. Mazour, *Finland between East and West* (Princeton, 1956).

27. *Canadian Slavonic Papers* (Toronto, 1956 ff., annual); *Est et Ouest* (Paris, 1949 ff., semimonthly); *Slavic and East-European Studies* (Montreal, 1956 ff., quarterly); *Europe de l'Est et Union*

Soviétique (Paris, 1957 ff., quarterly); *Jahrbücher für Geschichte Osteuropas* (Munich, 1953 ff., quarterly); *Osteuropa* (Stuttgart, 1951 ff., monthly); *Revue des Etudes Slaves* (Paris, 1921 ff., annual); *Die Slavische Rundschau* (Munich, 1956 ff., bimonthly); *Slavonic and East European Review* (London, 1922 ff., semiannual); *Soviet Studies* (Glasgow, 1949 ff., quarterly); *Die Welt der Slaven* (Munich, 1956 ff., quarterly).

28. For example: A. N. Kurat, *Isvec Kirali XII Karl 'in Türkiyede Kalisi ve bu siralarda Osmanli Imparatorlugu* [The residence in Turkey of King Charles XII of Sweden and the Ottoman empire at that time] (Istanbul, 1943), and *Rusya Tarihi* [History of Russia] (Ankara, 1948); M. N. Roy, *The Russian Revolution* (Calcutta, 1949); and M. R. Masani, *The Communist Party of India: A Short History* (New York, 1954).

29. See Peter Berton, Paul Langer, and Rodger Swearingen, *Japanese Training and Research in the Russian Field* (Los Angeles, 1956).

30. There is a valuable description of Russian collections in American libraries in Charles Morley, *Guide to Research in Russian History* (Syracuse, 1951).

3. ECONOMICS

1. *Review of Economics and Statistics*, XXIX, No. 4 (November, 1947).

2. See the reply to *Fortune* by E. Varga, *ibid.* (July, 1957); to G. Warren Nutter in *New Times*, June 15, 1957; to J. P. Hardt in *Elektrichestvo* (1957); to David Granick and to the Joint Economic Committee (U.S. Congress) in *Voprosy Ekonomiki*, XI (1957); and by academician Ostrovityanov to various critics of the Soviet index of industrial production in *The Times* (London), February 6, 1958. That this constitutes a definite policy, at least on the part of the Academy of Sciences of the U.S.S.R., is indicated in *Voprosy Ekonomiki*, XI (1957), 160.

3. Where the regimens of weights are drawn from years at different stages of industrialization, this index number phenomenon is now often referred to as the "Gerschenkron effect." For striking illustrations of the "effect," see Alexander Gerschenkron, *A Dollar Index of Soviet Machinery Output, 1927-28 to 1937* (Santa Monica: The RAND Corporation, 1951), chap. 4.

4. See Abram Bergson, *Soviet National Income and Product in*

1937 (New York, 1953), chap. 3, on the nature of the alternative standards.

5. This is essentially the approach of both Naum Jasny in his growth study, *The Soviet Economy during the Plan Era* (Stanford, 1951), and of the Bergson-RAND project currently in progress.

6. Demitri B. Shimkin, *Minerals: A Key to Soviet Power* (Cambridge, Mass., 1953), chap. IX; Francis Seton, *The Tempo of Soviet Industrial Expansion* (Manchester, 1957); Raymond P. Powell, *A Materials-Input Index of Soviet Construction, 1927/28 to 1955* (The RAND Corporation, Parts I and II, RM-1872 and RM-1873, 1957); D. Gale Johnson, *A Study of the Growth Potential of Agriculture of the USSR* (The RAND Corporation, RM-1561, 1955).

7. Naum Jasny, *The Socialized Agriculture of the USSR* (Stanford, 1949); M. Gardner Clark, *The Economics of Soviet Steel* (Cambridge, Mass., 1956); Holland Hunter, *Soviet Transportation Policy* (Cambridge, Mass., 1957).

8. Shimkin, *op. cit.*; John P. Hardt, *Economics of the Soviet Electric Power Industry* (Research Studies Institute, Air University [mimeographed], 1955); James H. Blackman, *Transport Development and Locomotive Technology* ("Essays in Economics," No. 3, Bureau of Business and Economic Research, University of South Carolina, 1957); Timothy Sosnovy, *The Housing Problem in the Soviet Union*, Research Program on the U.S.S.R. (New York, 1954).

9. Solomon M. Schwarz, *Labor in the Soviet Union* (New York, 1951). At this point note should also be made of Walter Galenson's major statistical study, *Labor Productivity in Soviet and American Industry* (New York, 1954).

10. A helpful start in this direction is Jerzy Gliksman's *Postwar Trends in Soviet Labor Policy* (The RAND Corporation, P-754, 1955), and various articles by the same author.

11. Abram Bergson, *The Structure of Soviet Wages* (Cambridge, Mass., 1946).

12. Franklyn D. Holzman, *Soviet Taxation* (Cambridge, Mass., 1955); Raymond P. Powell, "Soviet Monetary Policy" (Ph.D. dissertation, University of California, 1952). Mikhail V. Condoide's *The Soviet Financial System* (Columbus, 1951) is less analytical.

13. Alexander Baykov, *The Development of the Soviet Economic System* (Cambridge, England, 1946); Maurice Dobb, *Soviet Economic Development since 1917* (New York, 1948). These two books are sometimes also thought of as basic textbooks. As such, they seem

to be much less in use in this country than the standard (and only) American textbook: Harry Schwartz, *Russia's Soviet Economy* (2d ed., New York, 1954).

14. Joseph S. Berliner, *Factory and Manager in the USSR* (Cambridge, Mass., 1957); David Granick, *Management of the Industrial Firm in the USSR* (New York, 1954). See also Gregory Bienstock *et al.*, *Management in Russian Industry and Agriculture* (New York, 1948); Alexander Vucinich, *Soviet Economic Institutions* (Stanford, 1952); and relevant sections of Raymond A. Bauer *et al.*, *How the Soviet System Works* (Cambridge, Mass., 1956). At this point may be also mentioned the helpful survey, based on secondary sources, of "The Organization of Economic Activity in the Soviet Union" by Andrew G. Frank (*Weltwirtschaftliches Archiv*, 78:1 [1957], 104-156).

15. Lazar Volin's numerous articles; Naum Jasny's *Socialized Agriculture, op. cit.* and many articles; Herbert Dinerstein, *Communism and the Russian Peasant* (Glencoe, Ill., 1955).

16. See Norman Kaplan, "Investment Alternatives in Soviet Economic Theory," *Journal of Political Economy*, LX, No. 2 (April, 1952), 133-44; and Gregory Grossman, "Scarce Capital and Soviet Doctrine," *Quarterly Journal of Economics*, LXVII, No. 3 (August, 1953), 311-43, as well as the literature cited in footnote 1 thereof. For more recent developments, see also A. Zauberman, "A Note on Soviet Capital Controversy," *ibid.*, LXIX, No. 3 (August, 1955), 445-51.

17. E. g., Gardner Clark, *op. cit.*, Blackman, *op. cit.* Also note Granick's work on technological choice in the metalworking industry still in progress with interim reports by him in "Economic Development and Productivity Analysis: the Case of Soviet Metalworking," *Quarterly Journal of Economics*, LXXI, No. 2 (May, 1957), 205-33, and "Organization and Technology in Soviet Metalworking: Some Conditioning Factors," *American Economic Review*, XLVII, No. 2 (May, 1957), 631-42.

18. Norman Kaplan, "Arithmancy, Theomancy, and the Soviet Economy," *Journal of Political Economy*, LXI, No. 2 (April, 1953), 110. The paragraph from which the quotation is taken is a plea for "a model of the Soviet economic system, a theory of 'perfect Soviet socialism' . . . ," with which the present author substantially agrees.

19. Naum Jasny, *The Soviet Price System* (Stanford, 1951) and *Soviet Prices of Producers' Goods* (Stanford, 1952).

20. For the meaning of these terms and their use see: Bergson, *Soviet National Income and Product in 1937, op. cit.*; Bergson and Hans Heymann, Jr., *Soviet National Income and Product, 1940-48* (New York, 1954); Oleg Hoeffding, *Soviet National Income and Product in 1928* (New York, 1954).

21. See *Soviet Studies*, October, 1956, and subsequent issues.

22. Bergson's studies in question are essentially the books by himself and his associates cited in note 20 above; Donald R. Hodgman, *Soviet Industrial Production, 1928-1951* (Cambridge, Mass., 1954), and "A New Production Index for Soviet Industry," *Review of Economics and Statistics*, XXXII, No. 4 (November, 1950), 325-338.

23. For example, many of the contributions to Abram Bergson (ed.), *Soviet Economic Growth* (Evanston, 1953); Norman Kaplan, *Capital Investments in the Soviet Union, 1924-1951* (The RAND Corporation, RM-735, 1951); Walter Galenson, *op. cit.*; Nicholas DeWitt, *Soviet Professional Manpower* (Washington, 1955).

24. Alexander Erlich, "Preobrazhenskii and the Economics of Soviet Industrialization," *Quarterly Journal of Economics*, LXIV, No. 1 (February, 1950), 57-88, and "Stalin's Views on Soviet Economic Development," in Ernest J. Simmons (ed.), *Continuity and Change in Russian and Soviet Thought* (Cambridge, Mass., 1955). A book-length study on the industrialization debates is now under preparation by the same author. Another postwar American publication on the economic theorizing of the twenties is Adam Kaufman, "The Origin of the 'Political Economy of Socialism'," *Soviet Studies*, IV, No. 3 (January, 1953), 243-72.

25. See, for example, the valuable recent study of the ideologies of industrialism in prerevolutionary Russia and in the postwar Soviet orbit by a sociologist: Reinhard Bendix, *Work and Authority in Industry* (New York, 1956), esp. chaps. 3 and 6.

26. "Study of Soviet Economic Growth," National Bureau of Economic Research, Inc., under the direction of G. Warren Nutter (originally under Raymond W. Goldsmith).

27. Under the supervision of Norman M. Kaplan, and with the collaboration of the Stanford Research Institute.

4. POLITICAL SCIENCE

1. A brief preliminary version of this paper was presented and discussed at a meeting of Soviet area specialists during the convention

of the American Political Science Association, New York, September, 1957.

2. Such topics are, of course, appropriate for the study of certain pre-Soviet Russian political institutions; indeed, one of the earliest scholarly works on Russia by an American, Samuel N. Harper's *The New Electoral Law for the Russian Duma* (Chicago, 1908), dealt with such a theme. In general, coverage of Tsarist political institutions is part of the general treatment of Russian history prior to the Revolution, and is not reviewed in this paper. Three works now in progress which promise to be of special interest to the student of comparative politics should, however, be mentioned: Marc Szeftel's "The Political Institutions of the Russian Constitutional Monarchy (1905-1917)"; C. E. Black's "The Founding of the Modern Russian State: The Administrative Reforms of Peter the Great;" and Serge Levitsky's "Studies in the Procedure of the Russian Duma."

3. A notable example of books in the first category is Malbone W. Graham, *New Governments of Eastern Europe* (New York, 1927).

4. See especially *Civic Training in Soviet Russia* (Chicago, 1929) and *The Government of the Soviet Union* (New York, 1938).

5. For a comprehensive list of studies published by American scholars in the Soviet area field since 1947, and of work now in progress, see *Soviet Studies in the United States: A Survey of American Social Science Research on Soviet Russia, 1947-1957* (prepared in mimeographed form by the External Research Staff, Department of State).

6. Meyer's work on Marxism deals largely with non-Russian schools of Marxist thought. A number of other books on Marxism are discussed in the section on political philosophy in the chapter reviewing research in Russian and Soviet philosophy and religion.

7. Bertram D. Wolfe, *Three Who Made a Revolution* (New York, 1948); Leonard Schapiro, *The Origin of the Communist Autocracy* (Cambridge, Mass., 1955).

8. "Stalin's Vision of Utopia," *Proceedings of the American Philosophical Society*, XCIX, No. 1 (January 27, 1955), 11-21.

9. "Stalin on Revolution," *Foreign Affairs*, XXVII, No. 2 (January, 1949), 175-214.

10. *The Prophet Armed: Trotsky, 1879-1921* (New York, 1954). Deutscher is preparing a continuation of this treatment of Trotsky; Sidney Heitman is preparing a history Ph.D. dissertation on Bukharin (Columbia University); another dissertation (J. E. Flaherty, "The Political Career of Nicholas Bukharin") was completed at New York

University in 1954. For information on dissertations in the Soviet field, I am indebted to the Research Program on the Communist Party of the Soviet Union, for which Kermit Mackenzie prepared a comprehensive list.

11. *Le Marxisme en Union Soviétique* (Paris, 1955).

12. *Dialectical Materialism: A Historical and Systematic Survey of Philosophy in the Soviet Union* (New York, 1958).

13. *Der Sowjetrussische dialektische Materialismus (Diamat)* (Bern, 1950).

14. *Soviet Marxism* (New York, 1958).

15. Most of the studies of "political behavior" fall under this heading. Essentially, however, "behavioral" studies are an approach or a method rather than a distinct subject matter, and consequently will not be considered separately here.

16. An important study of this nature, now nearing completion, is Robert V. Daniels' "A History of Opposition in the Russian Communist Party."

17. Julian Towster, *Political Power in the USSR* (New York, 1948); Barrington Moore, Jr., *Soviet Politics: The Dilemma of Power* (Cambridge, Mass., 1950); Boris Meissner, *Russland im Umbruch* (Frankfurt a.M., 1951); Merle Fainsod, *How Russia Is Ruled* (Cambridge, Mass., 1954); Raymond Bauer, Alex Inkeles, and Clyde Kluckhohn, *How the Soviet System Works* (Cambridge, Mass., 1956); John N. Hazard, *The Soviet System of Government* (Chicago, 1957).

18. The historian Sidney Harcave's study, *The Structure and Functioning of the Lower Party Organizations in the Soviet Union* (Technical Research Report Number 23 of the Human Resources Research Institute Project, "An Analysis of the Soviet Social System," Maxwell Air Force Base, Alabama, 1954); a study of the political indoctrination system of the Soviet Army prepared by the political scientist Louis Nemzer for the Department of the Army; Herbert Dinerstein, *Communism and the Russian Peasant*, and Dinerstein and Leon Gouré, *Moscow in Crisis* (the latter two studies published in a single volume, Glencoe, Ill., 1955).

19. A few solidly based articles of a monographic nature should be noted. See especially Louis Nemzer's "The Kremlin's Professional Staff," *American Political Science Review*, XLIV (March, 1950), 64-85; and Merle Fainsod's "Controls and Tensions in the Soviet System." *ibid.*, XLIV (June, 1950), 266-82.

20. This topic is to be the subject of a book-length monograph being written by Mark Neuweld: "The Central Organization of the Communist Party of the Soviet Union."

21. See note 18.

22. Merle Fainsod, *Smolensk under Soviet Rule* (Cambridge, Mass., 1958). See also John A. Armstrong, *The Soviet Bureaucratic Elite: A Case Study of the Ukrainian Apparatus* (New York, 1959); and a dissertation by M. Rywkin being prepared for the Department of Public Law and Government, Columbia University, on the Uzbek Party organization.

23. In addition to those mentioned in note 22 above, two British Ph.D. candidates are treating the subject: T. H. Rigby, "The Selection of Leading Personnel in the Soviet State and Communist Party," University of London; and S. Utechin, "The Formation of the Ruling Class in the Soviet Society," Oxford University.

24. The numerous studies of Soviet strategical doctrine, while of special interest to the political scientist analyzing international relations, are in themselves too peripheral to political science to be discussed here.

25. Otto Heilbrunn, *The Soviet Secret Services* (New York, 1956) and Robert Slusser and Simon Wolin, *The Soviet Secret Police* (New York, 1957).

26. Ernest V. Hollis, Jr., "Police Systems of Imperial and Soviet Russia, 1700-1938" (Department of Public Law and Government).

27. See note 22.

28. The psychologist, Raymond Bauer, has used the techniques of political psychology in his composite "portrait" of a Party secretary in *Nine Soviet Portraits* (New York, 1955).

29. See especially Alex Inkeles, *Public Opinion in Soviet Russia* (Cambridge, Mass., 1951); and a European study, Bruno Kalnins, *Der sowjetische Propagandastaat* (Stockholm, 1956). An earlier work is Arthur W. Just, *Die presse der Sowjetunion: Methoden diktatorischer Massenführung* (Berlin, 1931).

30. Naive or illiberal efforts to glorify the Soviet experience as something to be adopted wholesale have tended to obscure the practical advantages to be derived from the study of Soviet administrative practice. Apparently the Labor administrators in Great Britain did draw heavily on the Soviet experience, without being "corrupted" by it.

31. See note 17.

32. See especially David Granick's *Management of the Industrial Firm in the USSR* (New York, 1954). Among other "management" studies are Alexander Baykov, *The Development of the Soviet Economic System* (New York, 1947); Alexander Vucinich, *Soviet Economic Institutions* (Stanford, 1952); and Joseph S. Berliner, *Factory and Manager in the USSR* (Cambridge, Mass., 1957).

33. *Soviet Housing Law* (New Haven, 1939); *Law and Social Change in the USSR* (Toronto, 1953).

34. *Justice in Russia* (Cambridge, Mass., 1950); *Soviet Military Law and Administration* (Cambridge, Mass., 1955).

35. For example, George M. Kahin, *Nationalism and Revolution in Indonesia* (Ithaca, 1952).

36. The helpful study by John S. Curtiss, *The Russian Church and the Soviet State* (New York, 1953), deals chiefly with the period before 1935.

37. *Bolshevism in Turkestan, 1917-1927* (New York, 1957). Mary Kilbourne Matossian has published two articles on Soviet Armenia and has completed studies, as yet unpublished, on the Communist Party of Armenia and the impact of Soviet policies in Armenia.

38. Among these studies, Henry L. Roberts' *Russia and America* (New York, 1956) is especially important.

39. Among the most significant are: "Soviet Policy in the UN," *Proceedings of the Academy of Political Science*, XXII, No. 2 (January, 1947), 28-37; "Dismemberment of Germany: The Allied Negotiations from Yalta to Potsdam," *Foreign Affairs*, XXVIII, No. 3 (April, 1950), 487-98; "The Occupation of Germany: New Light on How the Zones Were Drawn," *ibid.*, XXVIII, No. 4 (July, 1950), 580-604; "Soviet Exploitation of National Conflicts in Eastern Europe," in *The Soviet Union: Background, Ideology, Reality*, ed. by W. Gurian (Notre Dame, 1951), pp. 67-84; "Soviet Foreign Policy: New Goals or New Manners?," *Foreign Affairs*, XXXIV, No. 4 (July, 1956), 541-53; "The Soviet Union and the United States: Problems and Prospects," *Annals of the American Academy of Political and Social Science*, CCCIII (January, 1956), 192-98; (co-author) "The Moscow-Peking Axis in World Politics," in *Moscow-Peking Axis: Strengths and Strains*, by Howard L. Boorman and others (New York, 1957), 198-227.

40. In his *Soviet Image of the United States* (New York, 1950).

41. A proposed history dissertation by Eugene Magerovsky (Columbia University) will examine this subject for the 1920's, when

much more material was made available. For a good summary of the
meager available information on the formulation of foreign policy
in the Soviet Union, see David T. Cattell's chapter in Philip W.
Buck and Martin B. Travis, Jr., *Control of Foreign Relations in
Modern Nations* (New York, 1957), pp. 656-84.

42. The most important collections dealing directly with the
U.S.S.R. are Jane Degras' *Soviet Documents on Foreign Policy*
(London, 1951-1952) and *The Communist International, 1919-1943*
(London, 1956——); Xenia J. Eudin and Harold H. Fisher, *Soviet
Russia and the West, 1920-1927*, and Xenia J. Eudin and Robert C.
North, *Soviet Russia and the East, 1920-1927* (both Stanford, 1957).
In addition, of course, the British, American, and German diplomatic
documents have been invaluable as sources on Soviet policy.

Among sources on Communist parties outside the U.S.S.R. as aux-
iliaries of Soviet foreign policy, the Canadian Royal Commission to
Investigate Disclosure of Secret and Confidential Information to Un-
authorized Persons, *The Report of the Royal Commission* (Ottawa,
1946) and the Australian Royal Commission on Espionage, *Report of
the Royal Commission on Espionage* (Sydney, 1955) are outstanding.

Jan Triska and Robert M. Slusser are completing a two-volume
work "The Soviet Government as a Treaty Partner: 1917-1957,"
which will contain an annotated calendar of treaties and an analysis
of Soviet theory and practice of treaty-making. See also the article by
Triska and Slusser, "Treaties and other Sources of Order in International Relations: The Soviet View," *The American Journal of
International Law*, LII, No. 4 (October, 1958), 699-726.

43. The principal work is Max Beloff's *The Foreign Policy of
Soviet Russia, 1929-1941* (2 vols.; London, 1947-49). Among studies
on special questions may be mentioned Gerhard L. Weinberg, *Germany and the Soviet Union, 1939-41* (Leyden, 1954) and David T.
Cattell, *Soviet Diplomacy and the Spanish Civil War* (Berkeley,
1957).

W. L. Mahaney, *The Soviet Union, the League of Nations, and
Disarmament* (Philadelphia, 1940); and T. A. Taracouzio, *The
Soviet Union and International Law* (New York, 1935) and *War
and Peace in Soviet Diplomacy* (New York, 1940) were early and
relatively successful efforts to examine Soviet policies toward international organization and law.

Alexander Dallin's *The German Occupation of Russia* (London,
1957) carries the story of German-Soviet relations through the war

period. Boris Meissner's *Russland, die Westmächte, und Deutschland* (Hamburg, 1954) is an examination of Soviet policy toward Germany since the closing period of the war.

Two studies dealing with Soviet war-time foreign relations, though written by scholars not connected with the Soviet area field, deserve special mention: Herbert Feis's *Churchill—Roosevelt—Stalin* (Princeton, 1956) and William H. McNeill's *America, Britain, and Russia* (London, 1953). Both are based primarily on the important body of memoir material concerning negotiations during the war.

44. Important studies of this type now in progress are Paul E. Zinner's "Communist Strategy and Tactics in Czechoslovakia from 1924 to 1952" and Richard V. Burks, "Communism in the European East."

45. *The Appeals of Communism* (Princeton, 1954).

46. M. Einaudi and others, *Communism in Western Europe* (Ithaca, 1951).

47. *Die KPD in der Weimarer Republik* (Offenbach a.M, 1948). There are, in addition, other useful works, such as Angelo Rossi's *Physiologie du parti communiste français* (Paris, 1948); and Franz Borkenau's *The Communist International* (London, 1938), together with later studies by the same authors.

48. On the somewhat different problem of direct Soviet-Chinese relations, the important survey *Moscow-Peking Axis: Strengths and Strains* (New York, 1957) by Howard Boorman *et al.*, and the numerous articles on border problems by William B. Ballis should be noted. See also R. C. North, *Moscow and Chinese Communists* (Stanford, 1953) and J. H. Kautsky, *Moscow and the Communist Party of India* (New York, 1956).

49. Particularly by the Harvard Refugee Interview Project. Continued efforts are needed to secure the most important testimony of the émigrés before it is lost forever through their deaths.

50. "Approaches to the Study of Political Power," *Political Science Quarterly*, LXV (June 1950), 161-80.

5. PHILOSOPHY AND RELIGION

1. T. G. Masaryk, *The Spirit of Russia*, trans. E. and C. Paul (2 vols.; New York, 1955; original German edition, 1913).

2. V. V. Zenkovsky, *A History of Russian Philosophy*, trans. G. L. Kline (2 vols.; New York and London, 1953; original Russian edition, Paris, 1948, 1950).

3. N. O. Lossky, *History of Russian Philosophy* (New York, 1951).

4. Benoit-P. Hepner, *Bakounine et le panslavisme revolutionnaire: Cinq essais sur l'histoire des idées en Russie et en Europe* (Paris, 1950); Herbert E. Bowman, *Vissarion Belinski (1811-1848): A Study in the Origins of Social Criticism in Russia* (Cambridge, Mass., 1954); Richard Hare, *Pioneers of Russian Social Thought: Studies of Non-Marxian Formation in Nineteenth-Century Russia and of Its Partial Revival in the Soviet Union* (London and New York, 1951); Leopold H. Haimson, *The Russian Marxists and the Origins of Bolshevism* (Cambridge, Mass., 1955).

5. Gustav A. Wetter, *Dialectical Materialism: A Historical and Systematic Survey of Philosophy in the Soviet Union* (New York, 1958).

6. I. M. Bocheński, *Der sowjetrussische dialektische Materialismus (Diamat)* (Bern, 1950; 2nd ed., 1956). It should be noted that Wetter, Bocheński, and Zenkovsky are all members of religious orders. However, this fact does not adversely affect the objectivity of their studies. Even Wetter, who offers the fullest "confession of faith," is careful to place it in a separate chapter at the end of his study.

7. H. B. Mayo, *Marxism and Democracy* (New York, 1955); Josef Maček, *An Essay on the Impact of Marxism* (Pittsburgh, 1955). Marxist-Leninist political and social theory is competently discussed by two recent British writers: John Plamenatz in *German Marxism and Russian Communism* (New York and London, 1954); and, more briefly, R. N. Carew Hunt in *The Theory and Practice of Communism* (London, 1950). To be noted also: Max G. Lange, *Marxismus Leninismus Stalinismus: Zur Kritik des dialektischen Materialismus* (Stuttgart, 1955).

8. Stanley W. Moore, *The Critique of Capitalist Democracy: An Introduction to the Theory of the State in Marx, Engels, and Lenin* (New York, 1957).

9. H. B. Acton, *The Illusion of the Epoch: Marxism-Leninism as a Philosophical Creed* (London, 1955).

10. B. Petrov (Vysheslavtsev), *Filosofskaya Nishcheta Marksizma* (Frankfurt am Main, 1952; 2nd ed., 1957). For an exposition and evaluation of this study, see G. L. Kline, "A Philosophical Critique of Soviet Marxism," *The Review of Metaphysics,* IX (1955), 90-105.

11. Alfred G. Meyer, *Leninism* (Cambridge, Mass., 1957).

12. Herbert A. Marcuse, *Soviet Marxism: A Critical Analysis* (New York, 1958).

13. Geroid T. Robinson, "Stalin's Vision of Utopia," *Proceedings of the American Philosophical Society*, XCIX, No. 1 (January 27, 1955), 11-21.

14. While its main focus is intellectual and cultural history, the *Festschrift* for Professor Michael Karpovich, *Russian Thought and Politics*, ed. Hugh McLean, Martin E. Malia, and George Fischer ("Harvard Slavic Studies," Vol. IV; Cambridge, Mass., 1957), contains several articles touching on philosophy (e.g., those by Malia and Barghoorn). Russian philosophy and religion are ably discussed, in a broad cultural context, by Wladimir Weidlé in his *Russia, Absent and Present* (New York, 1952; original French edition, 1949).

15. G. L. Kline, "Russian Philosophy" in *Dictionary of Russian Literature*, ed. William E. Harkins (New York, 1956), pp. 288-300; "Recent Soviet Philosophy," in *Annals of the American Academy of Political and Social Science*, CCCIII (1956), 126-38; "Current Soviet Morality" in *Encyclopedia of Morals*, ed. V. T. A. Ferm (New York, 1956), pp. 569-80. The last work represents a preliminary and highly condensed version of part of a book (now in progress) on Russian ethical and social theory.

16. G. L. Kline, *Spinoza in Soviet Philosophy* (London and New York, 1952).

17. Alexander Philipov, *Logic and Dialectic in the Soviet Union* (New York, 1952), with preface by Ernest Nagel. Kline has reviewed the Soviet literature in this field for the *Journal of Symbolic Logic* and for *Mathematical Reviews*, and has translated technical papers in probability theory and mathematical logic.

18. David Joravsky, "Soviet Marxism and the Philosophy of Natural Science, 1922-1929: The Rejection of Positivism" (doctoral dissertation, Columbia University, 1957).

19. G. L. Kline, "Darwinism and the Russian Orthodox Church" in *Continuity and Change in Russian and Soviet Thought*, ed. Ernest J. Simmons (Cambridge, Mass., 1955), pp. 307-28.

20. John S. Curtiss, *Church and State in Russia, 1900-1917* (New York, 1940); *The Russian Church and the Soviet State, 1917-1950* (New York, 1953).

21. N. S. Timasheff, *Religion in Soviet Russia, 1917-1942* (New York, 1943); *The Great Retreat* (New York 1946). Professor Timasheff brings his account into the postwar period in a long article on "Religion" in *The Soviet Union*, ed. Waldemar Gurian (Notre

Dame, 1951). He also has ready for publication a manuscript on "Religion and Antireligion in Russia since the Revolution."

22. Matthew Spinka, *The Church in Soviet Russia* (New York, 1956).

23. Alex Inkeles, "Family and Church in the Postwar U.S.S.R.," *Annals of the American Academy of Political and Social Science,* CCLXIII (1949), 33-51.

24. A pioneer study of religious beliefs and attitudes, based on the testimony of recent Soviet émigrés, is Ivan London and N. Poltoratsky, "Contemporary Religious Sentiment in the Soviet Union," published in *Psychological Reports,* Monograph Supplement 3, (1957).

25. Nicolai von Bubnoff, *Russische Religions-Philosophen* (Heidelberg, 1956). This volume contains selections from Ivan Kireyevsky, Leontyev, Rozanov, Nesmelov, Ye. Trubetskoy, and Shestov.

26. Kline has undertaken the first study, which is now nearing completion. See note 15.

27. Nicholas V. Riasanovsky, *Russia and the West in the Teachings of the Slavophiles* (Cambridge, Mass., 1952); Robert E. Mac-Master, "Danilevski: Scientist and Panslavist" (a Harvard dissertation, currently being reworked for book publication in 1959 or 1960); Dmitri Chyzhevsky, *Gegel' v Rossii* [Hegel in Russia] (Paris, 1939); for Hare, see note 4.

28. Isaiah Berlin, *The Hedgehog and the Fox: An Essay on Tolstoy's View of History* (New York, 1953).

29. Professor Peter K. Christoff is working on a study of nineteeth-century Slavophilism which will deal with such questions. It will also include translations of brief works by several Slavophile thinkers.

30. Another study of Mikhailovsky, by Mendel, is now in progress. Robert Belknap of Columbia has undertaken a study of Lunacharsky. Professor Frederick Barghoorn's Harvard dissertation on Pisarev (1941) deserves to be reworked for publication as a monograph. This is also true for Mrs. Miriam Haskell Berlin's Harvard dissertation on Nechayev and Tkachev (1957), although both of these studies straddle the border regions where philosophy, intellectual history, and political science converge.

31. Burton Rubin has a dissertation in progress at Columbia on the Marxian aesthetics of Plekhanov.

32. Kline has undertaken two such comparative studies: of Bugayev

and Whitehead (with special attention to ontology, cosmology, and philosophy of science), and of Bogdanov and Dewey (with special attention to theory of knowledge and experience). The essay on Bogdanov and Dewey will appear as an article or pair of articles in the *Journal of the History of Ideas;* that on Bugayev and Whitehead as a series of articles in the *Review of Metaphysics.* The author hopes eventually to publish both essays as a short book under the title, "Comparative Studies in Russian and Anglo-American Philosophy."

33. Emanuel Sarkisyanz, *Russland und der Messianismus des Orients: Sendungsbewusstsein und politischer Chiliasmus des Ostens* (Tübingen, 1955).

34. Alfred G. Meyer, "Historical Notes on Ideological Aspects of the Concept of Culture in Germany and Russia" and "The Use of the Term Culture in the Soviet Union," printed as appendices to *Culture: A Critical Review of Concepts and Definitions,* ed. Clyde Kluckhohn and A. L. Kroeber (Cambridge, Mass., 1952). pp. 207-12 and 213-17.

35. Though not well edited, an example of this type of anthology is *The Political Philosophy of Michael Bakunin: Scientific Anarchism,* ed. G. P. Maximoff (Glencoe, Ill., 1953).

36. An anthology of Rozanov's writings has reportedly been prepared in French for publication in 1959 or 1960.

6. SOCIAL RELATIONS

1. This study is primarily concerned with work done by sociologists, psychologists, and anthropologists, but the contributions of students in other relevant disciplines are also discussed. It is of some interest to sociologists and Russian area specialists that one of the first American scholars to write about the Russian revolutions with some firsthand knowledge was the sociologist Edward Alsworth Ross, who published *Russia in Upheaval* (New York, 1918), *The Bolshevik Revolution* (New York, 1921), and *The Russian Soviet Republic* (New York, 1923).

2. See some of the articles in a symposium of the *American Sociological Review,* IX, No. 3 (June, 1944), for examples of work in this vein.

3. See Alexander Vucinich, "The Structure of Factory Control in the Soviet Union," *ibid.,* XV, No. 2 (April, 1950), 179-86, for an example of this approach.

4. For example, *How the Soviet System Works* by Raymond Bauer, Alex Inkeles, and Clyde Kluckhohn (Cambridge, Mass., 1956).

5. For example, *Totalitarianism: Proceedings of a Conference Held at the American Academy of Arts and Sciences, March, 1953,* ed. Carl J. Friedrich (Cambridge, Mass., 1954).

6. Margaret Mead and Rhoda Métraux (eds.), *The Study of Culture at a Distance* (Chicago, 1953).

7. Nathan Leites, *A Study of Bolshevism* (Glencoe, Ill., 1953); Barrington Moore, Jr., *Soviet Politics: The Dilemma of Power* (Cambridge, Mass., 1951).

8. Frank Lorimer, "Recent Population Trends In the Soviet Union," *American Sociological Review*, IX, No. 3 (June, 1944), 219-22; and *The Population of the Soviet Union* (New York, 1947).

9. Warren Eason, "Population and Labor Force" in *Soviet Economic Growth*, ed. Abram Bergson (Evanston, 1953), pp. 101-26; and *Trends and Prospects of the Soviet Population and Labor Force* (the RAND Corporation [mimeographed], appendix B, December 17, 1952).

10. Nicholas Timasheff, *The Great Retreat* (New York, 1946); and Eugene Kulischer, "Recent Migration in the Soviet Union," *American Sociological Review*, IX, No. 3 (June, 1944), 223-28.

11. Eugene Kulischer and Michael Roof, "A New Look At The Soviet Population Structure of 1939," *American Sociological Review*, XXI, No. 3 (June, 1956), 280-90.

12. Nicholas DeWitt, *Soviet Professional Manpower* (Washington: National Science Foundation, 1955).

13. David Heer, "Differences Between Men and Women in Occupational Placement and in Attitudes toward Occupations," The Harvard Project (see note 22).

14. The author's evaluation of studies of Russian national character borrows heavily from two papers: Alex Inkeles and Daniel J. Levinson, "National Character: The Study of Modal Personality and Socio-cultural Systems," reprint of chapter 26 from G. Lindzey (ed.), *Handbook of Social Psychology*, II (Cambridge, Mass., 1954); and Daniel Bell, "Ten Theories in Search of Reality: The Prediction of Soviet Behavior in the Social Sciences," *World Politics*, X, No. 3 (April, 1958), 327-65.

15. E. Hanfman and H. Beir, "Psychological Patterns of Soviet Citizens: A Survey of Clinical Psychological Aspects of the Soviet

Defection," The Harvard Project; Henry Dicks, "Observations on Contemporary Russian Behavior," *Human Relations,* V, No. 2 (1952), 111-76; Nathan Leites, *A Study of Bolshevism* (Glencoe, Ill., 1953); H. Roseborough and H. Phillips, "A Comparative Analysis of the Response to a Sentence Completion Test of a Matched Sample of Americans and Former Russian Subjects," The Harvard Project; Raymond Bauer, *The New Man in Soviet Psychology* (Cambridge, Mass., 1952); Margaret Mead, *Soviet Attitudes toward Authority* (New York, 1951). The work done in this field has exclusively emphasized the character of the Great Russians. It is a failing of the field in general that none of these studies has explored personality patterns among members of the minority nationality groups of the Soviet Union.

16. Dicks stresses Russian "orality;" others do not. Hanfman fails to find a dominant need in Russians for submissiveness; Dicks does, etc.

17. Bauer's study, *The New Man in Soviet Psychology,* represents an outstanding contribution to the sociology of knowledge. Nowhere else in sociological literature is the interaction between a system of knowledge and political, ideological, and economic requirements so sensitively traced. As a matter of fact, because of its unique emphasis on the relation between ideology and social structure, the whole field of Soviet studies contains much valuable material for the study of the sociology of knowledge.

18. Bauer, Inkeles, and Kluckhohn, *How the Soviet System Works* (see note 4).

19. Raymond Bauer, "The Developmental History of the Political Attitudes of Individuals toward the Soviet Regime," The Harvard Project.

20. An exception is Edward Shils' essay, "Authoritarianism: 'Right' and 'Left,'" in *Studies in the Scope and Method of the Authoritarian Personality,* ed. Richard Christie and Marie Jahoda (Glencoe, Ill., 1954), pp. 24-49.

21. Geoffrey Gorer's swaddling hypothesis (dubbed "diaperology" by some critics) notwithstanding. See Gorer, *The People of Great Russia* (London, 1949).

22. The Harvard Project was sponsored by the United States Air Force and conducted by the Russian Research Center of Harvard University. During 1950 and 1951 interviews were conducted and questionnaires administered to Soviet émigrés in Europe and the United States. The project gathered data from 329 extended life-

history interviews, including detailed personality tests; 435 supplementary interviews; almost 10,000 questionnaires on special topics; 2,700 general questionnaires; and 100 interviews and tests administered for control purposes to a matched group of Americans. To date, over fifty specialized unpublished studies, about thirty-five published articles, and a summary book (see note 4) have emerged from the project. An over-all evaluation of this project is to be found in our discussion of the "Soviet Social System" later in this paper.

23. D. Gleicher and I. Caro, "Patterns of Ideological and Value Orientation among Former Soviet Citizens," The Harvard Project.

24. Frederick C. Barghoorn, The Soviet Image of the United States: A Study in Distortion (New York, 1950).

25. American sociologists will be amused (and appalled) to learn of the Soviet image of American sociology. See J. K. Musgrave, "Soviet Evaluation of American Sociology," American Sociological Review, XIV, No. 1 (February, 1949), 137-43.

26. Government studies have undoubtedly been made, but are not available to the public.

27. Alex Inkeles, "The Soviet Attack on the Voice of America: A Study in Propaganda Warfare," American Slavic and East European Review, XII, No. 3 (October, 1953), 319-42.

28. Alex Inkeles, Public Opinion in Soviet Russia: A Study in Mass Persuasion (Cambridge, Mass., 1953).

29. For an analysis of the situation in one medium, see John Rimberg, The Soviet Film Industry (New York, 1956).

30. Merle Fainsod, "Censorship in the U.S.S.R.," Problems of Communism, V, No. 2 (March-April, 1956), 12-19; and Leo Gruliow, "How the Soviet Newspaper Operates," ibid., 3-11.

31. Ivan London, "The Scientific Council on Problems of the Psychological Theory of Academician I. Pavlov: A Study in Control," Science, CXVI, No. 3002 (July 11, 1952), 23-27.

32. Alex Inkeles and Kent Geiger, "Critical Letters to the Editors of the Soviet Press: Social Characteristics and Interrelations of Critics and the Criticized," American Sociological Review, XVIII, No. 1 (February, 1953), 12-22; and "Critical Letters to the Editors of the Soviet Press: Areas and Modes of Complaint," ibid., XVII, No. 6 (December, 1952), 694-703.

33. Raymond Bauer and David Gleicher, "Word-of-Mouth Communication in the Soviet Union," Public Opinion Quarterly, XVII, No. 3 (Fall, 1953), 297-310.

34. Peter Rossi and Raymond Bauer, "Some Patterns of Soviet

Communications Behavior," *ibid.*, XVI, No. 4 (Winter, 1952-53), 653-65.

35. Harold Lasswell and Sergei Yakobson, "May Day Slogans in Soviet Russia, 1928-43," *Language of Politics*, ed. Harold Lasswell (New York, 1949), pp. 233-97; Nathan Leites, "The Third International on Its Changes in Policy," *ibid.*, pp. 298-333; and Nathan Leites and I. de Sola Pool, "The Response of Communist Propaganda to Frustration," *ibid.*, pp. 334-68.

36. G. Denicke, "Links With the Past in Communist Society" (Washington: Series 3, No. 84, External Research Staff, Department of State, 1952).

37. Irwin Sanders, *Final Technical Report, Research for Evaluation of Social Systems Analysis* (Prepared for the Officer Education Research Laboratory, Air Force Personnel and Training Research Center, Maxwell Air Force Base, Alabama, by Associates for International Research, Cambridge, Mass. [mimeographed], September 15, 1957).

38. In the introduction to Ernest J. Simmons (ed.), *Through the Glass of Soviet Literature* (New York, 1953).

39. In addition to the examples cited below, see many of the articles included in *ibid.*

40. Kathryn Feuer, "Evidences of Class Stratification and Social Mobility in Postwar Soviet Literature" (Master's thesis, Columbia University, 1954).

41. Vera Dunham, "The Party Secretary in Postwar and Post-Stalinist Soviet Literature" (unpublished paper for the Research Program on the History of the Communist Party of the Soviet Union).

42. See note 7 and Nathan Leites, *The Operational Code of the Politburo* (New York, 1951).

43. John Reshetar, *Problems of Analyzing and Predicting Soviet Behavior* (Garden City, 1955).

44. Bertram Wolfe, "The Durability of Soviet Despotism," *Commentary*, XXIV, No. 2 (August, 1957), 93-104.

45. Edith Bennett, "The Relationship of Age to Other Demographic Characteristics of the PPQ Sample"; David Gleicher, "The Meaning of Distortion: A Note on the Causes and Correlates of Hostility toward the Soviet Regime"; Edward Wasiolek, "Responses of Former Soviet Citizens to a Questionnaire vs. Life History Interview"; Daniel Rosenblatt, "Technical Report on Coding and

Reliability Studies"; Babette Whipple, "Munich-New York Comparisons as Validity Tests of the PPQ"; all are papers of the Harvard Project.

46. Mark Field, "Structural Strain in the Role of the Soviet Physician," *American Journal of Sociology*, LVIII, No. 5 (March, 1953), 493-502.

47. John Hazard, "Trends in the Soviet Treatment of Crime," *American Sociological Review*, V, No. 4 (August, 1940), 566-76; Mark Field, "Drink and Delinquency in the U.S.S.R.," *Problems of Communism*, IV, No. 3 (May-June, 1955), 29-37.

48. See Harold J. Berman, *Justice in Soviet Russia: An Interpretation of Soviet Law* (Cambridge, Mass., 1952), for some analysis in this vein.

49. Michael Luther and John Reshetar, "The Genesis of Soviet Nationality Policies," The Harvard Project; Timasheff, *The Great Retreat* (see note 10); Michael Pap, "The Ukrainian Problem" in *Soviet Imperialism: Origins and Tactics*, ed. Waldemar Gurian (Notre Dame, 1953), pp. 43-74.

50. John Reshetar, "National Deviation in the Soviet Union," The Harvard Project.

51. Frederick Barghoorn, *Soviet Russian Nationalism* (New York, 1956).

52. *Ibid.*; George Fischer, *Soviet Opposition to Stalin: A Case Study in World War II* (Cambridge, Mass., 1952); Gillian, Rosow, and Reshetar, "The Nationality Problem in the Soviet Union: The Ukrainian Case," The Harvard Project; Irving Rosow, "Educational Patterns in the Soviet Union," The Harvard Project; Reshetar, "National Deviation in the Soviet Union" (see note 50).

53. Pap, "The Ukrainian Problem" (see note 49); Merle Fainsod, *How Russia Is Ruled* (Cambridge, Mass., 1953).

54. Timasheff, *The Great Retreat* (see note 10); William Petersen, "The Evolution of Soviet Family Policy," *Problems of Communism*, V, No. 5 (September-October, 1956), 29-35; Berman, *Justice in Soviet Russia* (see note 48).

55. Kent Geiger, "The Solidarity of the Urban Slavic Family under the Soviet System," The Harvard Project.

56. Alex Inkeles, "Social Change & Social Character: The Role of Parental Mediation," *Journal of Social Issues*, XI, No. 2 (1955), 12-23.

57. Alice Rossi, "Generational Differences in the Soviet Union," The Harvard Project.

58. Alex Inkeles, "Stratification and Mobility in the Soviet Union," *American Sociological Review*, XV, No. 4 (August, 1950), 465-79; Nicholas Timasheff, "Vertical Social Mobility in Communist Society," *American Journal of Sociology*, L, No. 1 (July, 1944), 9-21; Robert Feldmesser, "Some Observations on Trends in Social Mobility in the Soviet Union and Their Implications," The Harvard Project; Feuer, "Evidences of Class Stratification and Social Mobility" (see note 40); Gabriel Grasberg, "Problems of Stratification," The Harvard Project; Kassof, Inkeles, Feldmesser, and Grasberg, "Stratification and Mobility in the Soviet Union: A Study of Social Class Cleavages in the U.S.S.R.," The Harvard Project; David Dallin, *The Changing World of Soviet Russia* (New Haven, 1956).

59. W. W. Kulski, "Classes in the 'Classless' State," *Problems of Communism*, IV, No. 1 (January-February, 1955), 20-28; Hugh Seton-Watson, "The Soviet Ruling Class," *ibid.*, V, No. 3 (May-June, 1956), 10-15; Barrington Moore, Jr., "The Communist Party of the Soviet Union, 1928-1944," *American Sociological Review*, IX, No. 3 (June, 1944), 267-78.

60. Robert Feldmesser, "The Persistence of Status Advantage in Soviet Russia," *American Journal of Sociology*, LIX, No. 1 (July, 1953), 19-27.

61. See note 7.

62. Bauer, Inkeles, and Kluckhohn, *How the Soviet System Works* (see note 4).

63. Robert Feldmesser, "Social Status and Access to Higher Education, A Comparison of the U. S. and the Soviet Union," *Harvard Educational Review*, XXVII, No. 2 (Spring, 1957), 92-106.

64. See note 58.

65. Alex Inkeles and Peter Rossi, "National Comparisons of Occupational Prestige," *American Journal of Sociology*, LXI, No. 4 (January, 1956), 329-39.

66. Alex Inkeles, "Images of Class Relations among Former Soviet Citizens," *Social Problems*, III, No. 3 (January, 1956), 181-96; Grasberg, "Problems of Stratification" (see note 58).

67. Milovan Djilas, *The New Class* (New York, 1957).

68. Robert Feldmesser of Brandeis University is grappling with these issues. For an initial statement, see his work cited in note 63.

69. David Granick, *Management of the Industrial Firm in the U.S.S.R.* (New York, 1954).

70. See, for example, the article by Vucinich cited in note 3.

71. Joseph Berliner, *Industrial Management in the U.S.S.R.* (Cambridge, Mass., 1957).

72. Gregory Bienstock, Solomon M. Schwarz, and Aaron Yugow, *Management in Russian Industry and Agriculture* (New York, 1944).

73. David Dallin and Boris Nicolaevsky, *Forced Labor in Soviet Russia* (New Haven, 1947); Barrington Moore, Jr., *Terror and Progress in the U.S.S.R.* (Cambridge, Mass., 1954).

74. There is a theory (especially pronounced in the work of Isaac Deutscher) that once industrialization has been fully achieved and a reasonable standard of living obtained, social forces will come into being which will conflict with the regime and will tend to change it. The change will take the direction either of greater "liberalization" or of Bonapartism. It will be engendered by a more politically conscious working class and by a managerial elite desiring stability, security, wealth, etc. All this is debatable, of course. The approach is interesting, though, as a kind of "reverse Marxism" (i.e., wealth and privilege leading to greater freedom).

75. Instead of studying conventional institutions such as the family, church, army, etc., the Harvard Project identified eight basic "operating characteristics": "Creating and Maintaining Myths," "Planning and Controlling," "Problem Solving, Over-commitment of Resources, and Storming," "Refusal to Allow Independent Concentrations of Power," "Terror and Forced Labor," "Informal Adjustive Mechanisms," "Rigidity-Flexibility," "Caution at Major Risks in Foreign Affairs." As with conventional institutions, however, the analysis emphasized interrelatedness, adjustive mechanisms, functional and dysfunctional, etc.

76. Bauer, Inkeles, and Kluckhohn, *How the Soviet System Works* (see note 4).

77. Again, this discussion borrows heavily from Daniel Bell's analysis of several theories of Soviet behavior (see note 14).

78. For an example of the use of the power and command variable in an analysis of Soviet institutions and ideology, see D. Tomasic, "Interrelations between Bolshevik Ideology and the Structure of Soviet Society," *American Sociological Review*, XVI, No. 2 (April, 1951), 137-48.

79. W. W. Rostow, *The Dynamics of Soviet Society* (Cambridge, Mass., 1953). This study also seeks to specify strengths and weaknesses in the system.

80. For a sophisticated analysis of the relation of terror and

monopoly of control to other features of the Soviet system, see
Barrington Moore, Jr., *Terror and Progress in the U.S.S.R.* (see
note 73), and Merle Fainsod, *How Russia Is Ruled* (Cambridge,
Mass., 1955).

81. Zbigniew Brzezinski, *The Permanent Purge* (Cambridge,
Mass., 1956). This study, incidentally, contains an excellent definition of totalitarianism: ". . . a system where technologically advanced
instruments of political power are wielded without restraint by centralized leadership of an elite movement, for the purpose of effect-
ing a total social revolution, on the basis of certain arbitrary ideological assumptions proclaimed by the leadership, in an atmosphere of
coerced unanimity of the entire population."

82. Alex Inkeles, "The Totalitarian Mystique: Some Impressions
of the Dynamics of Totalitarian Society," The Harvard Project.

83. Mark Field, "The Academy of the Social Sciences of the Soviet
Union," *American Journal of Sociology*, LVI, No. 2 (September,
1950), 137-41.

84. George S. Counts, *The Challenge of Soviet Education* (New
York, 1957).

85. Nicholas Timasheff, *Religion in Soviet Russia, 1917-1942*
(New York, 1942).

86. Wolfe, "The Durability of Soviet Despotism" (see note 44).

87. Marshall Shulman, "Is the Soviet Union Changing?," *Problems of Communism*, V, No. 3 (May-June, 1956), 16-23.

88. Moore, *Terror and Progress* (see note 73).

89. Moore, *Soviet Politics* (see note 7).

90. Timasheff, *The Great Retreat* (see note 10).

91. Alex Inkeles, "Social Changes in Soviet Russia," The Harvard
Project.

7. SCIENCE

1. F. G. Benedict, "Russian Research in Metabolism," *Science*,
XXIX (March 5, 1909), 394-95.

2. Alexander Petrunkevich, "Russia's Contribution to Science,"
Transactions of the Connecticut Academy of Arts and Sciences,
XXIII (1920), 611-41; A. Hrdlička, "Scientific Work in Russia,"
Science, LV (June 9, 1922), 618-19; H. J. Muller, "Observations of
Biological Science in Russia," *Scientific Monthly*, XVI (May, 1923),
539-52; V. Kellogg, "Relief for Russian Scientists," *Science*, LVIII

(October 5, 1923), 264-65; W. Seifriz, "Science in Russia Today," *Scientific Monthly*, XXVI (May, 1928), 433-48.

3. For example, Julian S. Huxley, *Heredity East and West: Lysenko and World Science* (New York, 1949).

4. P. P. Lazarev, *Ocherki po Istorii Russkoi Nauki* [Essays in the history of Russian science] (Moscow, 1950); T. I. Rainov, *Nauka v Rossii XI-XVII vekov* [Science in Russia from the eleventh to the seventeenth centuries] (Parts 1-3; Moscow, 1940); I. S. Galkin, ed., *Rol' Russkoi Nauki v Razvitii Mirovoi Nauki i Kulturi* [The role of Russian science in the development of world science and culture] (3 vols.), in the *Uchenye Zapiski Moskovskovo Gosudarstvennovo Universiteta* [Learned Papers of Moscow State University], Nos. 91-92, 103-104, 106-107 (1946).

5. Academy of Sciences of the U.S.S.R., *Yubileinyi Sbornik Posvyaschchenny Tridtsatiletiyu Velikoi Oktyabr'skoi Sotsialisticheskoi Revolyutsii* [Jubilee anthology dedicated to the thirtieth anniversary of the great October socialist revolution] (2 vols.; Moscow, 1947). Volume one reviews progress in mathematics; physics, geophysics, and astronomy; and chemistry. Volume two covers geology, mineralogy, and soil sciences; biological sciences; history; and language and literature.

6. For example, V. A. Riazanovsky, *Razvitiye Russkoi Nauchnoi Mysli XVII-XIX st.* [The development of Russian scientific thought from the seventeenth to the nineteenth centuries] (New York, 1949); A. Lipski, "The Foundation of the Russian Academy of Sciences," *Isis*, XLIV (1953), 349-54.

7. B. N. Menshutkin, *Russia's Lomonosov* (Princeton, 1952).

8. Daniel Q. Posin, *Mendeleyev: The Story of a Great Scientist* (New York, 1948); Boris P. Babkin, *Pavlov: A Biography* (Chicago, 1949), written in exile by a former student; see also the special issue of the *Bulletin*, XXIV (1929), of the medical faculty of the Battle Creek (Mich.) Sanitorium, in honor of the eightieth birthday of Pavlov; V. N. Boldyrev, "Academician I. P. Pavlov," *American Journal of Digestion Diseases and Nutrition*, I (December, 1934), 747-54.

9. V. N. Ipatieff, *The Life of a Chemist* (Stanford, 1946); see also his "Modern Science in Russia," *Russian Review*, II (Spring, 1943), 68-80.

10. A study of scientific research and development in the Soviet

Union is currently being undertaken by the Center for International Studies at M.I.T. for the National Science Foundation.

11. Alexander Vucinich, *The Soviet Academy of Sciences* (Stanford, 1956); George C. Guins, "The Academy of Sciences of the USSR," *Russian Review*, XII (1952), 269-71; Iakov Budanov, "Tekhnicheskiye Instituti v SSSR" [Technical institutes in the U.S.S.R.], No. 26 in the Mimeographed Series of the Research Program on the U.S.S.R. (New York, 1952).

12. W. W. Leontief, Sr., "Scientific and Technological Research in Russia," *Russian Review*, IV (1943), 70-72.

13. Nicholas DeWitt, *Soviet Professional Manpower* (Washington, 1955); Alexander G. Korol, *Soviet Education for Science and Technology* (Cambridge, Mass., 1957); Leon Trilling, "Soviet Engineering Education," *Aviation Week*, LXV (August 20, 1956), 50-63, and (September 3, 1956), 58-79; John Turkevich, "The Soviet's Scientific Elite," *The Saturday Review of Literature*, XXXIX (March 24, 1956), 60-62, "Soviet Science and Education," in *The Challenge of Soviet Industrial Growth* (Princeton, 1957), 25-45, and "The Scientist in the USSR," *Atlantic Monthly*, CCI (January, 1958), 45-49.

14. V. P. Marchenko, *Planirovaniye Nauchnoi Raboty v SSSR* [The planning of scientific work in the U.S.S.R.] (Munich, 1953), prepared under the auspices of the Institute for the Study of the U.S.S.R.

15. For two excellent studies of this problem in the United States, see Don K. Price, *Government and Science* (New York, 1954); and A. Hunter Dupree, *Science in the Federal Government* (Cambridge, Mass., 1957).

16. L. S. Feuer, "Dialectical Materialism and Soviet Science," *Philosophy of Science*, XVI (April, 1949), 105-24; David Joravsky, "Soviet Views on the History of Science," *Isis*, XLVI (March, 1955), 3-13, and his "Soviet Marxism and Biology before Lysenko," *Journal of the History of Ideas*, XX, No. 1 (January, 1959), 85-104; and Gustav Wetter, "Dialectical Materialism and Natural Science," *Soviet Survey*, No. 23 (January-March, 1958), 51-59. See also the doctoral dissertation of David Joravsky on "Soviet Marxism and the Philosophy of Natural Science, 1922-1929: The Rejection of Positivism" (Columbia University, 1957), and the following papers prepared under the auspices of the Research Program on the History of the Communist Party of the Soviet Union: Maxim M. Mikulak,

"Soviet Philosophical-Cosmological Thought"; Stanislaw Kownacki, "Dialectical Materialism and Soviet Theoretical Physics"; and Michael Samygin, "Terror in the Academy of Sciences."

17. Conway Zirkle (ed.), *Death of a Science in Russia* (Philadelphia, 1949).

18. *Soviet Science,* arranged by Conway Zirkle and Howard A. Meyerhoff, and edited by Ruth C. Christman (Washington, 1952).

19. Russell L. Ackoff, "Scientific Method and Social Science: East and West," *ibid.,* 48-56; Lazar Volin, "Science and Intellectual Freedom in Russia," *ibid.,* 85-99; Conway Zirkle, "An Appraisal of Science in the USSR," *ibid.,* 100-108; John Turkevich, "The Progress of Soviet Science," *Foreign Affairs,* XXXII (April, 1954), 430-39, "Soviet Science in the Post-Stalin Era," *Annals of the American Academy of Political and Social Science,* CCCIII (January, 1956), 139-51, and "How Good is Russian Science?" *Fortune,* LV (February, 1957), 117-21.

20. Theodosius Dobzhansky, "Russian Genetics," *Soviet Science,* 1-7; W. Horsley Gannt, "Russian Physiology and Pathology," *ibid.,* 8-39; Ivan D. London, "Russian Psychology and Psychiatry," *ibid.,* 40-47; J. S. Joffe, "Russia's Contribution to Soil Science," *ibid.,* 57-69; John Turkevich, "Soviet Physics and Chemistry," *ibid.,* 70-79; J. R. Kline, "Soviet Mathematics," *ibid.,* 80-84; Raymond A. Bauer, *The New Man in Soviet Psychology* (Cambridge, Mass., 1952); G. L. Stebbins, "New Look in Soviet Genetics," *Science,* CXXIII (April 27, 1956), 721-22; M. J. Ruggles and A. Kramish, *The Soviet Union and the Atom* (Santa Monica, 1956).

21. Edward Podolsky, "Some Achievements of Soviet Medical Research," *Russian Review,* VI (Autumn, 1946), 77-83; and Saul Herner, "American Use of Soviet Medical Research," *Science,* CXXVIII, 3314 (July 4, 1958), 9-15. There are also several books on medicine: Henry E. Sigerist, with Julia Older, *Medicine and Health in the Soviet Union* (New York, 1947); I. Lazarévitch, *La Médicine en U.R.S.S.* (Paris, 1953); and especially Mark G. Field, *Doctor and Patient in Soviet Russia* (Cambridge, Mass., 1957).

22. Andrew R. MacAndrew (comp.), *A Glossary of Russian Technical Terms Used in Metallurgy* (New York, 1953); Ludmilla Ignatiev Callaham, *Russian-English Technical and Chemical Dictionary* (New York, 1957); Eugene A. Carpovich, *Russian-English Atomic Dictionary* (New York, 1957); James Perry, *Scientific Russian* (New York, 1951).

23. U. S. Library of Congress, *Bibliography of Translations from Russian Scientific and Technical Literature* (monthly); Special Libraries Association, *Translation Monthly;* Great Britain, Department of Scientific and Industrial Research, *Translated Contents List of Russian Periodicals* (monthly). See also A. E. Stubbs, "The Dissemination of Knowledge of Soviet Scientific Works in Western Countries," *Proceedings* of the Association of Special Libraries and Information Bureaux (London), IX (November, 1957), 333-40; and National Science Foundation, *Providing U.S. Scientists with Soviet Scientific Information* (Washington, 1958).

24. Translations are listed in U. S. Library of Congress, *East and East Central Europe: Periodicals in English and Other West European Languages,* comp. by Paul L. Horecky and Janina Wojcicka (Washington, 1958).

25. R. E. O'Dette, "Russian Translation," *Science,* CXXV (March 29, 1957), 579-85; and S. A. Wilde, "On Scientific Russian: Its Study and Translation," *American Scientist,* XLVI, No. 3 (September, 1958), 222-25.

26. For example, J. G. Crowther, *Science in Soviet Russia* (London, 1930); *Soviet Science* (Harmondsworth, England, 1942); P. H. Hudson and R. H. Richens, *Genetics in the Soviet Union* (Cambridge, England, 1946); Eric Ashby, *Scientist in Russia* (London, 1947).

27. Arnold Buchholz, *Ideologie und Forschung in den Sowjetischen Naturwissenschaft* (Stuttgart, 1953); and Gustav A. Wetter, *Der Dialektische Materialismus und das Problem der Entstehung des Lebens: Zur Theorie von A. I. Oparin* (Munich-Salzburg-Cologne, 1958).

28. For example, A. E. Fersman, *Twenty-five Years of Soviet Natural Science* (Moscow, 1944); S. I. Vavilov, *The Progress of Soviet Science* (Moscow, 1951).

29. M. J. Ruggles and A. Kramish, cited above in note 20.

30. See, for example, the extensive attention to Russian science in Mary A. B. Brazier (ed.), *The Central Nervous System and Behavior* (New York, 1958), pp. 23-231, resulting from a conference sponsored by the Josiah Macy, Jr., Foundation.

8. GEOGRAPHY

1. Professor John A. Morrison, at the University of Chicago, and Professor George B. Cressey, at Syracuse University.

2. George B. Cressey, *The Basis of Soviet Strength* (New York, 1945); *How Strong Is Russia? A Geographical Appraisal* (Syracuse, 1954).

3. Theodore Shabad, *Geography of the USSR: A Regional Survey* (New York, 1951). His research on Soviet population, undertaken while with the RAND Corporation, was issued under the title: *Population of Major Cities of the USSR* (Santa Monica: RAND Corporation, 1952). Shabad's technique for arriving at estimates of the 1947 and 1950 Soviet population allowed for a margin of error, as he himself acknowledged, but it is doubtful if the author anticipated so wide a margin as was revealed by the publication of *Narodnoye Khozyaistvo S.S.S.R.* [National economy of the U.S.S.R.] (Moscow, 1956).

4. Nicholas Tiho Mirov, *Geography of Russia* (New York, 1951).

5. L. S. Berg, *Natural Regions of the USSR* (New York, 1950); S. S. Balzak, V. F. Vasyutin, and Ya. G. Feigin, *Economic Geography of the USSR* (New York, 1949).

6. S. P. Suslov, *Fizicheskaya geografiya SSSR, Azyatskaya chast'* [Physical geography of the U.S.S.R., Asiatic part] (Moscow, 1954).

7. Werner Leimbach, *Die Sowjetunion; Natur, Volk und Wirtschaft* (Stuttgart, 1950); Erich Thiel, *Sowjet-Fernost; eine Landesund Wirtschaftskundliche Übersicht* (München, 1953); *The Soviet Far East* (New York, 1957); see also Heinrich Hassman, *Oil in the Soviet Union: History, Geography, Problems* (Princeton, 1953).

8. Georges Jorré, *The Soviet Union, the Land and Its People* (New York, 1950); Pierre George, *U.R.S.S., Haute-Asie, Iran* (Paris, 1947); James S. Gregory and D. W. Shave, *The USSR: A Geographical Survey* (London, 1944); G.D.B. Gray, *Soviet Land: the Country, Its People and Their Work* (London, 1947).

9. John A. Morrison, "The Evolution of the Territorial-Administrative System of the USSR," *The American Quarterly on the Soviet Union*, I, No. 3 (October, 1938), 25-46; Theodore Shabad, "The Soviet Concept of Economic Regionalization," *The Geographical Review*, XLIII, No. 2 (April, 1953), 214-22; also his "Political-Administrative Divisions of the USSR," *The Geographical Review*, XXXVI, No. 2 (April, 1946), 303-11; Demitri B. Shimkin, "Economic Regionalization in the Soviet Union," *The Geographical Review*, XLII, No. 3 (October, 1952), 591-614.

10. Chauncy D. Harris, "The Cities of the Soviet Union," *The Geographical Review*, XXXV, No. 1 (January, 1945), 107-21; for his study of the Soviet city as a center of assimilation, see "Ethnic

Groups in Cities of the Soviet Union," *ibid.*, XXXV, No. 3 (July, 1945), 466-73.

11. *Izvestia Vsesoyuznovo Geograficheskovo Obshchestvo* [Journal of the All-Union Geographical Society], LXXIX, No. 2 (1947), 218.

12. George B. Cressey, "The Geographic Base for Agricultural Planning," pp. 334-36, in "Soil Conservation in the USSR," *Land Economics*, XXV (1949), 333-64; Chauncy D. Harris, "Soviet Agricultural Resources Reappraised," *Journal of Farm Economics*, XXXVIII, No. 2 (May, 1956), 258-73.

13. W. A. Douglas Jackson, "The Virgin and Idle Lands of Western Siberia and Northern Kazakhstan: A Geographical Appraisal," *The Geographical Review*, XLVI, No. 1 (January, 1956), 1-19; "Durum Wheat and the Expansion of Dry Farming in the Soviet Union," *Annals of the Association of American Geographers*, XLVI, No. 4 (December, 1956), 405-10. In progress are additional studies by Jackson, involving Soviet experience with wheat culture in the non-chernozem zone of the north European part of the country and attempts to expand agriculture generally in eastern Siberia and the Soviet Far East. Jackson's studies are to be combined with other unpublished studies of agricultural change in a monograph on Soviet agricultural geography.

14. Neil C. Field, "The Amu Darya: A Study in Resource Geography," *The Geographical Review*, XLIV, No. 4 (October, 1954), 528-42; "The Role of Irrigation in the South European USSR in Soviet Agricultural Growth" (Ph. D. dissertation, University of Washington, 1956).

15. Allan L. Rodgers, "The Pasture—Small Grains—Livestock Region of North European Russia," in *Proceedings* of the Eighth General Assembly and Seventeenth International Congress of the International Geographical Union (Washington, 1952), pp. 662-67.

16. John A. Morrison, "Russia and Warm Water, A Fallacious Generalization and Its Consequences," *Proceedings*, U. S. Naval Institute, LXXVIII, No. 11 (November, 1952), 1169-79.

17. George A. Taskin, "The Falling Level of the Caspian Sea in Relation to the Soviet Economy," *The Geographical Review*, XLIV, No. 4 (October, 1954), 508-27.

18. Allan L. Rodgers, "Changing Locational Patterns in the Soviet Pulp and Paper Industry," *Annals of the Association of American Geographers*, XLV, No. 1 (March, 1955), 85-104.

19. Demitri B. Shimkin, *Minerals, A Key to Soviet Power* (Cambridge, Mass., 1953); Lazar Volin, *A Survey of Soviet Russian Agriculture*, U.S. Department of Agriculture, Agriculture Monograph No. 5 (Washington, 1951); Michael Y. Nuttonson, *Ecological Crop Geography of the Ukraine and the Ukrainian Agro-Climatic Analogues in North America*, American Institute of Crop Ecology (Washington, 1947); *Agricultural Climatology of Siberia, Natural Belts, and Agro-Climatic Analogues in North America*, American Institute of Crop Ecology (Washington, 1950); *Wheat-Climate Relationships and the Use of Phenology in Ascertaining the Thermal and Photo-Thermal Requirements of Wheat*, American Institute of Crop Ecology (Washington, 1955); Frank Lorimer, *The Population of the Soviet Union: History and Prospects*, League of Nations (Geneva, 1946).

20. *Soviet Geography: A Bibliography*, Part I, USSR Geography by Subject; Part II, Administrative, Natural and Economic Regions (Washington: Library of Congress Reference Department, 1951).

9. LITERATURE

1. D. S. Mirsky, *A History of Russian Literature, Comprising a History of Russian Literature and Contemporary Russian Literature*, edited and abridged by Francis J. Whitfield (New York, 1949).

2. Marc L. Slonim, *The Epic of Russian Literature, from Its Origins through Tolstoy* (New York, 1950); and *Modern Russian Literature* (New York, 1953).

3. Ernest J. Simmons, *Leo Tolstoy* (Boston, 1946).

4. David Magarshack, *Chekhov, A Life* (London, 1952); *Chekhov the Dramatist* (New York, 1952); *Turgenev, A Life* (New York, 1954); *Gogol* (New York, 1957).

5. Janko Lavrin, *Tolstoy: An Approach* (New York, 1946); *Pushkin and Russian Literature* (London, 1947); *N. V. Gogol, 1809-1852: A Centenary Survey* (London, 1951); *Goncharov* (New Haven, 1954).

6. W. H. Bruford, *Chekhov and His Russia* (London, 1947).

7. Ronald Hingley, *Chekhov, a Biographical and Critical Study* (London, 1950).

8. Herbert Bowman, *Vissarion Belinski, 1811-1848: A Study in the Origins of Social Criticism in Russia* (Cambridge, Mass., 1954).

9. Avrahm Yarmolinsky, *Dostoevsky: His Life and Art* (2nd ed., revised and enlarged; New York, 1957).

10. Henri Grégoire, Roman Jakobson, Marc Szeftel, *La Geste du Prince Igor', épopée russe du douzième siècle* (New York, 1948).

11. Roman Jakobson and Ernest J. Simmons (eds.), *Russian Epic Studies* (Philadelphia, 1949).

12. Kathryn Feuer, "Tolstoy's Literary Method in *War and Peace*."

13. Ralph E. Matlaw, *The Brothers Karamazov: Novelistic Technique* (Musagetes, No. 2; The Hague, 1957).

14. Robert Belknap, "The Narrative Structure of *The Brothers Karamazov*."

15. André Mazon, *Un Maître du roman russe: Ivan Gontcharov* (Paris, 1914).

16. Dmitri Chyzhevsky, *On Romanticism in Slavic Literature* (Musagetes, No. 1; The Hague, 1957).

17. We are helped by articles such as Kenneth Harper's "Criticism of the Natural School in the 1840's," *American Slavic and East European Review*, XV, No. 3 (October, 1956), 400-14.

18. An excellent piece of German scholarship is A. Rammelmeyer, "Dostojevskijs Begegnung mit Belinskij," *Zeitschrift fur slavische Philologie*, XXI (1952), 1-21; 273-92.

19. Waclaw Lednicki, *Russia, Poland and the West: Essays in Literary and Cultural History* (New York, 1954).

20. George Gibian, *Tolstoy and Shakespeare* (The Hague, 1957).

21. Ernest J. Simmons, *English Literature and Culture in Russia, 1553-1840* (Cambridge, Mass., 1935). Mention should also be made of Ludmilla Turkevich's study, *Cervantes in Russia* (Princeton, 1950).

22. V. Seduro, *Dostoevsky in Russian Literary Criticism, 1846-1956* (New York, 1957).

23. Renato Poggioli, *The Phoenix and the Spider* (Cambridge, Mass., 1957).

24. P. Yershov (ed.), *Letters of Gorky and Andreev, 1899-1912* (New York, 1957).

25. Marc L. Slonim, *Modern Russian Literature* (New York, 1953).

26. Gleb Struve, *Soviet Russian Literature, 1917-1950* (Norman, Okla., 1951). A revised and enlarged edition has appeared more recently in German translation: *Geschichte der Sowjetliteratur* (Munich, 1957).

27. *Continuity and Change in Russian and Soviet Thought*, edited with an introduction by Ernest J. Simmons (Cambridge, Mass., 1955).

28. Edward J. Brown, *The Proletarian Episode in Russian Literature, 1928-1932* (New York, 1953).

29. George Luckyj, *Literary Politics in the Soviet Ukraine, 1917-1934* (New York, 1956).

30. *Through the Glass of Soviet Literature*, edited with an introduction by Ernest J. Simmons (New York, 1953).

31. Victor Erlich, *Russian Formalism; History—Doctrine* (The Hague, 1955).

32. Ernest J. Simmons, *Russian Fiction and Soviet Ideology: Introduction to Fedin, Leonov, and Sholokhov* (New York, 1958).

33. *Harvard Slavic Studies*, I-IV (Cambridge, 1953-1957). The four volumes published up to the time this is written contain interesting material on Gorky, Soviet war poetry, and Ukrainian literature, as well as articles on Dostoevsky, Bunin, and other figures.

34. Initials used in referring to the proletarian writers' groups of the thirties.

35. Alexander Kaun, *Maxim Gorky and His Russia* (New York, 1931).

36. N. Matsuev, *Khudozhestvennaya Literatura, Russkaya i Perevodnaya, 1938-1953 gg. Bibliografiya* [Artistic literature, Russian and translated, 1938-1953, a bibliography] I (1938-1945) (Moscow, 1956).

37. Oleg Maslennikov, *The Frenzied Poets: Andrey Biely and the Russian Symbolists* (Berkeley, 1952).

38. V. Zavalishin, *Early Soviet Writers* (New York, 1958).

10. LINGUISTICS

1. Alfred Senn, "The Original Homeland of the Baltic People," and Roman Smal-Stocki, "The Original Homeland of the Slavic People." See *Publications of the Modern Language Association of America*, LXV (1950), 63.

2. *La Geste du Prince Igor'*. . . . Texte établi, traduit et commenté sous la direction d'Henri Grégoire, de Roman Jakobson et de Marc Szeftel, assistés de J. A. Joffe (*Annuaire de l'Institut de philologie et d'histoire orientales et slaves*, Tome VIII, New York, 1948). Professor Shevelov, in his comments on the present essay, has observed:

"The only field in which American Slavic research in linguistics has yielded significant results has been the examination of the *Igor' Tale* and contiguous problems. But . . . this field less than any other meets the justified requirement . . . that American Slavic linguists concentrate their efforts primarily on those questions which cannot be adequately studied in the Slavic countries. The problem of the *Igor' Tale*, which has been raised in Moscow to an issue of Russian national pride and patriotism, is a problem which, whatever may be the endeavors and intentions of American scholars, is doomed to be dependent, not guiding, and is bound to move in channels and along lines set in Moscow."

3. This record of periodical and monographic publication cannot, however, stand comparison with the contributions of some other non-Slavic countries, such as France, Germany, and Sweden.

4. See E. Colin Cherry, Morris Halle, and Roman Jakobson, "Toward the Logical Description of Languages in Their Phonemic Aspect," *Language*, XXIX (1953), 34-46.

5. In *Harvard Slavic Studies*, I (1953).

6. *Orbis*, III (1954), 43-57.

7. I am indebted to Professor Shevelov for his suggestion of some of the major studies that remain to be undertaken.

II. MUSIC

1. As of February, 1958, the coverage of the major pre-1917 Russian composers whose works are available on long-playing records could be characterized as follows: Balakirev, good; Borodin, good; Cui, poor; Dargomyzhsky, poor; Glazunov, fair; Glinka, fair; Ippolitov-Ivanov, fair; Liadov, good; Musorgsky, excellent; Rimsky-Korsakov, excellent; Rubinstein, fair; Scriabin, good; Taneev, fair; Tchaikovsky, excellent.

The situation with regard to the leading post-1917 émigrés can be characterized as follows: Gretchaninoff, nothing; Rachmaninoff, excellent; Stravinsky, excellent.

2. Post-1917 Russian (Soviet) composers whose works are currently available on long-playing records include the following: Fikret Amirov; Arno Babadzhanian; Nikolai Chaikin; Boris Chaikovsky; Reinhold Glière (many works); Otar Gordelli; Vera Gorodskaia; Dmitri Kabalevsky (many works); Basil Kalinikov; Kara Karaev; Aram Khachaturian (many works); Karen Khachaturian; Tikhon Khrennikov; Alexis Machavariani; Nikolai Medtner; Nikolai Mias-

kovsky (several works); Aleksandr Mossolov; Gavril Popov; Nikolai Rakov; Lazar Sarian; Yuri Shishakov; Aleksandr Spendiarov; Otar Taktakishvili; Armen Tigranian; Sergei Vassilenko; and Vladimir Vlassov. Recordings of compositions by two post-1917 composers— Sergei Prokofiev and Dmitri Shostakovich—rival in number and variety those of the most popular pre-1917 or émigré composers.

3. Only a few general historical surveys of Russian music have been published, none entirely adequate. M. Montagu-Nathan's *A History of Russian Music* (New York, 1914), good for its time, is now out of date. M. D. Calvocoressi's *Survey of Russian Music* (New York, 1944) is a competent brief introduction. The most recent one-volume treatment, R. A. Leonard's *History of Russian Music* (New York, 1956), is reasonably satisfactory although the author makes no direct use of Russian language sources and omits any musical citations.

Biographical coverage is highly uneven. No full-length biographical or critical studies of the following composers have been published in English in the last forty years: Balakirev, Cui, Dargomyzhsky, Glazunov, Ippolitov-Ivanov, Glinka, Khachaturian, Liadov, Rebikov, Serov, and Taneev. The most recent book on Borodin (by G. E. H. Abraham) is over twenty years old; on Nikolai and Anton Rubinstein (by Catherine Drinker Bowen) over fifteen; on Scriabin (by Alfred J. Swan) over thirty. Except for translations of studies first published in the Soviet Union, there are no books in English on Miaskovsky and Prokofiev. On Gretchaninoff, there is only the composer's autobiography, *My Life* (New York, 1952).

The situation with regard to a few Russian composers is better. Musorgsky has been the subject of several excellent books. The biography by M. D. Calvocoressi (New York, 1951), not to be confused with earlier studies (1919 and 1946) by the same author, is a work of fundamental importance; it overshadows the French study by Rostislav Hofman (Paris, 1952) and the German biography by Oskar von Riesemann, translated by Paul England (New York, 1929). Of particular value is *The Musorgsky Reader,* ed. Jay Leyda and Sergei Bertensson (New York, 1947), a biography in letters and documents.

On Rachmaninoff there are a number of excellent studies. The most recent is the biography by Sergei Bertensson and Jay Leyda (New York, 1956). Also valuable are John Culshaw's *Rachmaninov, the Man and His Music* (London, 1950), V. I. Seroff's *Rachmaninoff* (New York, 1950), and to a lesser extent the older studies by Antoni Gronowicz (New York, 1946, a translation) and W. R. Lyle (London, 1939). The composer's *Recollections* (London, 1934, translated from the German) are still indispensable.

The only good study of Rimsky-Korsakoff available is the one by G. E. H. Abraham (London, 1945). There is an excellent translation, however, of the classic autobiography, *My Musical Life,* based on the revised 3rd Russian edition (New York, 1942). In addition, two of the composer's technical treatises are available in English translation: *Principles of Orchestration,* ed. Maximilian Steinberg (3rd ed.; London, 1938) and *Practical Manual of Harmony,* translated from the 12th Russian edition by Joseph Achron (New York, 1930).

On Shostakovich, surprisingly enough, there is only one non-Soviet work, the useful study by V. I. Seroff (New York, 1943), which includes material provided by the composer's aunt, Nadejda Galli-Shohat. The more recent book by I. I. Martynov (New York, 1947) is a translation of a Soviet study.

The list of books on Stravinsky and his music is a long one. Of prime importance are the composer's autobiography (first published in French; English translation, New York, 1936) and his *Poetics of Music* (French edition 1942, English edition 1947, both Cambridge, Mass.). A bibliography to 1940 has been compiled by Paul David Magriel in *Bulletin of Bibliography,* XVII, No. 1 (January-April, 1940), 8-9; No. 2 (May-August, 1940), 31-33.

As is perhaps inevitable in the case of such a protean artist, whose career is still unfolding, none of the many useful studies so far published can claim to be definitive. The following volumes may be mentioned: Rollo H. Myers, *Introduction to the Music of Stravinsky* (London, 1950); Eric Walter White, *Stravinsky's Sacrifice to Apollo* (London, 1930); V. M. Beliaev, *Igor Stravinsky's "Les Noces"* (London, 1928); and Merle Armitage's *Stravinsky* (New York, 1936). European studies include the following: Italian, Alfredo Casella (Brescia, 1947); Belgian, Paul Collaer (Brussels, 1930); German, Herbert Fleischer (Berlin, 1931); Swiss, Leon Oleggini, *Connaissance de Stravinsky* (Lausanne, 1952), and C. R. Ramuz, *Souvenirs d'Igor Stravinsky* (Paris, 1929); and French, André Schaeffner (1931) and Boris Schloeser (1929). The composer's son has published *Le Message d'Igor Stravinsky* (Paris, 1948).

Less extensive is the published literature on Tchaikovsky. The composer's *Diaries* have been made available in translation (New York, 1945). The best biography, a model of musicological research and style, is Herbert Weinstock's *Tchaikovsky* (New York, 1943),

which supersedes the biography by the composer's brother, M. I.
Tchaikovsky, *Life and Letters of Peter Ilich Tchaikovsky* (New
York, 1924, an abridged translation). A popular biography, *Beloved
Friend*, by Catherine Drinker Bowen and Barbara von Meck (New
York, 1937), deals primarily with the relation between the composer
and his patroness, Madame Nadejda von Meck. Other useful studies
are those by G. E. H. Abraham (new ed.; London, 1949), A. Grono-
wicz (New York, 1946), and E. Evans (rev. ed.; New York, 1935).
The best critical studies of the music are by Eric Blom, dealing with
the orchestral works (London, 1927; new ed., 1948), and by G. E. H.
Abraham (New York, 1946). The somewhat oddly titled book,
Russian Symphony: Thoughts about Tchaikovsky (New York, 1947),
is a translation of a volume of essays on Tchaikovsky by various
Soviet musicians and writers, including B. V. Asafiev, Dmitri Shostakovich, and Yuri Keldysh.

To some extent the deficiencies in biographical and critical studies
which have been pointed out above are remedied by shorter treatments of individual composers available in collective volumes. Thus,
the able and industrious English critic G. E. H. Abraham has dealt
with the Soviet composers Shostakovich, Prokofiev, Khachaturian,
Knipper, Shebalin, Kabalevsky, Dzerzhinsky, and Shaporin in his
book, *Eight Soviet Composers* (London, 1946), and with some of
the major nineteenth-century composers in *On Russian Music* (New
York, 1939) and *Studies in Russian Music* (London, 1935). The
same writer has collaborated with M. D. Calvocoressi in *Masters of
Russian Music* (New York, 1936). Less scholarly, but useful, is
the book by V. I. Seroff, *The Mighty Five* (New York, 1948), dealing with the nineteenth-century pleiade around Musorgsky.

A number of valuable documentary translations from Soviet musical politics are given in Nicolas Slonimsky's *Music Since 1900* (3rd
ed.; New York, 1949). Useful summary articles by the same author
are "Development of Soviet Music" in *Research Bulletin on the
Soviet Union*, II, No. 4 (April 30, 1937), 31-36, and "The Changing
Style of Soviet Music" in the *Journal of the American Musicological
Society* (hereinafter cited as *JAMS*), III (1950) 236-55.

As part of the Russian translation project of the American Council
of Learned Societies, translations were undertaken of two standard
Soviet historical works on music, B. V. Asafiev's *Russkaya Muzyka ot
Nachala XIX Veka* [Russian music from the beginning of the nine-
teenth century] (Moscow, 1930) and Nikolai Findeisen's *Ocherki po
Istorii Muzyki v Rossii s Drevneishikh Vremyon do Kontsa XVIII*

Veka [Essays on the history of music in Russia from the earliest times to the end of the eighteenth century] (Moscow, 1928-1929). Owing to lack of funds, the work by Asafiev was put out in paper covers with a minimum of editorial revision, while that by Findeisen was left in manuscript. (On the whole music translation project and on the deficiencies of the Asafiev translation, see the review by Judah A. Joffe, *Music Library Association Notes*, XII, No. 1, 2nd series (December, 1945).

Other translations of Soviet studies, undertaken commercially, include, in addition to those mentioned previously in this note: I. V. Nestyev on Prokofiev (New York, 1946) and A. A. Ikonnikov on Miaskovsky (New York, 1946).

A unique place in Western studies of music in Russia during the past four decades is occupied by two magistral works by the Swiss scholar, R. A. Mooser. His *magnum opus*, a landmark in musicology but apparently almost unknown to Russian area specialists, is *Annales de la musique et des musiciens en Russie au 18e siècle* (3 vols.; Geneva, 1948-1951). This "monumental assemblage of source materials" (E. O. D. Downes in *JAMS*, IX [1956], 47) has been severely criticized, however, by a musicologist who specializes in Slavic music for "disparag [ing] the whole Russian past, disposing of it as a state of barbarism," and as a "truly monumental work . . . on the crazy Italian eighteenth century," rather than a study of *Russian* music (review by Alfred J. Swan, *JAMS*, I [1949], 51-52). Mooser's three volumes are nevertheless a mine of information for anyone concerned with the origins of modern Russian culture.

On a less imposing scale but equally indispensable for the period is the same author's *L'opéra-comique français en Russie au XVIIIe siècle* (Geneva, 1951); for a review, with valuable data on the author's background and sources, see *JAMS*, IX (1956), 46-47.

Of the few other serious scholarly historical studies may be mentioned Elsa Mahler's *Altrussische Volkslieder aus den Pečoryland* (Basel, 1951) and C. Stief's *Studies in the Russian Historical Song* (Stockholm, 1953). Studies of this caliber by American scholars are conspicuously lacking.

4. The works which fall in this category are included in note 3.

5. The 1948 decree on music by the Communist Party, for example, gave rise to an extensive discussion. Alexander Werth's *Musical Uproar in Moscow* (London, 1949) retains its value as a record of the debate. Juri Jelagin's *Taming of the Arts* (New York, 1951), although it deals primarily with the theater, is of great interest

for the light it casts on the situation of music and musicians in the Soviet system. An unclassifiable but noteworthy book is Truman Capote's *The Muses Are Heard: An Account of the Porgy and Bess Visit to Leningrad* (New York, 1956).

6. The publication of various Soviet studies in translation has been mentioned in note 3. One may add I. F. Boelza's *Handbook of Soviet Musicians* (London, 1942); A. D. Bush's *Music in the Soviet Union* (London, 1944); R. Moisenco's *Realist Music* (London, 1949); and the same author's *Twenty Soviet Composers* (London, 1942).

7. Most of the articles in *Grove's* make careful use of Soviet materials. Facts are used without accompanying propaganda, and Soviet evaluations, where used, are generally counterbalanced by quotations from Western critics. Of the smaller music handbooks, perhaps the only one which calls for separate mention is Percy Scholes' *Oxford Companion to Music* (Oxford, 1938).

8. The following articles may serve as examples of the three types of material mentioned: (a) Reviews of Shostakovich's Violin Concerto in *Music Review,* November, 1956; *Music Times,* October, 1956; *Musical Opinion,* April, 1956; *Musical America,* January, 1956; *Saturday Review of Literature,* January 14, 1956; *Time,* January 9, 1956. (b) Reviews of the performances of *Porgy and Bess* in Moscow and Leningrad in *Etude,* March 15, 1956; *Musical Courier,* March 1, 1956; *Saturday Review of Literature,* January 14, 1956; *Musical America,* January 15, 1956. For Soviet musicians in the United States, "The Soviet Invasion of Our Concert Halls," *Reporter,* March 22, 1956. (c) Walter Howard Rubsamen, "Political and Ideological Censorship of Opera," 1941 (read at the American Musicological Society Annual Meeting, 1941); see the same author's review of several books on Russian music in *JAMS,* IV (1951), 268-72; Marc Soriano, "Les Problèmes de la musique et le Marxisme," *La Pensée,* new series, No. 56 (1954), 77-88; Robert C. Tucker, "Music in the Soviet Union," *Musical Opinion,* March, 1955; J. Briggs, "Soviet Party Line in Song," *New York Times,* June 17, 1956, Section 2; editorial, "Reform from the Bottom," *Musical America,* LXXVI, No. 9 (July, 1956), 4; I. Stern, "A Violinist's Look at Russia," *New York Times,* July 8, 1956, Section 2; Y. Arbatsky, "Soviet Attitude towards Music: An Analysis Based in Part on Secret Archives," *Musical Quarterly,* XLIII (July, 1957), 295-315; Jean-Michel Hayos, "Art et communisme," *Schweizerische Musikzeitung,* XCVIII, No. 7-8 (July 15, 1958), 293-96.

9. The results of a survey of musicological resources and studies in

the United States sponsored by the committee in musicology of the American Council of Learned Societies (appointed in 1929) were published in W. O. Strunk's *State and Resources of Musicology in the United States* (American Council of Learned Societies Bulletin No. 19, 1932). Later bibliographies sponsored by the committee include *Report on Publication and Research in Musicology and Allied Fields in the United States, 1932-1938* (Washington, 1938) and *A Bibliography of Periodical Literature in Musicology and Allied Fields* (A.C.L.S. Bulletins No. 1, 1938-1939, and No. 2, 1939-1940). Musicological studies suffered some interruption during World War II, but were resumed with new vigor thereafter, with the establishment of a central organ, *The Journal of the American Musicological Society* (*JAMS*), and the broadening of general interest in music and musicology.

10. The following titles will serve as characteristic examples of the articles on Russian music in specialized musicological journals: Alfred J. Swan, "The Nature of the Russian Folk-song," *Musical Quarterly*, XIX (1943), 499-503; *idem*, "Old Byzantine and Russian Liturgical Chant," *Bulletin of the American Musicological Society*, No. 8 (1945), 22-23; *idem*, "Harmonizations of the Old Russian Chants," *JAMS*, II (1949), 83-86; Bruno Nettl, "Ukrainian Polyphonic Folksongs," abstract in *JAMS*, VII (1954), 167-68; Alfred J. Swan, "Russian Liturgical Music and its Relation to Twentieth-century Ideals," *Music and Letters*, XXXIX, No. 3 (July, 1958), 265-74. Mention should also be made of the article by Dragotin Cvetko, "The Renaissance in Slovene Music," in the British *Slavonic and East European Review*, XXXVI, No. 86 (December, 1957), 27-36.

11. In the course of making this survey, the author has compiled a list of American master's essays and doctoral dissertations in musicology concerned with some aspect of Russian music (based principally on the bibliographical works cited in note 9, on annual lists of doctoral dissertations in musicology for 1953-1954, 1955, and 1956 in *JAMS*, and on *A List of Doctoral Dissertations in Musicology and Allied Fields* [Denton, Texas, 1951]). Since 1920, a period of almost forty years, only nine master's essays and nine doctoral dissertations in musicology have dealt with Russian music; one dissertation is still in progress. Moreover, only twelve of the forty institutions in the United States which sponsor doctoral degrees in music are represented in this list, and there is no indication of systematic attention to the study of Russian music in any institution.

12. Harald Heckmann, "Musikwissenschaftliche Unternehmun-

gen in Deutschland seit 1945," *Acta musicologica*, XXIX, fasc. ii/iii (1957).

13. Prospectus of the Congress, Cologne, June, 1958. Compare the report on the 1956 Congress in Hamburg (Gesellschaft für Musikforschung, *Bericht über den internationalen musikwissenschaftlichen Kongress Hamburg 1956* [Kassel and Basel, 1957]), from which it would appear that although the Congress found time to explore such esoteric topics as "The Gilds of Blind Musicians in Japan" and "Robber Folk Songs in the Tatra Mountain Area," no one at the Congress spoke on any subject connected with Russian music.

14. Andrei Olkhovsky, *Music Under the Soviets: The Agony of an Art* (New York, 1955).

15. Robert M. Slusser, "Soviet Music since the Death of Stalin," *Annals of the American Academy of Social and Political Science*, CCCIII (January, 1956), 116-25.

12. ARCHITECTURE AND MINOR ARTS

1. George Heard Hamilton, *The Art and Architecture of Russia*, (Baltimore, 1954). Other volumes on this subject in English include C. G. E. Bunt, *Russian Art from Scyths to Soviets* (New York, 1956); Tamara Talbot Rice, *Russian Art* (Baltimore, 1949); D. Talbot Rice (ed.), *Russian Art* (London, 1935); D. R. Buxton, *Russian Medieval Architecture* (Cambridge, England, 1934); G. K. Lukomsky, *History of Modern Russian Painting* (London, 1945); Arthur Voyce, *The Moscow Kremlin* (Berkeley, 1954). Voyce has also prepared a volume on "The Russian Decorative Arts and Crafts." As in other fields, Soviet scholars of the arts have contributed some basic research on earlier historic periods. One Soviet history has been translated into English: M. Alpatov, *The Russian Impact on Art* (New York, 1950). This book is increasingly useful the more remote it becomes from contemporary problems.

2. Alfred Hamilton Barr, Jr., "Notes on Russian Architecture," *The Arts*, XV, No. 2 (February, 1929), 99-105. For Barr's later observations on a related topic, see his "Is Modern Art Communistic?," *New York Times Magazine*, December 14, 1952, pp. 22-23, 28-29.

3. Robert Byron, "The Russian Scene, I. The Foundations," *Architectural Review*, LXXI, No. 426 (May, 1932), 174-200; and Edward Carter, "Soviet Architecture To-day," *ibid.*, XCII, No. 551 (November, 1942), 107-14.

4. Frank Lloyd Wright, "Architecture and Life in the U.S.S.R.," *Architectural Record*, LXXXII, No. 4 (October, 1937), 58-63.

5. Talbot Faulkner Hamlin, "Style Developments in Soviet Architecture," *American Quarterly on the Soviet Union*, I, No. 1 (April, 1938), 17-21. See also his later articles on "The Development of Russian Architecture," *Magazine of Art*, XXXVIII, No. 4 (April, 1945), 128-32; No. 5 (May, 1945), 180-85.

6. See, for example, Lionel Brett, "The Architecture of Authority," *Architectural Review*, XCIX, No. 593 (May, 1946), 131-34.

7. An article utilizing some material from Paul Willen's Master's essay is his "Soviet Architecture: Progress and Reaction," *Problems of Communism*, III, No. 1 (January-February, 1954), 24-34. For a discussion of recent problems in Soviet architecture, see the same author's "New Era in Soviet Architecture?," *ibid.*, V, No. 4 (July-August, 1956), 29-33; and H. A. Meek, "Retreat to Moscow," *Architectural Review*, CXIII, No. 675 (March, 1953), 143-51.

8. For additional British articles useful in tracing the history of Soviet architecture, see David Arkin, "Architecture," *Art in the U.S.S.R.*, ed. C. G. Home (London, 1935), pp. 12-26; Peter Blake, "The Soviet Architectural Purge," *Architectural Record*, CVI, No. 3 (September, 1949), 127-29; Arthur Link, "Soviet Architecture," *Soviet Cultural Relations Journal*, Spring, 1949, pp. 31-32; Berthold Lubetkin, "The Russian Scene, II. The Builders," *Architectural Review*, LXXI, No. 2 (May, 1932), 201-8.

9. Hamilton, *The Art and Architecture of Russia*, p. 266.

10. M. N. Tsapenko, *O Realisticheskikh Osnovakh Sovetskoi Arkhitektury* [Concerning the realistic bases of Soviet architecture] (Moscow, 1952).

13. POSTSCRIPT

1. Paul F. Lazarsfeld and Wagner Thielens, Jr., *The Academic Mind: Social Scientists in a Time of Crisis* (Glencoe, Ill., 1958), 97-98, 219-20.

2. Marshall D. Shulman, "Changing Appreciation of the Soviet Problem," *World Politics*, X, No. 4 (July, 1958), 509. Also Harold J. Berman, "The Devil and Soviet Russia," *The American Scholar*, XXVII, No. 2 (Spring, 1958), 147-52, and Alex Inkeles, "The Challenge of a Stable Russia," *The Antioch Review*, XVIII, No. 2 (Summer, 1958), 133-44.

INDEX OF AUTHORS